Implementing Project Portfolio Management

A Companion Guide to
The Standard for Portfolio Management

Dr. Te Wu, PMP, PgMP, PfMP

Dr. Panos Chatzipanos, P.Eng, RPP

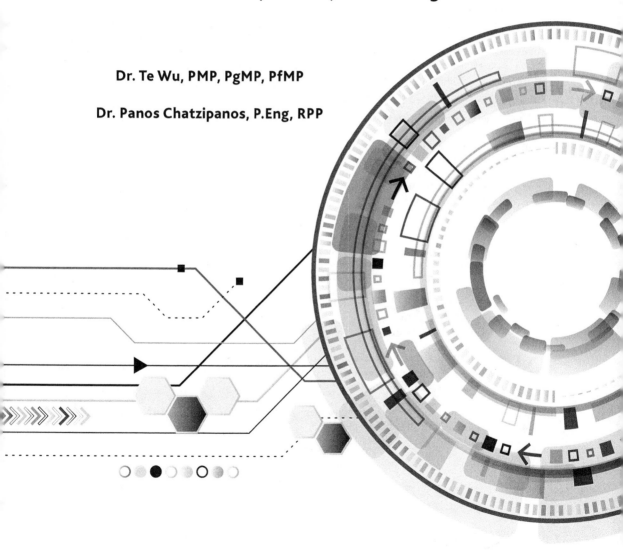

Library of Congress Cataloging-in-Publication Data has been applied for.

ISBN: 978-1-62825-557-7

Published by: Project Management Institute, Inc.
14 Campus Boulevard
Newtown Square, Pennsylvania 19073-3299 USA
Phone: +1 610 356 4600
Fax: +1 610 356 4647
Email: customercare@pmi.org
Internet: www.PMI.org

To place a Trade Order or for pricing information, please contact Independent Publishers Group:

Independent Publishers Group
Order Department
814 North Franklin Street
Chicago, IL 60610 USA
Phone: +1 800 888 4741
Fax: +1 312 337 5985
Email: orders@ipgbook.com (For orders only)

For all other inquiries, please contact the PMI Book Service Center.
PMI Book Service Center
P.O. Box 932683, Atlanta, GA 31193-2683 USA
Phone: +1 866 276 4764 (within the U.S. or Canada) or
+1 770 280 4129 (globally)
Fax: +1 770 280 4113
Email: info@bookorders.pmi.org

10 9 8 7 6 5 4 3 2

This book is dedicated the community of project portfolio management professionals

Table of Contents

List of Tables

List of Figures

Introduction

Purpose of this Book

> *A mind needs books as a sword needs a whetstone if it is to keep its edge.*
> — **George R. R. Martin**

The Standard for Portfolio Management – Fourth Edition is a major update to the third edition. There are three major changes: 1) The new book is now a principle-based standard in which the applicability has achieved greater universality; 2) The breadth of the new standard is broader, encompassing a portfolio life cycle, aligning with complexity and system theories, portfolio stakeholder management, and portfolio value management; and 3) The depth has also been increased to include a section on capability and capacity, a major rework on governance management, and significant insights in value management and stakeholder management. As a principle-based standard, the "how" of portfolio management is largely removed. While the "how" is context specific and therefore cannot be standardized, there is nevertheless value in understanding the various approaches. *Implementing Project Portfolio Management: A Companion Guide to The Standard for Portfolio Management* was written to address the "hows" that support the "what" of portfolio management.

As a companion guide to the current standard, this book is designed for three primary audience groups:

- **Business executives** – Part 1 of the book includes Chapter 1, which provides a comprehensive but high-level description of portfolio management, including the what, why, who, and how. Other groups are encouraged to review Part 1 as well, to achieve an executive-level understanding of portfolio management.

- **Portfolio leaders and practitioners** – Part 2 of the book, Chapters 2 to 8, offers an in-depth examination of the various performance domains discussed in *The Standard for Portfolio Management* – Fourth Edition. In addition, this book goes beyond the standard with additional domains and concepts that are in practice today. Each chapter offers new insights on how to apply the principles covered in the standard. As appropriate, selective tools and templates are introduced.
- **Portfolio thinkers** – Part 3, Chapters 9 to 13, is designed for tinkerers and inquisitive professionals who want to look ahead and see the future of portfolios and some areas of latest development. Part 3 is a true work in progress.

Portfolio management is a growing field, still in relative infancy. Over the course of the coming years, the authors and contributors of this book firmly believe that portfolio management will achieve significant adoption in organizations. Thus, we have published a website in which the authors and contributors will provide updates to this book. For more information, visit www.implementppm.com.

Establishing the Core Team for the Project Management Institute's Portfolio Management Core Team for the Fourth Edition (by Gary Sikma and Dave Ross)

Development of *The Standard for Portfolio Management* – Fourth Edition began in the summer of 2015. The primary group responsible, the core committee, was comprised of the chair, vice chair, and 10 committee members. As directed by the PMI Standards Member Advisory Group in the project charter, the new standard departed from the previous version, now placing emphasis on principles of portfolio management (the "what") as opposed to the processes (the "how"). Over 125 portfolio, program, and project management practitioners volunteered to serve on the core committee.

Since this version of the standard would be significantly different from its predecessors, the criteria used for selecting committee members emphasized experience in being responsible for a portfolio or organization's profit-and-loss or equivalent results. In addition, it was deemed important that the committee reflect a wide diversity of industry and cultural backgrounds. Résumés of the volunteers were compared against the selection criteria and a list of candidates was compiled for telephone interviews. At the end of the interview process, 10 core committee members were selected. As a result, all members of the core committee had senior executive management experience (including several CEOs) or leadership positions in significant portfolios within their organizations. Industries represented included technology, construction, manufacturing, finance, government, and academia. Several members also consulted in a number of these fields. Seven of the committee were from North America, and five were from Europe. Of those 12, two also had extensive experience in Asia and the Middle East. The core committee was supported by subcommittees comprised of 11 experienced PMI standards volunteers with demonstrated expertise in portfolio management.

Terminology and Convention

As a companion guide to portfolio management, this book is primarily grounded with *The Standard for Portfolio Management* – Fourth Edition. However, there are important concepts, processes, tools, and techniques from other Project Management Institute publications, including *The Standard for Portfolio Management* – Third Edition and *Navigating Complexity: A Practice Guide*.

The following table contains the standard acronyms for the various publications referenced in the companion guide.

Publication	Acronym
Implement Project Portfolio Management: A Companion Guide to The Standard for Portfolio Management	Companion Guide
Navigating Complexity: A Practice Guide	Navigating Complexity
The Standard for Portfolio Management – Third Edition	PfM Standard (3.0)
The Standard for Portfolio Management – Fourth Edition	PfM Standard

Supporting Website

Even though PMI is currently on the fourth edition of *The Standard for Portfolio Management*, the discipline is still emerging to establish its unique contributions, principles, knowledge domains, processes, practices, tools, and techniques. As portfolio management is a work in progress, the contributors to this book expect and hope that the discipline grows with greater adoption and new development. Therefore, we also created a website dedicated to the study and practice of portfolio management. Visit the website at implementppm.com.

The chief objectives of the website are the following:

- Create a community for project portfolio management practitioners to share knowledge, practices, and ideas to further the field;
- Download selective tools, techniques, and templates described in the book;
- Participate in project portfolio management-related surveys and studies;
- Enrich the reader's knowledge of the latest developments; and
- Provide additional resources to those who are seeking to attain PMI's Portfolio Management Professional (PfMP)® certification.

For those who wish to share ideas or contribute content (e.g., articles, blogs, templates, and other ideas) to this community, please contact us at ideas@implementppm.com.

Part I
An Executive Guide to Portfolio Management

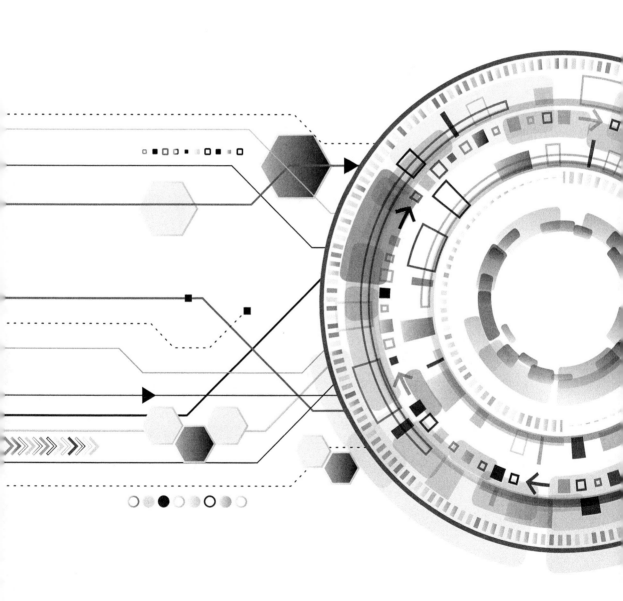

Understanding Portfolio Management

by Te Wu

[
A goal without a plan is just a wish.
— **Antoine de Saint-Exupery**
]

1.1. A Case for Portfolio Management

In our current, intensely competitive environment, organizations confront a variety of difficult choices, particularly regarding major investments. To achieve success, organizations must not only have strong concepts, but also the ability to implement those ideas to achieve the intended business value. This means that having the idea is not enough; organizations must also possess the potential to prioritize and select which plans to implement, provide strong governance during a plan's life span, nurture the implementation of the plan, and execute it deftly. Just look at the world around us: There is an ample number of good and even great ideas, as evidenced by bold initiatives ranging from driverless vehicles to an entirely new economy based on apps. Regardless of industry, good ideas are commonplace. The strategic differentiation rarely, if ever, will be achieved on ideas alone. Moreover, this is truer today than ever before, as competition leaves very little room for errors. What sets successful organizations apart is their strategic business execution ability that harnesses their ideas and turns them into tangible benefits. Successful organizations use portfolio management.

Project management has been the discipline of choice for business execution. Since its founding as a formal school of study in the 1950s, project management has itself become the preeminent approach to implementing one-time and often complex initiatives. Yet the results are mixed at best. A 2015 PMI study showed that of every US$1 billion spent on projects, about US$122 million was wasted. However, a more recent PMI study in 2016 showed significant improvement. Will this trend continue? Not likely. The Standish Group, which has been studying information technology projects since 1994, has placed the success rate less than 33 percent for nearly every single year since inception. In 2015, the success rate was about 29 percent—dismal by any standard.

When examined under closer scrutiny, the problem of success can be largely divided into two areas: 1) doing the *right* projects; and 2) doing the projects *right*. Project management—and by extension, program management—has mostly been focused on the second problem of "doing the projects right." When organizations apply a more disciplined approach to project management, the improvements are significant. For example, in the latter PMI study, published in 2016, when project management culture is a high priority, 71 percent of projects met their original goals and business intent versus 52 percent of projects when project management culture was a low priority. This improvement of almost 20 percent translates to a huge amount of savings.

Yet, "doing the project right" is only half of the equation. Are the right projects being done in the first place? For example, how many of you have ever questioned the importance of the projects you've worked on?

The importance of portfolio management became more evident when the Project Management Institute (PMI) introduced *The Standard for Portfolio Management* in 2006. Then in 2014, PMI launched a new certification, the Portfolio Management Professional (PfMP)®. This new professional certification sits atop the project management career ladder, helping to highlight the importance of the discipline while instilling project, program, and portfolio management as relevant topics in the boardroom. Portfolio management has finally arrived. The most recent work, which prompted the development of this book, is the latest update to *The Standard for Portfolio Management*, now in the fourth edition. The authors and contributors are all core committee members, including both the chair and vice chair, responsible for refreshing the current standard to keep up with the changing times.

1.2. Defining Portfolios and Portfolio Management

A portfolio is a logical group of components managed together to achieve certain strategic objectives. These components can be projects, programs, subsidiary components, and related operational activities. They may be related, such as targeting the same customers, or unrelated, such as projects from multiple functional areas. Even though components can be unrelated, as there are no dependencies or direct impact between these components, there is an underlying logic why these components are grouped in one portfolio versus another.

For example, a company may have an enterprise portfolio composed of large projects and programs. As these components require significant capital or operational expenditures, which is the underlying logic, the sponsoring organization wants a more dedicated focus on their management. However, aside from the budget size, these components can be from different areas of the organization, without any other relationships. Since portfolios are artificial constructs created to improve the efficient and effective management of these endeavors, an organization can have many portfolios; the number might depend on a multitude of factors, such as organization size, complexity, culture, capability, project and program intensity, and resources, to name a few. The strength of the underlying logic and the relationship of the components, as well as the desired outcome, often drive the major focus of portfolio management.

Portfolio management is the centralized management of portfolios by applying the principles, knowledge, and skills to achieve the intended business objectives. These can be strategic (e.g., long term, long lasting, with broad implications to the organization's mission and vision) or tactical (e.g., short term, immediate impact, with impact to near-term operations). Portfolio managers are chiefly responsible for guiding the portfolio management processes. This includes the identification, categorization, evaluation, selection and approval, prioritization, optimization, authorization, implementation, eventual transitioning or termination of portfolios, and management of the business value.

In practicality, portfolios of highly related components typically require more intensely focused management to achieve a high degree of synergy and coordination. Portfolios of unrelated components are typically grouped for convenience or to share certain resources. Aside from resource sharing and perhaps some minor integration management activities, the level of synergy and coordination is weak. For example, a portfolio of revenue-producing projects for a particular product line is likely to have a stronger centralized portfolio management setup than another portfolio composed of unrelated components assembled for convenience. All things being equal, unrelated portfolios have less structure and intensity within the portfolio management processes.

1.3. Relationship between Portfolio Management and Organization

Organizations have been practicing portfolio management since the dawn of business strategy as a focal area of concern. This occurs at all levels of organizations, from the enterprise to business units to departments and even teams. Executives and managers have implicitly recognized the importance of strategic choice, and when confronting the constraint of limited resources, these choices generally reflect some optimal balance of competing factors. Rigorous and process-driven organizations are likely to have specific business processes to generate new ideas, validate these ideas before committing serious resources, and implementing these ideas as projects or operational enhancements. In advanced organizations, approved business cases are evaluated for the benefits attained. Organizations practicing one or more of these activities are already using some aspects of portfolio management.

The contemporary challenges confronting organizations require them to adopt a more systematic approach to portfolio management. What may start out as a specific capability of ideation or prioritizing projects before approval or overseeing the implementation of a logical bundle of projects may address certain specific business needs. But to build sustainable capabilities addressing both strategic and tactical considerations, organizations need to reconsider portfolio management and how to incorporate it as a core competency in the organization. At the same time, to achieve greater value, the breadth of portfolio management needs to be broadened to include ideation to operations where business value is realized and the depth of portfolio management capabilities, such as capability and capacity planning, governance, and value management are also increased. Today's portfolio management is now much more than finding the best ideas, but also ensuring that they achieve the desired value.

Portfolio management today can take many forms. At the most strategic level, some companies build an "office of strategic investments" to bridge planning with execution. Most organizations establish a range of portfolio management capabilities and house them in enterprise or departmental-level project management offices (PMOs). At the more tactical end of the spectrum, organizations may create a portfolio management capability in an operational department for managing initiatives that lead to continuous improvement. Based on our experience, large and complex organizations can have up to 60 PMOs, with a handful of them having portfolio management capabilities. What is your organization like? What works best for your organization?

1.4. Relationship between Portfolio, Program, and Project Management

Portfolios are extensive collections of investment choices or endeavors to change the organization. These endeavors often take the form of programs, projects, quasi-projects (like continuous improvement initiatives), and operational activities. Collectively, these endeavors form the components of a portfolio. Portfolios are *artificial* constructs—they are formed to help organizations better manage a collection of related components. Thus, the nature of the portfolio (e.g., size, budget, focus, resources, etc.) depends on internal and external factors—internal factors, such as organizational culture, maturity, capability, and investment intensity; external factors, such as industry and its maturity, related industries that provide substitutions, macroeconomic environments, and regulatory and political settings.

As artificial constructs designed for effective management, portfolios can be flexible mechanisms for organizations to implement strategic and tactical components. In general, portfolios can contain multiple components across the life cycle. A robust portfolio is likely to have strong ideas in the pipeline, robust business cases waiting for approval, valuable programs and projects in implementation, completed components transitioning into operations, and successful components in operations realizing the intended benefits. Some programs may, in turn, contain smaller subsidiary programs and projects. Even some larger projects may include subsidiary projects. How well these components are managed throughout their life cycle can directly affect the health of the entire organization.

From a hierarchy of organization activities, portfolio management is at the crossroads of planning, operating, and changing. Table 1 illustrates relative positions of portfolio management among organizational activities:

Table 1.   Hierarchy of Organizational Activities[1]

Level	Pillars		Name	Description
10	Planning		Corporate or Enterprise Strategy	This is the highest level of business strategy, since the focus is the entire enterprise. Questions at this level mainly pertain to the firm's identity, purpose, and direction.
9			Organization Strategy	Following the corporate or enterprise strategy, an organization addresses the question of how it is to evolve to meet its business objectives. While mostly internally focused, it is built upon a realistic assessment of the external and internal environments.
8			Business Unit Strategy	Depending on the organization, a business unit can be a product line, a territory, or other profit centers. Here, the strategy is less about coordination among the operating units and more about developing and sustaining advantages to advance its products and services.
7			Functional Strategy	This is largely the realm of strategies for specific business objectives, such as sales, marketing, operations, product management, information technology, etc.
6		Changing	Portfolio	Even though portfolios can exist at all levels of the organization, this is where abstract planning starts to diminish and the hard work of getting things done starts. In addition, most portfolios cross functional lines and require a clear strategy.
5			Program	Programs can be seen as logical constructs of significant work components (other programs, projects, and operational initiatives) that require an organization to change. It is logical because of its relatedness and/or its interdependencies. In PMI's definition, programs focus on delivering business benefits.
4			Project	Projects are typically more specific, concentrating on deliverables and outcomes. Portfolios, programs, and projects are at the heart of the "changing" pillar.
3		Operating	Operational Initiatives	Operational initiatives are generally enhancement activities designed for the continuous improvement of operations. Occasionally, operational initiatives can be large and important to the overall business. In those cases, they are often managed as a part of programs.
2			Specific Teams	Specific teams are functional work units with highly defined expertise that are the building blocks for operational initiatives, projects, or programs. For example, a team in software development can be development, QA, deployment, or business analysis.
1			Tasks and Activities	These are specific tasks and activities that operate the business and its routine processes. For example, for sales, it can be making cold calls. For developers, it is coding.

1.5. How to Make Portfolio Management Work—Essential Principles of Portfolio Management

In *The Standard for Portfolio Management* – Fourth Edition, Section 1.7 lists eight fundamental principles of portfolio management without much description. The goal of this section is to elaborate on these ideas to both clarify and make them more executable. The eight principles are:

1. Strive to achieve excellence in strategic execution
2. Enhance transparency, responsibility, accountability, sustainability, and fairness
3. Balance portfolio value against the overall risk
4. Ensure that investments in portfolio components are aligned with the organizational strategy
5. Obtain and maintain the sponsorship and engagement of senior management and key stakeholders
6. Exercise active and decisive leadership for the optimization of resource utilization
7. Foster a culture that embraces change and risk
8. Navigate complexity to enable successful outcomes

1.5.1. Strive to achieve excellence in strategic execution

Today, most organizations have many wonderful ideas, but few of them are ultimately achieved. The challenges are many, such as limited resources, poor investment decisions, weak portfolio governance, and inadequate program and project management disciplines. For organizations, even the best ideas are worthless unless they can be successfully implemented to achieve the benefits. As a bridge between planning and execution, portfolio management is the first discipline in the project-program-portfolio management hierarchy to systemically manage these endeavors and tackle the complexities and intricacies of implementation. Portfolio management is the discipline that enables organizations to make optimal investment decisions of portfolio components and to oversee the performance of these components to achieve their intended value. By creating a sustainable environment for success to occur, portfolio management is the front line of achieving execution excellence.

1.5.2. Enhance transparency, responsibility, accountability, sustainability, and fairness

Effective portfolio management requires the appropriate governance of portfolio-level activities. Perhaps the most important outcome of governance is establishing the legitimacy of decisions where disenchanted executives, who otherwise would not support or endorse portfolio decisions, will abide by the governance team's decisions and implement them without significant issues. This is vital for the portfolio management team because portfolio decisions can be controversial when the interest of one party is pitted against an entrenched interest in another party. By establishing transparent processes where decision making is fair and where the decision makers have defined responsibilities and accountabilities, even controversial decisions can enjoy much higher degrees of support across the portfolio team.

1.5.3. Balance portfolio value against overall risks

At a portfolio level, uncertainties are prevalent. Commonly, risks can be inherent in the organization's operational environment, the internal uncertainties of capability and capacity, or the aggressiveness of the organization's strategy. Risks can bubble up from specific projects, programs, and operations. For portfolio managers, perhaps the biggest challenge is to create a sufficiently steady environment in which the portfolio management team and the component team can successfully implement and perform their work. This requires a delicate balancing act in which portfolios must manage the knowns and the unknowns to achieve the business value despite uncertainties. Taking on too many risks may jeopardize the target value; taking on too few risks may not maximize the value creation capabilities of the portfolio. Thus, portfolio managers are often walking a tightrope between analysis paralysis and acting upon what appears to be imperfect data.

1.5.4. Ensure that investments in portfolio components are aligned with organizational strategy

Strategic management can be divided in many ways. A simple, and yet effective, framework to examine strategic management is comprised of these four dimensions: planning, formulation, implementation, and evaluation. Planning is understanding the organization and determining its direction. Formulation is distilling the plan into specific goals and objectives. Implementation of the strategic plan with evaluation is the final dimension of monitoring and controlling for the desired outcome. Portfolio management spans across strategic formulation, implementation, and partially into evaluation. Serving as a bridge that connects strategic planning with the rest, portfolio management provides the pivotal discipline of aligning implementation and strategy. When applying appropriate portfolio, program, and project management in unison, organizations have a much higher likelihood of "doing the right things, in the right way."

1.5.5. Obtain and maintain the sponsorship and engagement of senior management and key stakeholders

Organizationally, portfolios are significant investments of resources. When implemented in conjunction with program, project, and operational management, portfolios represent the largest "container," wherein their cost can be a significant percentage of an organization's investment. This means the importance of having strong and steady sponsorship and engagement from senior executives is often magnified many times over as compared with project management. The success of portfolio managers is often dependent on engaging the key stakeholders, converting them from blockers to supporters, and maintaining that level of support throughout the portfolio life cycle.

1.5.6. Exercise active and decisive leadership for the optimization of resource utilization

One of the most important roles of the portfolio manager is to manage organizational resources; more specifically, the capability and capacity of important resources. Capability refers to the extent or ability to perform work effectively and efficiently, and capacity refers to the maximum amount in which the capability can be performed. As resources are often expensive and scarce, especially the precious assets, portfolio managers often must make difficult trade-off decisions. Effective portfolio managers should, therefore, be proactive, hands-on, and ready to be decisive.

1.5.7. Foster a culture that embraces change and risk

Portfolios, programs, and projects are vehicles for the planning and implementation of organizational changes, and change can be risky.

The large-scale change that often occurs at the portfolio level requires continuous navigation of the organization as it moves from the as-is state to the desired future state. As an organization leader, portfolio managers are intimately involved with and are often the champions of change by confronting challenges and tackling risks.

1.5.8. Navigate complexity to enable successful outcomes

Portfolios are often complex systems with intricate and complicated details, a multitude of interdependencies, and potential technical and organizational unknowns. To successfully achieve their goals and objectives, portfolio managers require advanced technical and soft skills to navigate many "land mines" across multiple organizational levels of challenges. These advanced soft skills include managing politics, dealing with difficult personalities, communicating effectively with stakeholders at all levels, facilitating problem-solving sessions to resolve issues, motivating the portfolio component teams, and making difficult decisions, especially where there is imperfect information, just to name a few.

1.6. How to Be an Effective Portfolio Manager

Portfolio managers are senior organizational leaders responsible for the establishment and implementation of portfolio management. Depending on the maturity of the organization's processes, portfolio management can be established across the entire life cycle of portfolios, including initiation, planning, execution, and optimization.

Strong portfolio managers master both the technical and soft skills. The technical skills focus mainly on strategic management; financial and value management; data analysis of all types, from the macroeconomic to hyperlocal marketing data (for example); and the processes of making sound decisions for establishing portfolio management processes. Soft skills are perhaps even more important than technical skills since the implementation of portfolio processes are delicate and require a high degree of organizational savvy and interpersonal talents. Successful portfolio managers often possess those skills that have broader applications, such as leadership, negotiation, diplomacy, business instinct, and the willingness to make difficult decisions.

Table 2 outlines some of the key skills needed for each performance domain.

Table 2.   Key Portfolio Management Technical and Soft Skills by Performance Domain

Performance Domain	Technical Skills	Soft Skills
Strategic Management	• Strategic planning • Industry and organization analysis • Data analysis • Financial acumen • Roadmapping • Portfolio optimization techniques • Process of making sound decisions and deriving business judgment	• Business instinct • Negotiation • Interpretation (including reading between the lines) • Working with senior management and customers
Governance	• Process development, especially governance-related processes • Performance metrics • Roles and responsibilities	• Communication (notably active listening) • Diplomacy • Leadership (of component teams) • Conflict resolution
Capacity and Capability Management	• Capacity analysis and planning • Supply chain management • Resource allocation • Demand optimization • Reporting and analytics	• Capability development (especially human resources, such as talent management) • Balancing capability and capacity • Making difficult decisions
Stakeholder Engagement	• Stakeholder analysis and prioritization • Stakeholder engagement planning • Communication requirement analysis and planning	• Elicitation techniques to identify stakeholders • Managing expectations • Converting blockers to supporters • Navigating politics
Value Management	• Benefit realization management • Measuring, assessing, and reporting value • Portfolio financial management • Requirements management	• Perspective • Holistic thinking • Trade-off analysis • Exploring synergy • Managing change
Risk Management	• Risk management plan (including risk planning, identification, assessment, and response planning) • Risk register • Risk implementation process	• Risk appetite • Developing appropriate risk mind-set • Working with other organizational resources on managing risk • Managing unknown unknowns

Part II
A Practitioner's Guide to Portfolio Management

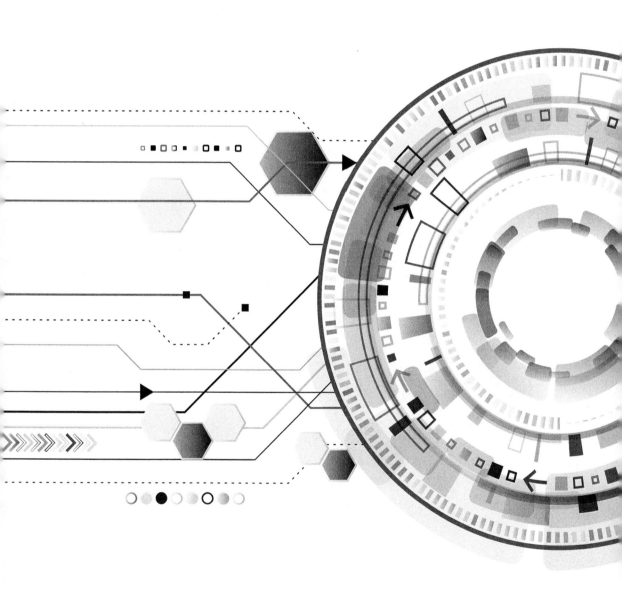

## CHAPTER 2

The Portfolio Life Cycle

by Panos Chatzipanos

> The external world is changing drastically, and enterprises and products will have a short life cycle if they don't change. So, we have to react to market trends. Nothing lasts forever in today's world.
> — **Li Ning**

Portfolio management establishes the principles, processes, and practices that align all change initiatives within the organization with strategy. Standardized portfolio management underpins project selection, prioritization, resourcing, and execution success. Thus, it is a paramount enabler for executive management to implement strategy and attain strategic objectives. Portfolio management is a core management function for the whole organization. Its primary purpose is to execute strategy effectively and realize strategic goals efficiently. In other words, portfolio management is a standardized management framework that bridges the space between strategy, change initiatives leading to strategic objectives, and their successful execution. It is performed in an organizational environment which is usually much broader than the portfolio itself. The following fundamental principles, as described in the PfM Standard, are paramount throughout the portfolio life cycle:[2]

- Strive to achieve excellence in strategic execution;
- Enhance transparency, responsibility, accountability, sustainability, and fairness;
- Balance portfolio value against overall risks;
- Ensure the alignment of the investments in portfolio components with the organization's strategy;
- Obtain and maintain the sponsorship and engagement of senior management and key stakeholders;
- Exercise active and decisive leadership for the optimization of resource utilization;
- Foster a culture that embraces change and risk; and
- Navigate complexity to enable successful outcomes.

Following the PfM Standard, the purpose of these principles, which are applicable throughout the portfolio life cycle, is to guide portfolio management practitioners in the conceptualization, establishment, implementation, and ongoing management of portfolio(s) in their organizations.

2.1. The Portfolio Life Cycle within the Organizational Environment

Execution of portfolio components leads to the achievement of organizational objectives. Sustained alignment of all portfolio components to strategic goals during the entire life cycle of the portfolio is a crucial function of portfolio management. Organizational strategy and objectives determine the means of attaining the goals through organizational activities: programs, projects, and operations. Portfolio management is the platform that connects organizational strategy to achievement of strategic objectives. As such, it maintains that all governance and management levels are connected, since this will ensure that initiatives support the organizational strategy. A portfolio is an integrated system consisting of components, each having specific purposes and characteristics, interacting with each other and their environment. Each component, when changed, affects other components of the portfolio to which it is connected. A portfolio managed in a complex environment usually exhibits behaviors that more closely resemble not just those of a single system, but rather those of a complex system of systems. In such systems, characteristics such as ambiguity, nonproportionality, and emergence may develop.

To build resilience and system stability, dependencies must be thoroughly understood by portfolio management practitioners. This as equally true of the interfaces between individual portfolio components, and between portfolio components and their environment. Programs and projects are the transient vehicles that deliver change for the whole organization. A systems perspective allows for better understanding of the goals of the change initiatives as well as of the vehicles delivering these goals—portfolio components. The systemic behavior of the portfolio plus the complexity encountered within the portfolio and its environment are discussed in Chapters 10 and 11 of this book. Portfolio management requires clearly defined and well-understood strategic objectives to properly focus the work. Poor definition of portfolio components is often accompanied by mistaken expectations and unrealistic assumptions. Thus, a well-defined strategic plan is also crucial to successful portfolio management.

Regular alignment of initiatives to strategic objectives is paramount, since organizations can undergo frequent strategy redefinition due to stakeholder pressure for greater profitability, changing market conditions, and the imperative to balance the needs for change with the needs of ongoing operations. The executive level decides, each time, on changes in strategy and on strategic objectives. Portfolio governance, throughout its life cycle, will follow the strategic plan. That plan must address how the organization's strengths and core competencies will be best used to:

- Manage resources;
- Create value;
- Engage stakeholders;
- Capitalize on opportunities and minimize the impact of threats;
- Navigate complexity;
- Respond to the ever-increasing environmental change (for example, in the market, legal, and regulatory environments); and
- Concentrate on critical operational activities.

The portfolio manager regularly communicates recommendations for governance actions; for example, deciding which portfolio components should proceed, be terminated, or suspended. Further, through the review of strategic, tactical, and operational capabilities and the performance of gap analysis, portfolio management may provide feedback that is essential for disciplined planning and management of resource demands. The portfolio manager also reviews the portfolio for balance toward risk, sequences portfolio components to account for deficiencies and their effects, maximizes efficient use of common constraint resources, and negotiates agreements with key stakeholders. Further, in many organizations, the portfolio manager participates in strategic planning and the organizational risk analysis team. If these organizational functions determine that a strategic objective is no longer valid, the portfolio manager recommends the reassessment of any portfolio components that are under implementation to achieve the obsolete strategic objective.

Once a portfolio component is authorized, the program manager or the project manager assumes management of the portfolio components to ensure that the work is done effectively and efficiently. The responsible program/project manager will manage the component per standardized program or project management processes and good practices (e.g., scope, schedule, budget, resources, as well as benefits realization for a program), and provide feedback to the portfolio manager.

Defining the boundaries for each of the portfolio components provides clarity for all stakeholders. Portfolio components do not exist in isolation. Each portfolio is a system of interrelated components, and simultaneously a part of the whole organizational system.

For this reason, portfolio managers must:

- Understand each portfolio component (feasibility, clear deliverables, added value, constraints, etc.);
- Understand relationships between components (the strategy as well as the strategic objectives of the organization);
- Understand the portfolio environment;
- Understand the entire portfolio ecosystem;
- Prepare for portfolio ecosystem changes, following strategic change management processes;
- Evaluate, prioritize, and approve changes; and
- Implement changes, overseeing their performance.

Priorities must be set through an appropriate value optimization process. Optimization is the process of making a portfolio as effective as possible by maximizing available conditions, constraints, and resources.

Typically, the primary goal of portfolio optimization is to ensure that all available resources are best applied to the appropriate active components of the portfolio. Risks need to be considered and balanced continuously. Feedback must be provided from all portfolio components so that portfolio adjustment, if necessary, can be performed simultaneously. Based on component feedback, the portfolio management iteration cycle incorporates the following cognitive behaviors and actions: awareness, recognition, monitoring, metrics, trigger points, review of information, corrective actions, flexibility, two-way communication with portfolio governance, and adaptability. It is important to note that each iteration increases a systemic view and complexity awareness; thus, a better understanding of the whole is achieved.

This approach further increases awareness of the overall portfolio risk. The portfolio manager does not only have to sum up the individual risks of portfolio components. The portfolio manager must consider further risks arising from the interactions of the individual risks to comprehend dependencies determining the overall portfolio risk. Thus, the portfolio manager must recognize dependencies as well as causes and effects that interconnections between portfolio components (such as the portfolio stakeholders, the portfolio environment, and so forth) introduce at any time during the portfolio life cycle. Such awareness allows the practitioner to introduce contingencies for emergent issues and risks arising from the aforementioned dependencies.

2.2. Portfolio Life Cycle Management Framework

The portfolio life cycle may be defined as the evolving set of changes that occur throughout the existence of the portfolio and to its components (subsidiary portfolios, programs, projects, and operations), within a continuous time frame. In today's global market, within the portfolio life cycle, outcomes from every portfolio component need to be very adaptive and flexible to constantly changing needs from internal and external influences so organizations can remain competitive and financially stable. If several portfolios exist in an organization, these can be centralized or decentralized with regard to their management, within the established governance structure. For example, a research and development portfolio might be decentralized and the other portfolios in the organization may be centrally managed. The establishment of appropriate controls required to manage a portfolio should be based on the flexibility and nature of the portfolio components and on the organizational project management maturity. Within the organization, each portfolio within its life cycle sustains ongoing change until it is decommissioned.

Portfolios usually have long life cycles; their stages primarily include initiation, planning, execution, and optimization as well as portfolio transformation and decommissioning. As the portfolio progresses, information is passed within and between stages as an ongoing and non-sequential process. Figure 1, taken from the PfM Standard[3], illustrates this flow of information and decisions.

An example of the portfolio life cycle major activities, as depicted in the PfM Standard, is presented in Figure 2.

Major factors that influence the portfolio life cycle include the definition of benefits and values derived from portfolio components. The defining value derived from products and/or services from key stakeholders' perspectives helps to directly eliminate non-value-added activities that

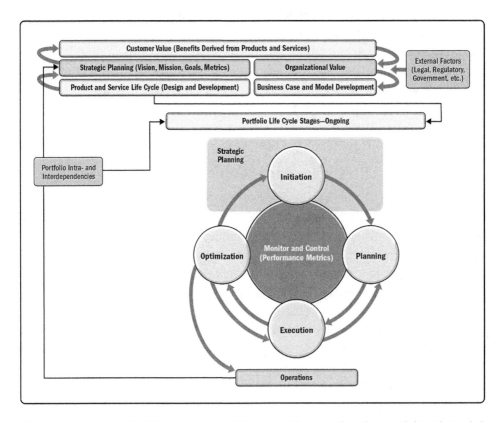

Figure 1. An Example of Information and Decision Flows within the Portfolio Life Cycle[4]

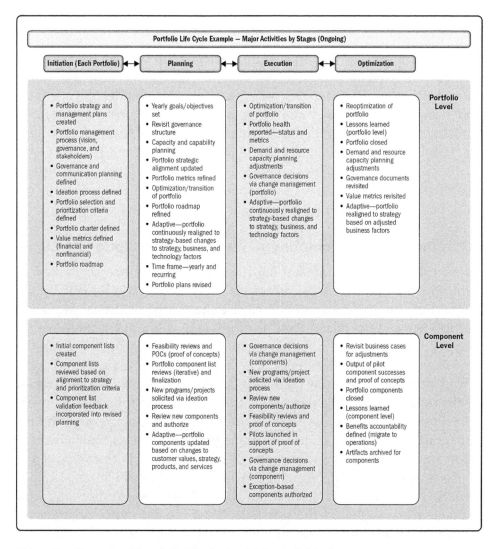

Figure 2. Example of Portfolio Life Cycle's Major Activities[5]

portfolio components may unintentionally serve. This process encompasses mapping the value stream. Moreover, such a process helps toward determining which portfolio components have minimal contribution to strategic objectives and add little or no benefits. Strategic planning, organizational performance metrics, and product and service design are all important inputs into the portfolio life cycle process. Under this process, the value stream should always be monitored. All stages within the portfolio after initiation must be flexible and adaptable. This means that as decisions are made, they can be changed and updated in real time to adapt to internal and external environmental factors. Supportive functions are utilized via integration management to keep the portfolio aligned with governance and top management decisions. Such functions, with their corresponding processes, include stakeholder engagement and risk and dependency management. These processes are defined and aligned to the portfolio in the initiation stage. Stakeholder engagement and risk management are discussed respectively in Chapters 6 and 8 of this book. Dependency management will be discussed further in this chapter.

2.3. The Portfolio Component Stages and Portfolio Life Cycle

Organizations have many standard and recurring processes. External requirements (such as fiscal reporting) or internal requirements (such as quarterly budget revisions) may drive these organizational processes and influence the application of portfolio management within the organization. While portfolio management is a continuous activity (unlike project or program management, which have a scheduled start and end), certain other activities may follow a recurring time frame, as determined by the organization. The purpose is to integrate portfolio management activities with the business activities of the organization through the application of organizational project management practices, which include the management of the whole portfolio in stages for its components. These stages, for each component, usually are: Identification, Evaluation, Selection, Prioritization, Resourcing, Balancing, Authorizing, and Managing. All stages in the portfolio life cycle are cyclic or iterative. Performance monitoring during the execution phase of the portfolio is obviously of paramount importance. Adjustments to the portfolio mix are required when disruptions to the organization inevitably occur. Once established, portfolio management is an ongoing practice.

During the portfolio initiation stage, processes determining how the organizational strategy and objectives will be implemented in the portfolio are established. From these, the portfolio strategic plan is derived, together with the structure and roadmap. These are primary inputs to the management plan. These processes are most active at the time the organization identifies and updates its strategic goals, near-term budgets, and plans. Subsequent processes must be set toward managing and optimizing the portfolio. These usually include processes and procedures for categorizing, evaluating, selecting for inclusion, modifying, balancing, prioritizing, resourcing, authorizing, and managing components. All these processes aim toward continuous alignment of the mix of components to the organization's strategy. Traditionally, these processes are used to administer all portfolio activities. Moreover, processes that determine how to monitor strategic changes, how to track and review portfolio performance indicators for alignment, how to determine key performance indicators for the components of the portfolio, and how to verify values that are delivered to the organization from the portfolio also have to be agreed upon and authorized.

There is a strong linkage between portfolio management and the iterative process cycle of determining the organizational strategy, aligning all portfolio components to that strategy, and monitoring the results of these decisions. Thus, the whole function of portfolio management acts as a series of interrelated processes between organizational strategy and portfolio components that are part of the tactical work to deliver on the strategic objectives of the organization. Portfolio management processes and good practices include:

- An adaptive approach (fluid, flexible, ad hoc) – new components are reviewed as required based on situational critical needs;
- Prioritization – components are reprioritized as needed based on these changes and business needs;
- Change management – changes proposed are reviewed based ongoing business and business support needs;
- Portfolio health is reported via regular status and metrics analysis;
- Exception-based components are authorized as needed;
- Integration management – communications, financial, and risk management are ongoing, supportive processes;
- Iterative replanning/decommissioning – portfolio components are canceled or closed as planned. This can include entire subordinate portfolio(s) or program(s) if several components related together are closed/canceled;
- Portfolios are re-optimized based on changes;
- Lessons learned are performed at regular intervals, based on component's delivery and performance metrics;
- Demand and resource capacity and capability planning is adjusted as necessary;

- Finalized portfolio components are moved to operations and benefits are assessed based on execution outcomes; and
- Outcomes of pilot components or prototypes, as well as finished components, are evaluated for the possible initiation of new components.

2.3.1. Initiation stage

Ideation – This is the business process in which new ideas are raised and discussed initially. It is the creative process of generating, developing, and communicating new ideas for change initiatives that are targeted at producing benefits for the organization. Some key elements outlined during the ideation process are an opportunity statement, financial cost estimate and financial impact (revenue/benefits), stakeholder impact, and key risks and dependencies. It is usually a one or two-page proposal. As part of the ideation process, a feasibility analysis can be conducted, which would assess in more detail the risks, costs, and revenue potential of the opportunity. This could also be a high-level business case. The next step is usually a "proof of concept" (POC). This could mean a pilot of a product, for example, or creation of a prototype to review more in-depth the feasibility of the idea based on customer perception, costs of the pilot, and revenue potential. This could also include consideration of a high-level business case.

Initiation – This is the phase when top management of the organization decides to establish and apply a portfolio management framework in the organization or in one of its business units. The portfolio governance framework is also set up during this period. Major decisions are made, such as communications planning, prioritization criteria, portfolio metrics, and a portfolio risk management plan. A first draft of the portfolio charter is created during the initiation phase. Further, a portfolio management plan is created to define how the portfolio will be implemented, monitored, and controlled to meet strategic objectives.

2.3.2. Planning phase

Strategic planning is an iterative process to be examined frequently. The portfolio is always optimized during cyclic periods. Portfolio metrics are reviewed to ensure they're tied to realistic objectives and envisioned benefits at all levels. They are also reviewed when major change proposals for individual portfolio components affecting their scope, budget, and schedule are received. Additionally, prioritization criteria are reviewed based on new components introduced since the last strategic planning reassessment. Needs are compared against available resources and demand, and resource capacity gap analysis and availability plans are set, based on the requirements of the portfolio. Changes are proposed and authorized based on such criteria. Finally, the portfolio management plan is reviewed and updated based on the relevant component status of the period, as well as overall portfolio risks, issues, and dependencies.

2.3.3. Portfolio execution phase

The portfolio execution phase includes the monitoring and controlling processes applied to various components. The health of the portfolio is communicated through regular status reports and by comparing the component performance metrics established during the planning phase. Changes in the organizational environment may necessitate the reprioritization of components or the introduction of new ones into the portfolio. These new components are reviewed as required based on unplanned critical needs or positive outcomes of proofs of concept, pilots, or feasibility studies.

The objectives of the execution phase, as discussed in the following chapters of this book, primarily include:

- The management of the successful delivery of all portfolio components;
- The competent resolution of risks and issues within the portfolio and its components. This includes component dependency management;
- The governance and management of the overall portfolio plus guidance for individual component management, particularly resource and communication management, and on stakeholder engagement;
- The monitoring of the components' benefits realization potential; and
- Managing portfolio assets and resources.

Portfolio execution is performed through its various components and operations. The health of the portfolio is reported through regular status reports and by reviewing the component performance metrics that were established during the planning phase. Identifying portfolio risks begins with an evaluation of the portfolio environment: What decision criteria have been established? What assumptions have been made regarding the organization's current processes and decision points that may increase the risk for the portfolio? Practitioners should perform this evaluation iteratively, as they plan, assess, and manage their portfolio management approach.

In programs and projects where high complexity is encountered, even the smallest deviation could trigger an unexpected series of events with unforeseen consequences. Senior management and practitioners should be sensitive to any indications that something may be amiss. Complexity is further discussed in Chapter 11 of this book.

Once recognition of complexity and possible effects is achieved, and once a holistic picture of the portfolio system is visualized, a business case for each authorized component should be prepared. Then the portfolio "funnel" (component selection) process will be reapplied. Transparent communication of factual key information reduces complexity. The portfolio manager must constantly strive for an environment of trust and be vigilant for key stakeholders reluctant to demand the information streams needed for timely decisions. Proposed changes are reviewed based on ongoing organizational needs. Monitoring and controlling processes are critical supportive activities for monitoring the portfolio performance and recommending changes to the component mix, performance, and compliance with organizational standards. In addition to enabling corrective actions and providing input for portfolio governance, a further purpose of monitoring and controlling is to understand when changes need to be made to the portfolio or the management processes. These processes include information analysis, documentation, communication of the results, relevant decisions, and support of the resulting actions.

2.4. Portfolio Management Information System (PMIS)

The portfolio management information system (PMIS) consists of the tools and techniques used to gather, integrate, visualize, preserve, and disseminate the outputs of organizational portfolio management. The PMIS used to support all aspects of portfolio management may be integrated with business management tools (the organization's enterprise resource planning, or ERP system, the business process management system, tools to measure and optimize business processes, process modeling tools, etc.), and may be manual or automated depending on the needs of the organization.

Automated tools may include commercial project portfolio management (PPM) applications, as well as an information-gathering and administration system with interfaces to other automated systems. The portfolio management information system is often a collection of spreadsheets rather than automated tools. An effective PMIS enables the portfolio manager to define, analyze, design, produce, and manage information systems to support a successful portfolio, and includes tools and processes such as:

- Software tools;
- Document repositories and version control systems;
- Change or configuration management systems;
- Workflow management;
- Risk database and analysis tools;
- Integrated business process management tools and tools that enable integration with other applications;
- Financial management processes and systems;
- Earned value management processes and tools;
- Enterprise resource planning tools;
- Communication management processes and tools; and
- Knowledge management tools and techniques required to support portfolio management.

The PMIS should be a comprehensive, documented, dynamic set of policies, principles, tools, and controls for portfolio management. The PMIS, when properly implemented, provides direction and integrates information from individual project/program management systems. The implementation of an effective PMIS provides a way to routinely analyze and quantify the value added by each portfolio component and provides input for component valuation and prioritization.

Specifically, the PMIS allows portfolio managers to evaluate:

- Which projects will best support the organization's strategies and goals?
- Is each portfolio component providing the anticipated results, as demonstrated by the portfolio metrics?
- Does each portfolio component have appropriate resources to be successfully completed?

A comprehensive PMIS should contain processes that address continuing performance issues for ongoing components as well as processes that concentrate on the portfolio's evolution, including a selection of new projects and portfolio component termination procedures.

2.5. Governance within the Portfolio Life Cycle

Portfolio governance provides the framework for making decisions, providing oversight, ensuring controls, and overseeing integration within the components. Governance is critical providing accountability, optimizing investments, and reporting issues to executives. It ensures the correct alignment of components to achieve the organizational strategy. Portfolio governance is responsible for decisions regarding resources (e.g., human, financial, material, equipment), and alignment to investment decisions and priorities while existing organizational constraints are being considered (*Governance of Portfolios, Programs, and Projects: A Practice Guide*, PMI, 2016). An example of a portfolio governance organization is presented in the following figure:

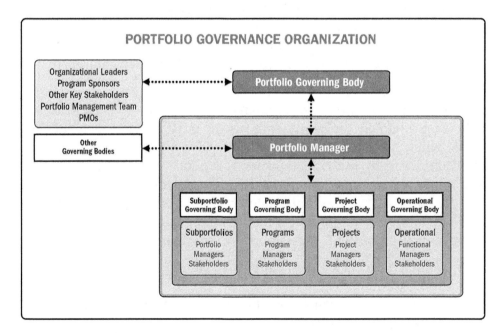

Figure 3.   Example of Portfolio Governance Organization[6]

Portfolio management governance is the structure and exercise of authority for the efforts and portfolios within the portfolio management domain. The components of portfolio management governance are:

- A set of governance principles;
- A governance framework or structure;
- Leadership, commitment, and support from the top;
- Controls implementation;
- Capability enablement;
- Description of decision-making authority;
- Communication of strategic objectives; and
- Governing roles and responsibilities.

To balance risk and efficiency, it is important to consider the complexity encountered within the portfolio environment, as well as the complexity carried over by the portfolio components as the portfolio governance structure, resources, and processes are designed and implemented. By choosing a flexible and proactive approach toward enforcing the governance principles and processes, an organization can achieve a high level of efficiency for its portfolio management function. The portfolio governance domain is further detailed in Chapter 4 of this book.

2.6. Portfolio Stakeholders

Portfolio stakeholders are individuals or groups whose interests may be positively or negatively affected by the components or the implementation of portfolio management. They may also exert influence over the portfolio, components, applied principles and practices, and most importantly, on decisions regarding the portfolio and its management. The level of involvement by stakeholders may vary from organization to organization or from portfolio to portfolio within an organization. Depending on the size and type of the organization as well as project and program management practices, certain stakeholders may be specifically identified according to the goals and risk management strategies for the portfolio. Close communication with portfolio stakeholders, navigating through the complexity introduced by component interdependencies, and the management of risk and emergent issues rising from stakeholder behavior, is paramount to the portfolio life cycle. Stakeholders may include but are not limited to the CEO and other executives, functional management, operations management, legal, finance, human resources, PMO, program/project teams as well as external stakeholders influencing organizational objectives.

Portfolio managers should focus on ensuring key stakeholders are aligned with and are actively supporting the portfolio's goals. Different views will often be encountered; each stakeholder is focusing on the components that affect that individual stakeholder. The portfolio manager strives to achieve balance and steer communications toward driving holistic understanding and consensus. The principal message is how the portfolio and its key components tie to organizational strategy. There should always be a direct link from the lowest level of defined goals and objectives to the organizational strategy. For any component mismatch, there needs to be a verification of scope. All approved change initiatives (portfolio components) and the scope defined within those initiatives should support the overarching organizational goals.

2.7. Portfolio Component Interdependencies and System Dynamics – Managing Dependencies and Component Interfaces

The portfolio system's functionality is primarily defined by component interactions, their subsystems' interactions, and interactions between these and external entities from the portfolio environment. Each interaction is constrained by structural, contextual, and behavioral dependencies that may greatly influence each component's behavior. Furthermore, these dependencies change over time. This subsection will examine how dependencies across various portfolio components are identified, analyzed, and managed. Dependencies may affect changes in a portfolio's components influencing, for example, scopes, time lines, costs, etc. Complexity increases considerably when dealing with dependencies within a set of portfolios. Dependencies of systems, subsystems, and components can be directional or bidirectional (sometimes referred to in the literature as interdependencies or mutual dependencies). They can be internal (i.e., from components of the portfolio system of reference) or external (i.e., resulting from interconnections of system components with other entities from the portfolio environment). In this book, the term *dependency* is used to describe all dependencies related to the portfolio system.

2.7.1. Dependencies across portfolio components

The effects of key dependencies may result in dramatic impacts; this may cause a strategic shift in an organization's portfolio structure and long-term direction. A dependency may be "a subordinate condition," (i.e., dependencies have hierarchies). An example of a hierarchical dependency is for a situation in which for A to occur, B must occur or be present—or not occur or be present. There are many types of dependencies within a portfolio. There are organizational dependencies, environmental dependencies, stakeholder dependencies, group dependencies, component dependencies, task dependencies, and so forth. Furthermore, dependencies within the portfolio evolve because components necessarily have varyingly scoped business cases and constraints. The ability to negotiate and creatively arrive at the best return on investment (ROI) of resources for the organization is paramount in managing dependencies at all levels within a portfolio or set of portfolios. Dependencies could also not be identified in documentation up front, and could be found during more detailed planning reviews, execution, or risk identification sessions. It may be possible that dependencies are not known until the time when these discussions occur. Dependencies may also co-evolve at various time periods within the portfolio life cycle.

2.7.2. Dependencies across other portfolios and their components

Dependencies may lie across various portfolios (and their respective components) within an organization. For example, if Portfolio A has to produce a new product by a certain date in order for Portfolio B to use that product in its multifaceted product customer market and beat the competition to market, then Portfolio B has a dependency on Portfolio A. Similarly, a portfolio's programs, projects, tasks, related operations, stakeholders' component teams, and so on may have interdependencies at every level. At the project level and for tasks, most dependencies tend to be technical, although the complexity introduced by the "human factor" should always be proactively accounted for. Dependencies at this level assist in building a critical path, and it is within the role of the project manager to prioritize the related resources and to deconflict as required. At the higher levels, program and portfolio managers need to coordinate across organizational constructs to ensure a coordinated approach. Practices to be followed include the following:

- Portfolio managers prioritize dependencies across their various portfolios and programs;
- Communication processes for identification and prioritization of dependencies should be similar to the governance structure of the organization;
- Governance, authority, and oversight trickle down the organizational levels while escalation acts as a feedback loop to incorporate change as the plan is executed; and
- Dependencies need to be identified, tracked, reported, prioritized, and managed.

Facilitation skills are critical to the portfolio, as are the negotiating skills of the portfolio manager. In cases with a conflict in the dependencies of multiple projects or programs, the effect of one course of action or another (grant one project or program the resource instead of the other) will most likely depend on the business outcome trade-off. The decision of how to proceed will usually be made at the portfolio governance level—that is, the level overseeing both projects/programs that are contending for the same resource—so, when briefing at that level, a clear statement on the business outcome will go much further than a technical, detail-oriented discussion. To facilitate the tracking of dependencies within portfolios, their components, and external entities, a dependency register or similar tool should be developed and managed at the portfolio level. Dependencies are an inherent risk and should be tracked in the portfolio risk register and cross-referenced in the dependency register.

Once the dependency register is developed, dependency diagrams or maps may be created. Dependencies are often depicted in time-based diagrams, where groups of "same-type" dependencies are shown on a common time scale, in network diagrams, in mind-map diagrams, and with other mapping tools. Time-scale diagrams for portfolios with many interrelated components can become quite complicated, particularly when several dependencies occur simultaneously. Network diagrams usually encompass representations of component importance (determined per key information, e.g., investment level, priority, strategic fit, ROI, etc.), represented by node size and color, and criticality of dependency or interdependency represented by arrow width and color.

Processes for managing dependencies should be clear and as simple as possible. A dependency review/validation cycle should be established and followed. New dependencies may be identified in each review cycle and terminated ones should be eliminated. In some organizations, the PMO keeps track of the dependency management repository. It is advisable that such a repository be available to all involved or interested in portfolio progress and performance. Dependencies may have considerable impacts on a number of portfolio component system parts, such as milestone/deliverable outcomes, financial benefits, assumptions at the portfolio level, mitigation/resolution plans as part of portfolio risk management plan or risk management plans within portfolio components, organization metrics within business/IT, resource capacity planning availabilities, and so on. Examples of external dependencies might come from legal, regulatory, economic, or governmental policies. Often, changes in a component's scope may affect other component activities, work packages, resources, and so forth down the timeline. For example, a small scope change for a subcontractor may have a serious impact on other contractors working down the timeline.

Dependencies should be considered when approving changes, because the cost of reversing a decision can have a severe financial impact on some components. An evaluation of such effects is recommended before decisions are taken. Further, at the portfolio level, resource dependencies are very important.

The following practices are advisable for dependency management:

- Multiple portfolios within an organization may require specific resources (funding, personnel, equipment, etc.) at specific times. Portfolio managers need to coordinate with one another to ensure that resources are available as planned in their portfolio resource plans and report to the enterprise portfolio governance for key decisions;
- Any delay in the availability of required resources is discussed as a potential risk and a mitigation plan should be developed and agreed upon; and
- If a resource is not available, the portfolio manager may decide to wait until it becomes available or decide to bring additional resources on board from outside the organization at an additional cost if that is preferred. Portfolio managers should remain aware of the status of resource dependencies

across various portfolios (portfolio-external resource dependencies), and the portfolio's components (portfolio-internal resource dependencies). As shared resources' availability changes, the portfolio plan should be updated to account for these changes.

2.7.3. The impact of dependencies on risk, scope, benefits, cost, and time

Dependencies can dramatically impact component schedule, cost, performance, and so on. Discussions with key stakeholders to identify dependencies and mapping each component and their key subsystem dependencies may help understand interrelationships and their possible effects, consequently enabling the planning of proactive actions. Dependencies can affect scope and component costs/benefits, add additional risk that impacts costs, and affect the timeline of portfolios.

2.7.4. The impact of dependencies on strategic business objectives

Strategic business objectives help the portfolio manager align efforts with the organization's mission priorities. Multiple portfolios and their components have multiple interconnections, feedback loops, and shared dependencies. For example, a new shift in an organization's mission to "be first to market with an innovative product" may cause multiple portfolios and their components to become dependent upon the critical subject matter expert (SME) resources within the organization. By explaining the change in mission, goals, and objectives, leaders can help portfolio managers properly prioritize available resources. This ensures that dependencies are well understood and agreed to by all parts of the organization, at the portfolio and component levels. Knowledge management is paramount here. In organizations, portfolio managers are positioned to bridge leadership vision with the organization's governance, standardization, visibility, control, decisions, and execution. Portfolio management connects strategic business objectives to execution. One way this is enabled is by allocating resources via the planning process and by incorporating dependencies into that planning cycle.

2.7.5. Navigating dependency issues

Different portfolio stakeholders tend to have diverging understandings of situations, contexts, behaviors, risks, priorities, and many other types of dependency causes, as well as of their effects. To create a common understanding, tools are used to explore the key stakeholders' multiple understandings and their implications. One useful tool for creating a common understanding is offered by the concept of frames. A frame is a collection of content, structure, and bias for action on a subject. Frame, or conditional framing, analysis aids in creating awareness and making sense of stakeholders' multiple understandings and desires that arise from different situations and phenomena, as well as of the cognitive biases to which they give rise. The relationship between cognitive biases and frames is both dynamic and reciprocal. Perceptions form parts of frames, which in turn, may shape and influence perceptions. Frame analysis helps the portfolio manager to "frame," that is, create a mental model of various groupings of the organizational construct (entities, components, structure, content, behavior) and determine dependencies across those groupings. Different scenarios of "how things are expected to work" are usually mapped.

Some aspects to consider in conditional framework analysis include:

- Cost and resources required for accomplishing or not accomplishing components need to be considered;
- Circular dependencies that can force components in or out if not adequately considered up front;
- Sets of component dependencies may be tested in different portfolio scenarios;
- Multiple dependency sets may be developed, and results compared; and
- Software packages may enhance this type of analysis.

Another useful technique is interdependency analysis. This technique is used to identify dependencies among portfolios, components, or external entities. Interdependency analysis identifies dependencies the portfolio has between itself and:

- Other portfolios within the organization;
- Components within the portfolio;
- Components within other portfolios; and
- The environment of the organization.

Dependencies to be analyzed may include:

- Resources;
- Finance;

- Quality;
- Risks; and
- Timelines.

Participants in this analysis may include all portfolio and component managers plus additional stakeholders supporting these portfolios. Further, both qualitative and quantitative dependency analysis techniques are used in, for example:

- Qualitative and quantitative approaches to studying the demand for resources against capacity and constraints to determine how best to allocate resources. When bottleneck resources or resource downtime are identified, resource leveling or component sequencing techniques can be applied. Resource leveling strives to smooth performance levels by managing bottleneck areas and communicating delayed schedules, if necessary. Recommended changes, requests for more resources, and updates are communicated to the governing body when resource leveling does not produce sufficient results.

- A quantitative analysis is usually performed when numerical data on the effects of certain dependencies and corresponding interactions are available, enabling the portfolio manager to compare probable outcomes over time and cost, arriving at statistical benchmarks and comparisons indicating preferred courses of action.

- Qualitative analysis, dependency analysis, review of resource schedules, and implementation of changes to improve capacity become quantitative when the number of full-time equivalents (FTEs) required and number of hours to be allocated for each component, and so on, are included in calculations.

- Trend analysis using historical data can be performed to determine whether resource requirements have been consistently underestimated or if resources are consistently over- or underperforming and adjustments need to be made.

The previous examples of existing tools and techniques are often used for dependency analysis. The appropriate tool or technique for the job will vary from situation to situation. Familiarity with the approach and availability of related software as well as other variables may affect a portfolio manager's decision regarding the preferred set of tools and techniques. Common issues that prevent exercising dependency management, which the portfolio manager may have to face and overcome, include:

- Lack of appreciation within senior management of the impact of dependency-related emergent problems, issues, and risks to portfolio components;
- Lack of clear managerial processes (identifying, documenting, resolving, or mitigating); and
- Lack of coordinated decisions (nonalignment to a common authority—portfolio governance—for all organizational component work).

It should also be noted that portfolio dependency management on certain key decisions may involve portfolio governance because related organizational operations, such as human resources, financial functions, enterprise architecture development, and so forth, are also usually involved.

Following dependency analysis and understanding how component interrelationships affect one another—usually by identifying, documenting, and mapping them—an organization can take appropriate actions based on its key portfolio's drivers. When demand is the primary driver, the organization needs to adjust the resource supply (through temporary and permanent resources). When the resource supply is relatively fixed, the organization needs to manage the project demand and sequence project work based on resource availability and component priority. In many cases, organizations will adjust resource supply and manage component demand simultaneously. Therefore, a key driver for portfolio management success is effective component dependency management. Dependency management must include identification of dependencies among portfolio components or with external entities, identified either within other portfolios or within the portfolio environment in general. Portfolio component dependencies should be analyzed and tracked on an ongoing basis.

2.8. Organizational Influences on Portfolio Management

Successful portfolio management requires all management levels to support and communicate the value of portfolio management to the organization and external stakeholders. When making portfolio decisions, organizations are influenced by a variety of constraints and dynamics brought by the stakeholders. Portfolio management is most successful when it balances stakeholder interests, both short term and long term, while staying aligned with the organizational strategy and objectives and considering resource constraints. Naturally, the organizational structure (e.g., functional, matrix, projectized) considerably influences the implementation of portfolio management and most importantly, the organizational maturity. The portfolio manager needs to make decisions in the best interest of the organizational strategy and objectives regardless of the impact to individual components, including termination. Examples of forces (flows and feedback loops as mentioned in previous sections, plus the application of the law of requisite variety, i.e., control systems) influencing portfolio management are specified in the following sections.

2.8.1. Organizational maturity

The organization as a whole should understand the need for portfolio management and commit its leadership, resources (i.e., people, capital, and equipment), processes, and tools to make it successful. It is important that the philosophy of portfolio management permeates the entire organization. This means that all other activities and processes take into account the impact on or influence of portfolio management, even if the effect is slight. For instance, general performance measures should be complementary with those used for assessing portfolio components. Portfolio governance has a leading role toward such compliance. The term organizational maturity may be applied to the acceptance of portfolio management in the same way as it may apply to program or project management. The level of application and the success of portfolio management are directly affected by the level of maturity in the organization. Lack of organizational support for portfolio management is a major obstacle to success. Portfolio management and the decisions resulting from it should be accepted at all levels within the organization. There is a threat that, while the concept and necessity of portfolio management are accepted by executives in the organization, the resulting decisions may not be. Acceptance of portfolio management principles and decisions throughout the organization are necessary for portfolio management success.

Another important element is the organization's ability to implement the changes recommended by portfolio management. The inability to execute change is distinct from lack of acceptance of the recommendations; it refers to an inability to implement the desired changes. Complexity introduced by change initiatives is usually exponentially analogous to the number of people impacted by that change. Moreover, not recognizing and formalizing the organization's ability to handle change enhances complexity and usually is an obstacle to realizing the benefits expected from portfolio management. Furthermore, each portfolio component manager should consistently apply the principles described in this chapter to facilitate and handle organizational change. The extent of change that the organization can accept may be one of the factors used to determine the appropriate mix of portfolio components. This is quite important since reaching strategic objectives usually entails some expected level of change to the organization's subsystems, such as people, resources, processes, products, and technologies. Figure 4 demonstrates the relationship between change initiatives and complexity.

Finally, organizational maturity includes effective metrics. Three important capability metrics for the whole domain of portfolio management in any organization are:

- Metrics on adherence to established principles and processes;
- Valuation of portfolio system structure; and
- Behavior, maturity, competence, and culture of the portfolio manager and team.

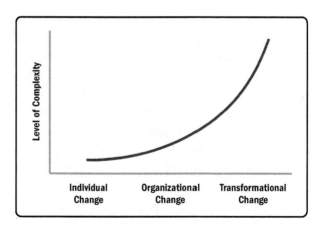

Figure 4.   Relationship between Change Initiatives and Complexity[7]

More specifically, portfolio management maturity assessment assesses the organizations in the following areas. This includes, but is not limited to:

- Strategic alignment;
- Portfolio management governance;
- Portfolio performance;
- Portfolio risk management; and
- Communications management.

A holistic approach has been proved to be quite important for the development and consistent implementation of these metrics.

2.8.2. Organizational impacts

This topic is closely related to organizational maturity described in Section 2.7.1. The distinction is that organizational impact refers to the impact that portfolio management has on the organization rather than on the organizational maturity in which portfolio management operates. First and foremost, portfolio management enables strategy execution. The probability of misalignment between strategic objectives and component-related work may increase without the presence of effective portfolio management. Further, portfolio management enables a holistic, contextual view of the whole organization and particularly when change influences the environment within which the organization operates. Portfolio management works bilaterally with strategy, and while strategy determines the portfolio and its management, portfolio management may influence toward adopting strategic objectives to a new emerging environment.

Effective portfolio management may also have a positive impact on the organization by facilitating tactical and operational planning, plus execution of strategic change initiatives in alignment with strategic goals. Conversely, the lack of efficient and effective processes and procedures in other functional areas of the organization may have a considerable impact on portfolio management. An example is the lack of an effective resource-assignment process to support the execution of projects and programs approved through portfolio management. Thus, executives and portfolio managers will need to factor organizational impacts into their corresponding plans and decisions and strive toward the application of the following essential principles for successful portfolio management.[8]

- Elevate portfolio management to a strategic level. It's imperative that senior management understands and supports the practice of portfolio management.

- Create a portfolio-minded culture. Senior management must be willing to show its support of portfolio management through communication, investment, dedicated resources, and effective sponsorship.
- Implement appropriate tools and practices. Senior management must understand the need to implement established portfolio management tools and practices and to standardize the practice of portfolio management throughout the organization.

2.9. The Portfolio Life Cycle – Further Considerations

Based on the considerations already presented, portfolio management is best established, developed, and implemented under a system-engineered organizational context. The following points include certain considerations for the practitioner to address, particularly during the development of the portfolio system, and then at regular intervals during the entire life cycle of the portfolio, until decommissioning.

2.9.1. Organizational framework for strategic execution

- Clear strategic objectives – This includes a well-defined strategy to achieve the objectives and a S.M.A.R.T. (specific, measurable, attainable, realistic, and timely) strategic plan, which is regularly reviewed;
- Validate and cross-check strategic objectives – Ensure the adequacy of the means and allocated resources to implement the strategic plan through the application of established portfolio management principles and practices;
- Portfolio governance – Apply, sponsor, and oversee portfolio management as a key part of the organization's strategic management cycle. Understand and communicate organizational constraints;
- Integration of business and portfolio management principles, processes, and practices, that is, integration of sets of activities to serve the specific portfolio objectives. Create buffers for key portfolio components;
- Correlation of portfolio management with the enterprise risk management framework and the organization's budgeting and profit-and-loss cycles;

- Making investment decisions – All portfolio components represent investments made or planned;
- Utilization of external resources – Oversee supply chain management;
- Lean approach – Applying systems thinking by imitating the principles that govern biological systems and predominant processes: flexibility (a critical control subsystem) and evolution (the most adaptable survive), create a repository of successful (effective and efficient) project portfolio adaptations; and
- When validated analysis points this way, terminate portfolio components. This is healthy; sometimes fewer portfolio components may lead to a more focused organization. No point in throwing good money after bad.

2.9.2. Portfolio considerations and characteristics

- Portfolio structure and capabilities – Look at the system from the outside as well as the inside. Examine and act based on both internal and external factors created by portfolio component interdependencies (reinforcing or balancing loops);
- Portfolio history – Create a repository of historical data, good practices, and lessons learned;
- Focus on the most important portfolio components, then try to cover the spectrum of components with the remaining resources. Insist on "kills" if audits point to such necessity. It is advisable for the selection of the most important portfolio components to fit the 20/80 Pareto principle;
- Portfolio component characteristics – Record components' contributions to and alignment with organizational objectives. Look for the effects of the interactions of the whole portfolio ecosystem;
- Record and monitor sustainable operational support activities, once portfolio components are authorized and prioritized;
- Understand component interdependencies with respect to available resources, and resourcing portfolio components correctly is paramount, particularly for the most important programs and projects of the organization. This is an area that most constraints and resulting bottlenecks are found;

- Be vigilant for complexity introduced from new, terminated, or delayed projects;
- Beware of requirements for planning changes due to ambiguity and changes in the portfolio ecosystem. Plans need to be monitored and adjusted accordingly;
- Portfolio component resources and capabilities need to be monitored and optimized continuously in a complex, dynamic environment;
- Create and utilize reports on expected benefits realization (iterative process). Project prioritization should follow a benefits hierarchy; and
- Portfolio management success depends primarily on executive management leadership, sponsorship, and strategy as well as portfolio management team talent, experience, and hard work.

Additionally, it is important to regularly perform consolidated risk assessments for the portfolio, to determine whether risk is within the acceptance criteria set by the organization. Since portfolios and their environments are dynamic, portfolio managers should review and adapt their portfolio risk management plans on a regular basis for the duration of the portfolio life cycle, considering each time the new issues, problems, and risks that have emerged due to the ever-present complexity. After all, it has been proved beyond any doubt that extreme events are ubiquitous in a wide range of human-made, dynamic systems, including portfolio systems.

CHAPTER 3

Portfolio Strategic Management

by Steve Butler, Te Wu, and
Panos Chatzipanos

> Tactics is the art of using troops in battle; strategy is
> the art of using battles to win the war.
> — **Carl von Clausewitz**

3.1. Strategy and Strategy Alignment

Organizational strategy is created by considering and asserting how an organization's primary goals will be pursued and attained. The portfolio management process encompasses a managerial framework for such top-level considerations. Strategic challenges need cohesive responses and coherent actions, and organizational goals need to cascade through strategic planning ending up as portfolios of change initiatives—mainly programs and projects. These become the vehicles for accomplishing the approved strategic objectives of the organization. Portfolio strategic management is the active alignment of the portfolio with the accepted organizational strategy, which includes the organization's mission and vision, goals and strategic objectives, and key performance indicators. It involves the management of intended and emergent initiatives, usually decided at the executive level. Strategic management consists of the ongoing activities and processes that organizations use to make the strategy happen, by aligning resources and activities with the mission, vision, and strategy. The system also provides strategic performance feedback to decision making and enables the strategic plan to evolve and grow within a disciplined framework as requirements and other circumstances change.

Organizations make strategic choices about which activities must be implemented in order to achieve success and deliver their vision. These strategic choices, once made, will form strategic portfolios, which will likely have a significant impact on the success of an organization. The process of deciding where best to focus finite resources in order to achieve strategic objectives is what is called portfolio strategic management. Determining the right strategy is essential to the overall organizational process. In a business environment, strategic alignment happens when all elements essential to a business, from market strategy to organizational structure, are arranged to support an organization's long-term purpose. Because business strategies and organizational structures change, realigning all these elements can be quite challenging. This makes portfolio strategic management challenging for anyone concerned.

By closely associating the portfolio value with the strategy, portfolio managers can directly contribute to the advancement of the organizational goals. Moreover, the successful implementation of strategy requires an assessment of the "right thing" being done. This continuous assessment needs a holistic understanding of the organizational environment, a consistent alignment of the portfolio components with organizational mission and goals, and a disciplined managerial framework for effective responses to the numerous challenges encountered during the portfolio life cycle.[9] This alignment enables a direct link between the implementation of the programs and projects and the organization strategy with portfolio management serving as the vital bridge. A 2015 PMI study shows that companies with mature portfolio management achieve 35 percent more of their programs successfully than organizations with minimally effective portfolio management.[10] In other words, companies with mature portfolio management waste less money and fail less often. Furthermore, sustainable competitive advantage requires organizational assets that are capable of providing continuous benefits, which cannot be quickly or easily copied by the competition. Portfolio management capabilities that have matured over time and practice and have been integrated with the organizational culture are not easy to copy. Research has proven that such an established framework is repeatedly associated with successful outcomes.[11]

Examined another way, the core purpose of portfolio management is the selection, prioritization, approval, resourcing, and realization of investments—change initiatives—(e.g., programs, projects, and other activities) that are executed under a proven successful framework of managerial principles, processes, and good practices. The portfolio manager will select, prioritize, and approve proposed portfolio components to begin, establishing criteria for governance actions, such as deciding when projects/programs should proceed, be terminated, or suspended prior to originally planned completion dates. Through the review of strategic, tactical, and operational capabilities and gaps, the portfolio management process provides feedback that is useful for the planning and management of resource demand and for monitoring the health of the portfolio. The portfolio manager should report portfolio performance as it relates to achieving the organizational strategy.

Studies have found that effective strategic alignment has a constructive impact on the portfolio management performance and vice versa. In short, strong alignment between portfolio management and strategy is paramount for organizations to achieve competitive advantage over their competitors. A necessary prerequisite to strong alignment is having a well-defined strategy. Numerous research results have documented that many organizations encounter major difficulties and often fail in implementing strategy. This starts by organizations not having a well-defined strategy. But even with good strategies, poor communication, stakeholder management, and execution can also jeopardize strategy execution.[12] Organizations cannot expect successful execution of their strategic objectives unless strategies can be clearly described, communicated, and understood. Strategy needs to be translated to understandable operational terms; the whole organization needs to be aligned to the strategy; the strategy must be translated into a continual business process; and all strategic change initiatives must be sponsored by executive leadership. A strategic plan needs to be carefully developed. The proper perspective for developing the strategic plan has been defined by Clausewitz in his famous saying: "the enemy of a good plan is the dream of a perfect plan."[13]

Therefore, both an effective strategy must be defined, and a S.M.A.R.T. strategic plan developed. Yet emphasis placed on creating the right strategy is not enough for successful business results. Making strategy work successfully is more difficult than making strategy.[14] Once the right strategy is created, the organization needs to have the ability to successfully execute its strategy. For this major organizational capability, research has proved that maturity in portfolio management is very important. Usually the problem is not bad strategy, but bad execution of strategy.[15] Problems with implementing strategy—the only sustainable way by which the organization may create value—usually have to do with the adopted managerial framework of execution, measuring and managing performance, stakeholder engagement, resources spread thin, and so forth. PMI research[16] indicates that maturity in portfolio management considerably enhances value creation.[17, 18, 19]

Portfolio management should be viewed as a dynamic process of strategic alignment and focus in which organizations constantly add, modify, complete, or terminate portfolio components. By applying a more centralized approach to managing a group of related projects and programs through portfolio management and potentially creating various portfolio scenarios to meet the challenge of environmental change, organizations enhance their strategic agility through advanced and thorough planning, identification, and analysis of risks at all organizational levels, reduction of conflicts and overlaps among portfolio components, and efficient allocation of precious resources.

The portfolio manager may evaluate the performance of portfolio components, and the portfolio as a whole, in relation to the key indicators and the organizational strategy and objectives. During a typical organization cycle, the portfolio manager monitors, evaluates, and validates portfolio components relative to the following:

- Alignment with organizational strategy and objectives;
- Viability as part of the portfolio, based on key performance indicators and an acceptable level of risk;
- Value/benefit and relationship to other portfolio components;
- Available resources and portfolio priorities; and
- Additions and deletions of portfolio components.

To achieve strong alignment, portfolio managers need to consider the following activities:

- Enabling well-defined strategy;
- Understanding the strategic risk appetite;
- Developing portfolio goals and strategic objectives;
- Creating the portfolio charter;
- Building the portfolio roadmap; and
- Managing strategic alignment—developing the strategic plan—managing strategic change.

3.2. Enabling Well-Defined Strategy

A well-defined organizational strategy enhances successful project portfolio management practices. The strength of the organizational strategy is generally revealed in its clarity of mission, the precision of the goals, the measurability of the objectives, soundness of the vision, and the thoroughness of communication. Strategic planning can be described as a disciplined activity that is used to set priorities, focus energy and resources in a potentially changing environment, establish agreement around intended outcomes/results, and ensure that employees and other stakeholders are working toward common goals. It effectively shapes and guides what an organization is; who it serves; and why, what, and when it does things over the short, medium, and longer terms. Effective strategic planning articulates not only where an organization is going, but how to get there and when and how to know when it gets there. The portfolio strategic plan, discussed in a following subsection, involves the evaluation of high-level organization strategy/investment decisions and defining the strategy in portfolio-related strategic goals and objectives.

Depending on organizations' history, culture, choices, and management styles, organizations have adopted different types of strategies. While a thorough discussion of strategy type is beyond the scope of this chapter, there are two types that form a continuum from up-front and detailed planning to more anticipative planning with the specifics that emerge over time. An extension of the emergent is the incorporation of organizational learning, which is sufficiently distinct to be considered as the third type of different strategy.

- A deliberate strategy is characterized by the thoroughness of planning at every level of the strategy development. Michael Porter's "Three Generic Strategies"[20] (e.g., cost leadership, differentiation, and focus) and "Five Forces Model"[21] (e.g., competitive rivalry, supplier power, buyer power, threat of substitution, threat of new entry) are examples of the deliberate strategy.
- An emergent strategy,[22] on the other hand, views that the real strategy or plan of action comes forth over time as even the best plans rarely survive the first major issues. Henry Mintzberg,[23] who developed this type of strategy, believes that the collisions of plans with reality are unavoidable, as no organization

can control the external environment. Therefore, instead of wasting time on the detailed planning, organizations should adopt a set of behaviors that are consistent with its principles and learn to adapt its plan with the reality. This emergence suggests a more incremental approach to strategy formulation and implementation, where results are regularly appraised against benefits, and changes are made and managed against the evolving picture of performance.

- An organizational learning strategy, as put forth by Chris Argyris,[24, 25] is a natural extension of the emergent strategy. Even a deliberate strategy can also incorporate organizational learning as it evolves the strategy. In organizational learning strategy, organizations can experience three types of learning: 1) Single-loop, or adaptive learning, occurs when organizations detect and correct their actions as necessary. This enables a continual course correction and adds to the knowledge of the firm, but without fundamental changes to how the organization performs its activities; 2) Double-loop, or generative learning, occurs when the organizations examine and change the existing processes and norms. This is viewed as higher-level learning; and 3) Deutero-learning, or learning about learning, encourages organizations to reconsider their current paradigm, leading to transformative changes.

The types of strategy significantly affect the design of portfolio management in organizations, as shown in Table 3.

Today, most organizations rarely adopt a single strategy type. However, there is usually a clear preference or leaning toward one strategy type over another. For portfolio managers looking to align portfolio management with the organizational strategy, understanding the type of strategy that their portfolios need to align with can provide vital insights on how to best structure their portfolio management overall process. Portfolios have a bilateral relationship with the corporate environment in which they evolve. Moreover, there may be multiple strategy-planning processes and practices. The integrated organizational strategy—usually a hybrid from the available theoretical models—once developed, needs to be approved and actively sponsored by executive management. Strategy should not be realized in a rigid manner. A certain amount of flexibility and adaptability always must be reached; consequently, a dynamic alignment process must be

Table 3.   Types of Strategy and Implication on Portfolio Management

#	Strategy Type	Implication on Portfolio Management
1	Deliberate Strategy	Organizations practicing deliberate strategy often have well-defined policies, processes, and procedures. New ideas and proposals are methodologically reviewed and progress to a predictive process of vetting and approval. The implementation also follows predictable paths. The strengths of a deliberate strategy with deliberate portfolio management process are clarity, consistency, and predictability. The challenge is tackling uncertainty, especially the unknown unknowns. When the situations are beyond what the clear guidelines can handle, the ability to adapt is often weak.
2	Emergent Strategy	With emergent organizations, firms often establish a well-defined direction and make a series of high-level choices, such as investment choices for their products and services. However, the details of the specific projects or components are often known much later in the process as the reality emerges—strategy becomes evident as events/evolving situations emerge with time. Strategy is rarely implemented in a rigid, normative manner. For portfolio management, there can be robust process, but there are also considerable discretions either with the portfolio governance or portfolio manager. The strength is greater adaptability, especially when genuine surprises occur. However, the weakness is that there can be a lack of rigid guidelines and strategies, which results in more discussions and deliberations.
3	Organizational Learning	While organizational learning can be incorporated into both deliberate and emergent strategy, it is much more compatible with the emergent strategy. The emphasis of organizational learning is the practice of single, double, and deutero learning, as organizations constantly seek ways to advance their organizational capabilities through learning. For portfolio management, much more emphasis is placed on reflection and reviews. The strengths are continuous improvement. However, when organizational learning is implemented poorly or excessively, this strategy can lead to a paralysis of actions, as organizations spend considerable effort learning for the sake of learning.

developed and followed by portfolio management practitioners. On the other hand, a formal strategy process is important, particularly at the initiation and planning phases; it brings discipline, clarity, and common understanding.

If the organizational strategic planning process determines that a goal is no longer valid for the organization, the portfolio manager should review the portfolio and recommend the reassessment of any portfolio components that are in place to achieve the obsolete goal. Organizations normally apply some form of control over portfolio components. For example, a phase-gate review is commonly applied to projects in those portfolios concentrating on research activities. Governance processes are often characterized by regular reviews at key decision milestones during the life of the major portfolio components. Senior stakeholders in governance roles analyze the risks and benefits associated with continuing each particular component. The purpose of such an analysis should be to assess the probability of success for various aspects of the component at multiple milestone points during the life cycle of that component. Such "gate analysis" is usually conducted at portfolio review meetings. For instance, the legal, engineering, financial, and commercial aspects of the product are included in the early-stage assessments when the immediate investment decision is about research and development. As the component execution progresses, the legal, engineering, scientific, and other aspects continue to be assessed. Assessment results support governance decision making and are stored as portfolio information.

In some organizations, it is possible, and even likely, that there is no well-defined strategy or the defined strategy is outdated or weak. For portfolio managers, this is an unfortunate but likely reality. In these situations, portfolio managers should work with their executives to define a workable strategy that can serve as the basis of support for the portfolio. In most cases, a hierarchy of strategic objectives is important for implementing strategy. Such a hierarchy may be a highly effective means of managing strategy and communicating it to the whole organization. A culture of achieving excellence in strategic execution is a huge organizational asset. A variety of methodologies, techniques, and performance management frameworks exist that are intended to manage strategic initiatives along the different phases of their life cycle. For example, strategies can be defined using strategic maps or goal models. Typically, strategic initiatives identify opportunities and enact change through a continuous process of monitoring and measurement to align operational performance with strategic targets.

A tool-supported methodology that can integrate goals, processes, and performance is essential to help management implement such initiatives by automating or semi-automating some of the implementations. Such a methodology mostly includes the business intelligence model, the portfolio strategic plan, the portfolio charter, the portfolio roadmap, and the processes of managing portfolio strategic alignment. The business intelligence model allows business users to conceptualize their business operations and strategies using concepts that are familiar to them, including actor, directive, intention, event, situation, indicator, influence, and process. It is drawn upon well-established concepts and practices in the business community, such as the balanced scorecard and strategy maps, as well as techniques from conceptual modeling and enterprise modeling, such as metamodeling, sensemaking, and goal-modeling techniques.

3.3. Understanding Strategic Risk Appetite

The factors of risk management, the maturity of project portfolio management, and organizational structure must also be taken into consideration to ensure an effective alignment of portfolios with organizational strategies. When it comes to risk management, a continuous balance between positive (or opportunity) and negative risk (or threat) must be achieved. This dynamic process involves taking advantage of the opportunities and the mitigation of threats. As already stated, the value of a portfolio regarding its effective alignment with the organizational strategy is the result of opportunity, risk management, and performance management. Comprehension of the strategic objectives and the envisioned added value obtained once the portfolio components are successfully executed is paramount in this context.

After determining the organizational strategy that can serve as the foundation for the portfolio, portfolio managers should determine the risk appetite of the sponsoring organization. This is a core consideration. Risk appetite is the amount of uncertainty that an organization is willing to accept to meet its strategy. Depending on the culture, history, position, tactical goals, and long-term vision, organizations can have very different risk appetites, even for organizations in the same industry. For example, in the case of two competing firms in the same industry, one firm is willing to explore cutting-edge technology and thus has a much higher risk appetite than the other firm, which focuses on proven technologies. As portfolio managers work with their executives on determining the risk appetite for the portfolio, it is important to understand and communicate that risk is pervasive, as sometimes the avoidance of action is riskier than tackling the challenges head-on.

More importantly, portfolio managers should focus on both the negative risks or threats and positive risks or opportunities. Their objective is to constantly balance risk by accepting the right amount of risk commensurate with the anticipated rewards. Under this dynamic balance during the whole portfolio life cycle, delivery of the optimum outcomes for the organization in the short, medium, and longer terms may be achieved. Portfolio governance may choose to actively embrace larger risks in anticipation of higher rewards. Organizational environment may contribute to portfolio risk considerably (e.g., poor management practices or an extensive number of portfolio components, i.e., negative risks, threats), integrated management systems or fully engaged key stakeholders (i.e., positive risks, opportunities). Disciplined risk management is critical for root cause correction of threats or capitalization of opportunities. Organizational risk appetite may vary during the portfolio life cycle, when, for example, the organizational environment evolves or the corrections of risk root causes mitigate threats. The portfolio manager must aggregate risk responses, provision certain resources as management reserves, and provide contingency plans to manage risk. Successful portfolio risk management usually allows for an increased risk appetite as the portfolio life cycle progresses.

Defining a specific risk threshold can be difficult, as there are myriad categories of risks. Organizations often have different tolerances and metrics for risks. Some common risk categories include financial, marketing, operational, human resources, customer, and innovation. Portfolio managers should examine these and other risk categories and work with their executives and teams to develop the maximum level of risk tolerance. Where quantitative measures are not feasible, the qualitative descriptions can also serve as important guidelines. How much risk an organization undertakes plays a larger part in whether that uncertain future outcome adds or deducts value from the organization. Risk appetite and risk tolerance[26] are directly linked with organizational strategy and are usually defined by top management. Portfolio strategic management incorporates risk appetite management, which is responsible for determining acceptable risk boundaries. The portfolio manager usually proposes to portfolio governance definitions of risk boundaries. In such cases, the portfolio management team is responsible for calculating and articulating risk tolerance, developing and submitting portfolio risk scenarios for balancing risks during daily management, making the trade-offs of risks and rewards, and for regularly making corrections—under an iterative process—between perceived and real risks.

Culture can be defined as a set of shared attitudes, values, goals, and practices. Chapter 13 of this book discusses cultural aspects in the context of portfolio management. With respect to change management and risk management, sound policies and procedures are a critical starting point; however, the best policies in the world will not help if the organization does not have a culture of mitigating or embracing risk, as appropriate. A strong risk culture should be promoted and reinforced constantly throughout an organization with clearly written, well-communicated, and readily accessible policies and procedures. The executive management team should be very clear about the organization's appetite for risk, and this should be regularly reviewed in line with the operating environment.

3.4. Developing Portfolio Goals, Strategic Objectives, and Strategic Plans

The portfolio strategic objectives serve to define a portfolio's value proposition and how it contributes to the organization's goals and objectives, provide the essential justification for a portfolio charter, and offer vital information for a portfolio strategic plan. As portfolios are collections of endeavors—change initiatives—contributing toward the achievement of strategic objectives, sound portfolios should have highly related goals. Since there is no natural limit on the number of portfolios per organization, it is far more important for organizations to create multiple portfolios, each with tightly connected goals. For example, in a growing financial services company, the senior executives agreed to create two portfolios at the enterprise level, each with three subsidiary portfolios, as shown in Table 4.

Table 4. Sample Strategic Goals

#	Portfolio	Subsidiary Portfolios	Strategic Goals and Objectives
1a	Revenue-Generating	New Product Development	Develop new products to develop new markets and enhance revenue and profitability.
1b		Product Enhancement (of existing products)	Enhance existing products and maximize their benefits to improve customer experience, increase market share, and enhance profitability.
1c		Product and Service Delivery	Improve how the products and services are distributed. Goals include improving customer experience, reducing the cost of service, and strengthening partners and supplier relationships.
2a	Internally Focused	Regulatory and Compliance	Meet regulatory and compliance requirements. Goals are to be compliant and ethical and avoid threats from poor compliance.
2b		Infrastructure (physical and information technology)	Provide suitable infrastructure to operate the business. Goals are more varied, but most focused on operational efficiency, information security, and employee well-being.
2c		Process Improvement	Continuously improve on the business processes to reduce waste, improve effectiveness, provide appropriate communication, and develop organizational resiliency.

The strategic goals and objectives serve as important inputs to the portfolio strategic plan. The portfolio strategic plan serves as a high-level organizational strategy distilled for the portfolio. It contains the portfolio's specific goals and strategic objectives, but also how the portfolio prioritizes the various factors of considerations. Key content includes the following:

- Portfolio vision and mission;
- Portfolio management structure and its relationship with organizational governance;
- Measurable goals and objectives;
- Funding mechanisms for the portfolio and the components;
- Initial portfolio value statement;
- Organizational and portfolio risk appetite and risk tolerance;
- Major stakeholders and communication requirements;
- Important constraints, assumptions, issues, risks, and dependencies;
- Initial resource requirement including high-level capacity and capability; and
- Portfolio priority and prioritization factors.

According to the PfM Standard,[1] the portfolio strategic plan "explains the key components of the portfolio management life cycle, describing the key initiation decisions, planning criteria, governance and optimization considerations, and execution elements. The portfolio strategic plan is used to align organizational and financial structure with priorities, mission, and objectives." A strategic plan may be considered as the deliverable that defines and explains how the components of the portfolio will be managed in order to deliver, measure, and communicate the results of each component within the scope of the portfolio. These functions take place in an evolving environment where strategy may change because of internal decisions, external constraints, or risk. It is used to align organizational and financial structure with priorities, mission, and objectives. It typically includes a vision and a mission statement, a description of the organization's long-term goals, objectives, and means by which the organization plans to achieve its goals and strategic objectives. The strategic plan may also identify external factors that might affect the achievement of long-term goals.

From a process perspective,[27] developing a portfolio strategic plan consists of aligning the organizational strategy to the strategic management of the portfolio. The organizational strategy and strategic objectives are aligned to the portfolio on the basis of the portfolio management objectives (e.g., component prioritization, allocation of funds, organizational benefits, performance expectations, resources, assumptions, constraints, dependencies, risks, requirements, etc.). The principal activities toward the development of the portfolio strategic plan are summarized in Table 5.

Table 5. Develop Strategic Plan – Inputs, Tools and Techniques, and Outputs

Artifacts	Description
Inputs	
Organizational Strategy and Objectives	Provide long-term direction, vision, goals, and objectives. Can take the form of a document containing the mission, vision, strategy, and objectives within the organization.
Inventory of Work	The minimum inventory of work acts as a starting point for developing a portfolio. It may be based on a prioritization of components.
Portfolio Process Assets	The process assets include plans, policies, procedures, and guidelines utilized by the portfolio manager. The tools used are benefits analysis and reporting.
Organizational Process Assets	Organizational assets may provide information and direction about the organizational strategy and objectives, vision and mission statements, prioritization, and resources.
Enterprise Environmental Factors	• May consist of corporate, environmental, and governmental variables. • Factors like organizational structure, stakeholder risk tolerances, marketplace conditions, and human resources may influence the organizational strategy and objectives to impact the process of developing the portfolio strategic plan.
Tools and Techniques	
Portfolio Component Inventory	• Based on the objectives, expected benefits, prioritization criteria, and performance, a portfolio manager defines the portfolio bearing in mind the strategic direction and prioritization. • This can be based on a list of work, and the detailing is done in order to reduce gaps in meeting objectives.
Strategic Alignment Analysis	• Focuses on the new or changing organizational strategy and objectives and indicates gaps in focus, investment, or alignment within the portfolio. • Factors that may need revision after analysis are obsolete goals, opportunities to be pursued, response to regulatory changes, etc.
Prioritization Analysis	• It is an approach that guides the ongoing decisions for components to be added, terminated, or changed. And it assists in balancing the component mix over time. • It contains parameters, such as alignment to strategic goals, ROI, investment risks, and dependencies. Examples include weighted ranking and scoring techniques.
Outputs	
Portfolio Strategic Plan (key contents are):	• Portfolio vision and objectives • Organizational structure • Performance metrics • Fund allocation, resource requirements, capacity, and capability • Portfolio benefits, performance results, and expected value • Stakeholder engagement—communication management • Assumptions, constraints, dependencies, and risks • Portfolio prioritization selected model • Portfolio risk tolerance
Portfolio Components Update	• Portfolio components are updated based on the developed portfolio strategic plan.

The Standard for Portfolio Management – Fourth Edition makes a distinction between goals and strategic objectives to emphasize that usually goals are more broad, abstract, and long term, while strategic objectives are more specific, tangible, and measurable. In portfolio management, goals may be thought of as the broad primary outcomes for creating the intended added value. Strategic planning includes all the steps to be taken to implement the strategy—the approach—to achieve the goal. The strategic objectives are the measurable milestones that need to be reached, usually serially (one after the other) under a performance management framework, toward executing strategy and achieving the goal(s). An organization's ambition is found in its mission and vision statements, which together describe the main thrust of the organization and its goal. Strategic objectives are the steps and accomplishments that the organization completes to realize that goal—they bridge the goal with specific outcomes. The strategic operating plan, and more specifically the strategic objectives, can be quite complicated to develop since they must practically create tangible, measurable outputs derived from aspiration (Vision – Mission) and the ultimate envisioned value (Goals).

3.5. Creating the Portfolio Charter

A portfolio charter is a formal agreement between the portfolio manager and the portfolio sponsor to formalize the creation of the portfolio. This document is perhaps one of the most important artifacts in portfolio management, as it serves as a written grant giving the portfolio manager (and by extension the portfolio management team) the authority and resources to initiate and manage the portfolio.

In creating the portfolio charter, the following elements should be considered:

- **Portfolio strategic plan** – When developing the portfolio charter and defining the portfolio structure, it is important to be guided by the portfolio strategic plan. The information in the portfolio strategic plan that is necessary for developing the portfolio charter includes the portfolio vision and objectives; the benefits expected; and the key risks, dependencies, and constraints. Within the portfolio strategic plan, the prioritization model is useful as a decision framework to structure the portfolio components.

- **Portfolio process assets** – To develop the portfolio charter, the portfolio manager should leverage the portfolio's plans, policies, procedures, and guidelines, and any existing documentation of stakeholder relationships, scope, benefits, and portfolio goals.
- **Enterprise environmental factors** – Enterprise environmental factors may consist of corporate, environmental, and governmental variables that may contribute to and constrain the process of developing the portfolio charter. The portfolio structure in the charter may need to align with the corporate accounting structure or with the functional structure of the organization (e.g., by organization unit or department).

For most portfolios, the development of the portfolio charter follows a standardized process. An example of such a process for a typical portfolio that includes the process inputs, tools and techniques, and outputs is given in Table 6.[19]

Table 6.   Develop Portfolio Charter – Inputs, Tools and Techniques, and Outputs

Artifacts	Description
Inputs	
Portfolio Strategic Plan	• It contains the portfolio vision and objectives, expected benefits, key risks, dependencies, and constraints. • It uses the prioritization model as a decision framework to structure the portfolio components.
Portfolio Process Assets	The process assets can be leveraged by the portfolio manager in order to develop the charter. These assets include the portfolio's goals, plans, policies, procedures, and guidelines.
Enterprise Environmental Factors	It may consist of corporate, environmental, and governmental variables that contribute to and constrain the process of developing the portfolio charter.
Tools and Techniques	
Scenario Analysis	• Based on a variety of assumptions, this is an analytical tool allowing decision makers to create numerous portfolio scenarios using combinations of potential and current components on the basis of their evaluated outcomes.
Capability and Capacity Analysis	It is based on the amount of work that can be performed with the availability of resources and the ability of the organization to utilize these resources bearing on the constraints it faces due to financial, skill set, or other capability concerns.
Outputs	
Portfolio Strategic Plan Updates	Updated to reflect resulting changes from defining the portfolio structure.
Portfolio Charter	A document that formally authorizes the portfolio manager to apply resources to components.
Portfolio Process Asset Updates	Process assets, such as formal and informal plans, policies, and guidelines may need to be updated.

3.6. Building the Portfolio Roadmap

A portfolio roadmap is a graphical illustration generally organized across a span of time that compresses and simplifies the overall portfolio plan, which typically has a horizon over multiple years. The beauty of a robust roadmap is that it provides a clear diagram illustrating the major components, their timing, and by association the realization of the strategic objectives and value to the organization. Roadmaps can also contain dependencies, challenges, and risks. The roadmap should be updated at least every six to 12 months and/or when major changes are made to the portfolio. For executives, a robust roadmap can serve as a vital communication and decision-making tool, as it is generally easy to understand and provides a rich array of information. For component team members, portfolio roadmaps can highlight important dependencies and constraints at the execution level. For other stakeholders, portfolio roadmaps establish common understanding and expectations. Portfolio roadmaps are constantly changing, being updated when new components are approved and existing projects are completed.

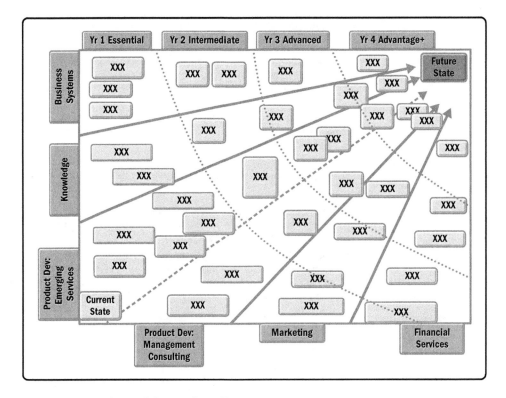

Figure 5. Sample Portfolio Roadmap[28]

Figure 5 is an illustrative portfolio roadmap. This portfolio strategy roadmap illustrates a four-year plan for a consulting service company to develop and improve existing operational capability.

- Year 1 is a limited pilot with a plan for full production in Year 2.
- Year 3 is about optimizing its processes so it is ready to manage other consulting service capabilities in Year 4 and beyond.

The portfolio roadmap may be thought of as a high-level schedule showing the strategic plan for all portfolio components to be executed during the portfolio life cycle. It also indicates dependencies between the components so that the portfolio manager can assess conflicts, gaps, and effects of component interactions. For most portfolios, the development of the portfolio roadmap follows a standardized process. An example[19] of such a process for a typical portfolio that includes the process inputs, tools and techniques, and outputs is given in Table 7.

Table 7. Develop Portfolio Roadmap – Inputs, Tools and Techniques, and Outputs

Artifacts	Description
Inputs	
Portfolio Strategic Plan	Reflects the organizational goals, objectives, and strategies necessary to enable alignment of the roadmap and for it to be built. The portfolio strategic plan provides the portfolio prioritization model that establishes the guidelines to prioritize portfolio components, enabling the portfolio roadmap to be built.
Portfolio Charter	It is needed to understand the portfolio structure, scope, constraints, dependencies, resources, and timeline in order to create the roadmap.
Portfolio	It contains the portfolio components and related information, which is referenced to define the roadmap. Examples of information referenced are prioritization, dependencies, timeline, and organization areas.
Tools and Techniques	
Interdependency Analysis	• It identifies the dependencies the portfolio may have with other portfolios or the portfolio environment. • It includes parameters such as resources, finance, quality, risks, timeline, etc. • Participants in this analysis may include executive-level and other key stakeholders.
Cost-Benefit Analysis	Used to quantify estimated costs and benefits, and lists qualitative considerations of alternate components in determining the best course of action for the portfolio.
Prioritization Analysis	It involves the comparison of strategic objectives, prioritization of objectives, and performing strategic assessments against current portfolios by the portfolio manager.
Outputs	
Portfolio Roadmap	Provides high-level strategic direction and information in a chronological view for portfolio management execution and enables dependencies within the portfolio to be established and evaluated.

3.7. Managing Strategic Alignment

One of the primary portfolio management functions is the activity of aligning resource demand with resource availability to achieve a set of strategic goals. A fully aligned portfolio strategy can be more than just helping organizations in the realization of their strategic goals and objectives. Strong alignment also improves the management of uncertainties and makes the most effective decisions related to organizational strategies. To achieve this, organizations need to understand the value of the portfolio, and portfolio managers must be given the due authority and responsibilities.

The alignment process begins with making sure that the right projects and programs have been selected. In this process, it is extremely important for executives to fully understand it is paramount that the organization should dynamically manage its portfolio regarding the initiatives that are pertinent to the organizational strategies. Aligning strategy of the organization with the portfolio is part science and part art. The science is the alignment of the key performance indicators between the organizational strategy and the portfolio strategic goals and objectives. Chances are, the more quantifiable these metrics are, the more accurate and "scientific" the alignment is likely to achieve. However, since many if not most strategies are also highly qualitative, the alignment requires the art of possibility. Following are seven activities to achieve a balance between the science and art of alignment:

- **Understanding strategic planning and execution** – Portfolio managers should understand how the organization develops its strategy, whether it is deliberate, emergent, organizational learning, or some other ways. As shown earlier, there are significant implications for the planning and execution, and a poor understanding will lead to ineffective translation of strategy to execution.
- **Clarifying the organizational goals and strategies** – As discussed earlier, successful portfolios require established organizational strategies with clear goals and objectives. Gaining clarity, especially at the specific level, ensures that the portfolio objectives are lined up with the organization's vital plans. Also, depending on the level of the organization in which the portfolio exists, it may be important to look at the organizational strategy at one level, or even multiple levels, to further enable alignment.

- **Development of a portfolio management office (PMO) or a project management office with portfolio management capability** – As organizations embark on portfolio management, it is important to create a centralized organization to sustain the proper functioning of portfolio management. A well-designed PMO enables organizational learning and continuous improvement as the PMO serves as a reservoir of knowledge. Furthermore, PMOs can also achieve economy of size and scope as the organization grows.
- **Development of evaluation criteria** – Portfolio managers should work with the sponsors and governance teams to establish the optimal evaluation criteria that are aligned with the organizational and portfolio strategies. Through the evaluation criteria, portfolio managers can objectively evaluate the portfolio components.
- **Enforcing a culture of accountability** – Even the best strategy and evaluation criteria will fail if organizations lack a culture of accountability in the portfolio and portfolio component business cases. For the proper alignment of the portfolio and its components, factual data and objective analysis must be applied with rigor and consistency. Otherwise, alignment may be based on false or exaggerated benefits, which would render the process ineffective.
- **Incorporation of risk management strategy** – Risks are pervasive. As portfolios are often significant undertakings for the sponsoring organization, it is important for portfolio managers to consider opportunities and threats that can either enhance or jeopardize the portfolio and its ability to realize value. Portfolio managers should work with executives earlier on to determine the risk appetite, tolerance, and threshold, which can serve as vital inputs to the alignment process.
- **Establishment of good governance** – Proper governance, including oversight, control, integration, and sound decision making, is critical to success. Oversight can be defined as direction, guidance, and leadership. Its basis regards getting involved via visible support and engagement in removing barriers and problem solving, and not just in the sense of being acquainted with the strategy without any directed course of action. Control is defined as reporting and monitoring of

core indicators of performance, including the lead indicators. These indicators include requirements volatility, incremental value delivered, and risk exposure. Integration is also important in the process of aligning portfolio management with organizational strategies. This integration can be expounded as strategy alignment as well as ownership of the organization regarding the changes that are being implemented by the portfolio. It is also important to note that this process must be directed by the portfolio governance. Lastly, decision making can be explained as the broad as well as day-to-day decisions that demand management and executive support for ensuring buy-in across the organization.

3.8. Managing Component Dependencies

Dependencies arise because different portfolio components operate with different business cases, timelines, and constraints; therefore, dependency management is really a very people-focused and potentially political process. To further the dependency management discussion in the previous chapter, a dependency is also an attribute of a portfolio component milestone. Beyond the identification of such dependencies, though, it is not useful to treat these dependencies as separate entities. The "dependent" component plan needs to show clearly, as a milestone, the point at which the component's project manager needs something from the "delivering" component. The specific dependencies discussed in this subsection are attributes of specific milestones. The project manager manages those milestones to agreed completion. The complexity arises because such dependencies influence other portfolio component performances; these other portfolio components are driven by different program or project management teams. Each manager has their own drivers and business case, and they must deliver to their own plan. Dependencies are largely associated with escalation. This means that to resolve a dependency conflict, they first have to line up with the governance structure. The governance structure is usually embodied in roles and meetings, which devolve authority to execute from the accountable and perform oversight to discharge that accountability. Escalations are what come back up the chain (i.e., "things that need to be sorted out"). Therefore, dependencies have to be defined to a point where they can be escalated effectively. Moreover, the PMO team, if a PMO exists, needs to understand the governance structure of the organization to understand how and where escalation of dependency issues is directed to. The escalation process for dependencies at the portfolio level should mirror the governance structure, which will already be in place.

Good dependency management hinges largely on the maturity of the organization, so speaking theoretically, if each project and program had a business case, we would look at those to see between which projects (and milestones within a project) a dependency may arise. In less-mature organizations, business cases are completed too late or not at all. In those cases, look at requirements documentation. If those are not available early enough, and the organization does not have a PMO, practitioners should consult the portfolio designers and the information architects. If all else fails, practitioners will have to wait until the dependency is obvious—usually a gap where something needs to be done. Another important aspect of dependency identification is to be clear about the business outcomes for the dependencies that influence components' performance. Often the resolution of contention in dependencies may come down to a priority call at the level of governance where the two components meet. At this level, the technicalities of this or that deliverable are not required, but the practitioner must be clear how the impact relates to ultimate business outcomes. Once the portfolio manager becomes aware of a likely dependency, it becomes the responsibility of the "dependent" project manager to drive the documentation and agreement of that dependency. A dependency log should be created and maintained, focused on solid data like baselined milestone dates.

3.9. Managing Portfolio Alignment to Organizational Strategy

Correctly aligning the portfolio to the organizational strategy enables the portfolio manager to effectively manage change in organizational strategy and to enhance the ability to accept and act on a significant strategic change that impacts portfolio planning and management. As strategy shifts, the "as-is" state must be compared with a "to-be" state (which may be evolutionary or incremental in nature), and the gap may result in a realignment of resources or adjustments in the portfolio component mix to support the strategic change. Change in portfolios is a normal occurrence, and depending on the significance of the changes, portfolio documents may need to be reworked to ensure continued alignment with the strategy. This repeated adaptation contrasts with the progressive elaboration required in project management. This process is an aligning process to identify the gap between as-is and to-be states and to analyze the impact and response to strategic changes and changes in resources (people, process, and assets/technology). The vehicles used to plan and execute the strategic change are the portfolio strategic plan and portfolio management plan.

3.9.1. Inputs required to manage portfolio alignment

- **Portfolio strategic plan** – When managing strategic change, it is important to understand the portfolio strategic plan to ensure inclusion of the correct components within those organization areas with the highest strategic value. Due to new strategic direction, before and during the portfolio changes, the executives' and key stakeholders' expectations and communication requirements must be considered.
- **Portfolio charter** – In managing strategic change, the original portfolio charter or revised charter, if applicable, should be reviewed to ensure the charter and portfolio remain in alignment and are updated as required.
- **Portfolio** – The portfolio is the means to the "to-be" vision. The list of current portfolio components is reviewed and evaluated to determine the required changes in the component mix and to align with the strategic direction.
- **Portfolio roadmap** – The portfolio roadmap provides the high-level strategic direction and information chronologically for portfolio management execution and to ensure that dependencies within the portfolio are established and evaluated. This is an essential component in enabling management of the portfolio and demonstrating a clear path from the "as-is" to the "to-be" states. Reviewing or updating the portfolio roadmap ensures that it is in sync with changes in strategic direction.
- **Portfolio process assets** – In managing strategic change, the portfolio manager references and is guided by the portfolio's plans, policies, procedures, and guidelines. Examples of assets may include analysis and assessment tools and templates.

3.9.2. Techniques used in aligning a portfolio to organizational strategy

- **Stakeholder analysis** – Stakeholder analysis is critical in managing strategic change because it helps to ensure continuity and align key stakeholder expectations with the changing strategy and resulting portfolio realignment. The techniques used to analyze stakeholder expectations and requirements may include interviewing senior executive stakeholders and analyzing requirements and expectations for strategic change. This may include identifying the stakeholders by individual or group, determining expectations, evolving conditions, newly recognized pain points, problems or desires, change impacts, issues, risk tolerance, and concerns.
- **Gap analysis** – A gap analysis is performed to compare the current portfolio mix and components with the new strategic direction and the "to-be" organizational vision. This is essential to properly manage strategic change. This analysis determines the gaps and changes needed in the portfolio mix so that components may be added, changed, or terminated.
- **Readiness assessment** – A readiness assessment is performed to assess how ready the organization is to perform the steps necessary to bridge the gap between the "as-is" portfolio state and the "to-be" state. The assessment determines the "if," "when," "what," and "how" of implementing the change and points out any needs not yet addressed that are required to affect the change.

3.9.3. Updates made when aligning a portfolio to a corporate strategy

- **Portfolio strategic plan updates** – The portfolio strategic plan is updated to reflect the outcome of the tools and techniques listed above and will need to be revisited when future strategic changes are made. Various elements of the portfolio strategic plan may need to change to reflect the organizational strategy change, such as the prioritization model, benefits, assumptions, constraints, dependencies, and risks.

- **Portfolio charter updates** – The portfolio charter is updated to reflect the outcome of the tools and techniques listed above and revisited when future strategic changes are made. The portfolio structure in the charter may need to change to reflect new strategic objectives, as well as key or major stakeholders and their communication requirements.
- **Portfolio updates** – When a strategic change is made, components may be added, delayed, or removed from the portfolio to enable alignment with the new strategy.
- **Portfolio roadmap updates** – Based on the impact of the strategic change, the portfolio roadmap is updated, taking into consideration the new "to-be" vision and resulting changes in the portfolio components, timeline, and dependencies.
- **Portfolio process assets updates** – If strategic changes impact portfolio plans and processes, the portfolio process assets are updated. These assets include information available from historic files on a previous strategic change to the portfolio-related people, processes and technology, performance metrics, risk management, and lessons learned databases.

3.10. Optimizing the Portfolio Management Process — Using Analytical Hierarchy Processing

The analytical hierarchy process (AHP) is a multicriteria decision aide involving a systematic procedure for dealing with complex decision-making problems in which many competing alternatives—projects, actions, and scenarios—exist. The alternatives are ranked using several quantitative and/or qualitative criteria, depending on how they contribute to achieving an overall goal. AHP is based on a hierarchical structuring of the elements that are involved in a decision problem. The hierarchy incorporates the knowledge, the experience, and the intuition of the decision maker for the specific problem. The simplest hierarchy consists of three levels. On the top of the hierarchy lies the decision's goal. On the second level, lie the criteria by which the alternatives (third level) will be evaluated. In more complex situations, the main goal can be broken down into subgoals or/and a criterion (or property) can be broken down into subcriteria.

People who are involved in the problem can use their goals and policies as additional levels. The hierarchy evaluation is based on pairwise comparisons, where two alternatives are compared concerning a criterion, and a numerical value to their relative weight is assigned. There are three approaches to the AHP method:

1. Decomposition: dividing a problem into smaller parts, the division process resolving some levels of a problem
2. Comparative judgment: assessing the relative importance of two elements and attaching relative priorities
3. Synthesis of priority: using a pairwise comparison matrix, the overall priority can be acquired by synthesizing between local priorities

The AHP method is useful where a problem cannot easily be assessed quantitatively, and centers on grouping the decision elements according to their common characteristics. This grouping process enables the ranking of the decision elements.

## CHAPTER 4

Portfolio Governance

by Nick Clemens

> Good governance requires working toward common ground. It isn't easy.
>
> — **Pete Hoekstra**

This chapter discusses portfolio governance. As defined within the PfM Standard, "Portfolio governance is a set of practices, functions, and processes within a framework based on a set of principles that are the fundamental norms, rules, or values that *guide* portfolio management activities to optimize investments and meet organizational strategic and operational goals."[29] The key phrase is "guide," as noted by the added emphasis in the above quote.

Governance is the guide that shapes or bounds management practices. With regard to management practices, the provision of bounds is critically important at the portfolio level because of the complex nature of the task of portfolio management. By bounding and guiding management processes, governance provides a simplifying structure for the execution of portfolio, program, and project management processes. Just as modeling reduces complexity, so analysis may be conducted on systems; governance as well reduces complexity so that management processes may be propagated throughout the portfolio management structure. Governance thus occurs at all levels of an organization.

PMI envisions three levels of organization within the program and project management space, and two more implied levels of the structure resulting from considerations outlined within PMI's *Organizational Project Management Maturity Model (OPM3®),* and PMI's foundational standards.[30] The explicit levels, as governed and defined by the PMI foundational standards are portfolio, program, and project. Beneath the project level is task or activity management, which contains work done within the work packages of a work breakdown structure (WBS). This level also contains small team[31] (about six to 10 individuals or less) actions, such as those associated with agile techniques, and is included in the project management space. The level above the portfolio contains senior executive bodies. The senior executive level of structure is outside the project, program, and portfolio space. Typical terms used to describe this level of governance are "the C-suite," senior staff, or the tongue-in-cheek, "the imperial staff."

The described PMI three-tier structure, or five as outlined above, is not an artifact of the PMI foundational standards. These standards merely describe the characteristics of the business environment. Other project or program management organizations have slightly modified structures but still seek to explain the structure as precisely laid out in the PMI foundational standards. For example, the International Project Management Association (IPMA) also has a three-tiered structure consisting of project(s), program(s), and multiple projects or portfolio(s). This three-tiered structure is contained within the domain of line organization/functional departments and an overarching layer defined as strategic/top management.[32] The U.S. federal government also acknowledges a three-tiered structure of project, program, and portfolio management within their acquisition management organizations. Without getting into the merits of various structures, we find that the structural definitions as laid out by PMI are elegantly straightforward. Figure 6 illustrates the three-tiered business structure.

Governance may be initiated within any of the levels pictured in the structure. It is possible to talk about governance within the task or small team domain. However, at this level, governance becomes focused on individual behaviors within the small team environment. Further governance behaviors are strongly bounded by the overlaying project governance. For example, agile teams of six or more individuals work within this small team domain. Governance within the agile team is strongly defined by the *Agile Manifesto* and implemented via various

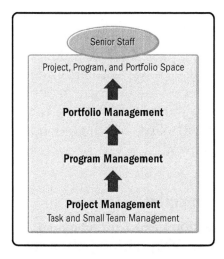

Figure 6. Three-Tiered Project, Program, and Portfolio Management Space

ceremonies or customs unique to that team and aligned to the *Agile Manifesto*.[33] These ceremonies or customs may take the form of specific agile approaches, such as Scrum, Kanban, or a combination of several agile techniques.[34] At the small team level, governance considerations are thus focused on the management of individuals, and, although important, not within the scope of this discussion.

At the project level and above, management considerations quickly expand geometrically as managers at the project level strive to manage, that is, monitor and control, the actions of multiple teams of varying size. It is at the project level were complexity begins to drive the management process and where small team ceremonies begin to break down. Governance thus takes on an increasing value as one moves up the management chain.

The rest of this governance discussion will be focused on portfolio governance considerations, its linkage to senior staff governance, and with the propagation of governance down through the project, program, and portfolio space. Task and small team governance considerations will not be covered. The execution of all effort or work relating to either operations or product development will be taken to occur within the project, program, and portfolio space. Thus, all work done by an organization will occur within the project, program, and portfolio space. This is not to say that the senior or executive staff does no work. Their role is primarily one of strategic oversite and governance formation. The implementation and execution of strategy within governance bounds is done by the portfolio managers through their respective programs and projects. Working now from the bottom up, it is through product delivery at the project level that programs deliver value to their respective organizations that then support the achievement of organizational strategic objectives. As stated in the PfM Standard, "A portfolio is a collection of projects, programs, subsidiary portfolios, and operations managed as a group to achieve strategic objectives."[35]

4.1. Governance Principles

As described within Section 1.7 of *The Standard of Portfolio Management – Fourth Edition*, there are eight principles relating to portfolio management; however, one principle directly relates to governance: "Enable transparency, responsibility, accountability, and fairness." Also, listed within Section 1.7 is a principle requiring the navigation of complexity, "to enable successful outcomes." Although listed last, this is a clear example of the common phrase, "last but not least." This last principle dealing with complexity is crucial because the project, program, and portfolio space have one single attribute if it has any, that is, "emerging complexity."[36]

The application of the principles of transparency, responsibility, accountability, and fairness to governance is taken as a given within the *The Standard for Portfolio Management*. This is not unreasonable; however, there is an underlying necessity for the application of these principles to the governance arena. Referring to Figure 1-3, portfolio management performance domains contained within Section 1.8.2 of the standard, we see that portfolio governance is one of six management domains that shapes the life of the portfolio. This shaping occurs throughout the portfolio life cycle as portfolio elements are initiated, planned, executed, optimized, and replanned. The goal of portfolio governance from a management perspective is outlined within the bulleted list following the figure where each of the domains are further explained. The governance domain is further elaborated within Section 1.8.2, as follows:

> Through open and transparent governance, including processes for categorizing, prioritizing, selecting, and approving portfolio components, key stakeholders are more likely to accept the decisions and agree with the process, even when they may not fully endorse the decisions made.[37]

From this we see a subordinated management purpose of governance beyond the aforementioned general purpose of guiding activities to optimize investments and meet strategic and operational goals. The management purpose as stated above is to facilitate the harmonization of decisions and processes between key stakeholders. It is through this harmonization process that strategic and operational goals are efficiently and effectively met. Simply stated, for project, program, and portfolio management to be effective, the top-down processes must operate in a harmonious fashion without rough spots or discord.

As seen in Figure 7, complexity interferes with the smooth functioning of management processes within the project, program, and portfolio space. Good governance process provides the "oil" that keeps the machinery of management within the project, program, and portfolio space operating smoothly. Moreover, to extend this analogy a bit further,

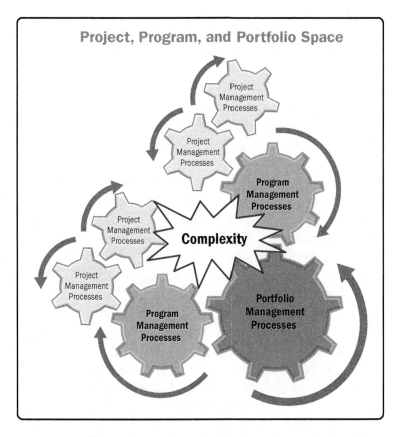

Figure 7. Restrictive Effects of Complexity on the Smooth Functioning of Management Processes

good governance keeps the "sand" of complexity from adding friction, as shown in Figure 7, to what should otherwise be a smoothly operating management process.

We will now look at each of the four governance principles expressed within the governance section of *The Standard for Portfolio Management* separately.

4.1.1. Transparency

Transparency involves providing information that is correct, unambiguous, and easily obtained. Generally, transparency is seen as a top-down function, as each level of the organization should achieve transparency for subordinate levels. However, transparency must also work across organizations so that peer structures also share directly in an open environment. Transparency is also seen as multidirectional. Information must flow both up and down and across organizations in all directions.

Transparency is synonymous with openness. Openness means that an organization's decision processes are known throughout the organization. The underlying assumption supporting the need for transparency is that minimally individuals will hold themselves accountable for their actions if those actions are public knowledge. It is also assumed that employees will also hold management accountable. However, when management holds hire and fire authority over subordinate employees, checks are problematic. In fact, even when protections are provided to subordinates via whistleblowing laws, employees generally choose not to raise issues.[38]

Transparency will not guarantee good decisions. However, it will maximize the probability that a poor decision will be identified early, and corrective action may be taken. Transparency will also contribute to a positive corporate climate. Senior executives should be particularly careful to provide transparency in their governance actions. The senior governing and related management processes above the portfolio level impact the entire organization through the portfolios managed. Good senior management decisions can, if executed incorrectly, adversely impact corporate climate and the subordinate management processes within managed portfolios, programs, and projects. For example, a company may be planning a restructuring to respond to a drop in market share or to better manage product development. This restructuring may not involve a reduction in the workforce. However, because of poor transparency on the part of the executive staff concerning this reorganization, rumors concerning layoffs and firing are circulating. As a result, after the reorganization, the company finds that it has lost a number of key staff and what should have been a positive experience to the company has now resulted in a lowering of company morale and a significant gap in needed employee resources.

4.1.2. Responsibility and accountability

Responsibility and accountability are often confused. In most cases, these two attributes go together. For example, a manager who is responsible for the execution of a program will also be held accountable should that program fail. However, a manager may delegate responsibility for a task to another person. In this case, that manager will hold the person delegated responsible for the successful outcome of that task. However, although the responsibility for the task has been delegated, the original manager is still accountable to higher management for all tasks being managed. The effect is that one can generally delegate responsibility but not accountability. One can hold others accountable, but that does not relieve them of their accountability.

Responsibility and accountability play a key role in governance. Governance, particularly at senior levels, is seen as an organizational function. For example, it is the board that establishes corporate governance, or the portfolio staff that writes governance and management policy. However, governance or policy that is made by individuals and organizations cannot be held responsible or accountable. Only individuals within an organization who make the governance and policy may be held responsible and accountable. Senior executives and managers on governing boards, along with subordinate management staff, must be careful to always accept responsibility and accountability in a transparent fashion.

4.1.3. Fairness

Fairness is subjective, as what is fair for one person or group may not be fair for another. Additionally, what may be considered fair by an individual, may not be fair for the group as a whole. Fairness at the portfolio and program level must be in the context of what is fair for the group or organization. When dealing with issues at the project or task level, individual considerations of fairness may come into play. However, at higher levels of management, whenever there is a conflict between the group and the individual, the group is usually considered above the individual.

A classic example of conflicting fairness considerations involves the approval of employee time off. Corporate governance may establish that time off will be considered based on corporate needs consistent with the needs of the employee. Governance acknowledges the possibility of conflicting needs between the organization and the employee and leaves it to policy guidance to sort out the issues. The policy may thus establish guidelines for the management of employee time off and direct managers to establish specific rules consistent with that guidance to explicitly tell employees how time off is requested, approved, and under what circumstances denied requests might be appealed.

Fairness, being subjective, requires the establishment of transparency and the acceptance of responsibility and accountability on the part of senior executives and managers. Thus, the attribute of fairness emerges[39] from the establishment of a transparent corporate climate and the willingness of individuals within the organization to openly accept responsibility and accountability. Because fairness emerges as a result of transparency and the acceptance of responsibility and accountability on the part of managers, it cannot be achieved in and of itself.

The attributes of transparency, responsibility, accountability, and fairness combine in changeable ways that result in an evolving corporate culture that encourages a certain approach to governance. The governance at various levels of an organization results in management structures that guide or bound how portfolios, programs, and projects are managed within the organization. The establishment of governance and management processes at the senior executive level and within the project, program, and portfolio space thus have a multidimensional property, which is a result of the complex nature of the project, program, and portfolio space. The principles of enabling transparency, responsibility, accountability, and fairness when taken together become more than just their constituent parts. Governance is thus seen as a complex system of systems that derives its fundamental complexity from the project, program, and portfolio space. By extension, project, program, and portfolio management are also complex processes and each is also a system of systems for the larger project, program, and portfolio management space.

4.2. Portfolio Governance Management

Within *The Standard for Program Management* – Fourth Edition, there is a distinction made between governance principles and management principles. Governance is seen as providing the underpinning for management principles. Management principles address how the organization produces work.[40] However, that is not to say that governance does not require management functions. This section will expand on the principles of governance management laid down in PMI's *The Standard for Program Management* and examine governance functions outlined within the standard. Within a particular organization, the governance functions would be implemented through management processes. These processes would be bounded or guided by the overarching governance structure established as part of the portfolio governance.

Figure 8: Portfolio Governance Domain illustrates the governance domain description provided in *The Standard for Portfolio Management* at Section 4.4.2. The illustration contains some additional elements not mentioned in the standard, but these additions are logical extensions based on the provided four governance functions. As pictured in Figure 8, the four governance functions are decision making, oversight, control, and integration. Working clockwise around the illustration, we see the oversight function as containing activities of an establishment of a corporate climate and supporting leadership and direction.

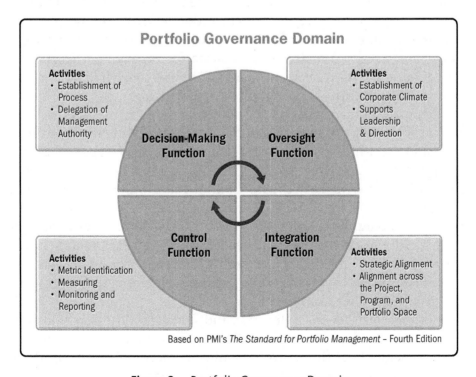

Figure 8. Portfolio Governance Domain

The addition of the establishment of a corporate climate derives from activities involving leadership and direction. The integration function contains the activities of strategic alignment and alignment within the project, program, and portfolio space. The addition of vertical and horizontal alignment activities within the project, program, and portfolio space is an extension of strategic alignment activities listed within the standard. Metric identification is added to the control function because of the important and central role that metrics selection plays in accurately measuring portfolio progress and achievement of goals. Finally, the activity of establishing processes is added to the decision-making function. The establishment of processes is how authority is delegated, and it is a necessary addition to the decision-making function.

Portfolio governance functions are carried out through the management efforts of individuals within the portfolio management team. At the portfolio level, work is usually completed through one of two methods. For matrixed organizational environments, some type of integrated or cross-functional team managed by an appropriate individual on the portfolio management staff completes work. For a functionally organized workplace, work is accomplished through staff offices headed by a staff chief or lead. Hybrid organizational structures are possible, but the fundamental point is that work is managed by the portfolio management staff no matter how that staff is organized.[41] For brevity throughout the rest of this section, we will refer to the portfolio management staff as the entity carrying out various functions.

The portfolio management staff must be ready to manage in all directions. The staff will be tasked by senior executive management from above and must be able to delegate and manage downward to subordinate portfolios, programs, projects, and operational efforts. The portfolio staff, and particularly the portfolio manager, must also be able to manage up to the senior staff. For example, senior management may overlook key data concerning a declining market share, or critical regulatory requirements may be unfunded within a certain program effort. The portfolio manager must be active and assertive in bringing this data to senior individuals within the organization so a quick decision concerning the way ahead can be made.

Another role of the portfolio staff, and specifically the portfolio manager, is to also bridge the gap between the senior executive staff and subordinate elements of the portfolio. Failure to accomplish this bridging function threatens transparency across the organization. The example reviewed in the transparency segment above about the corporate re-organization could have been a result of the failure of the portfolio management staff to effectively communicate the intention of senior management to lower levels within the portfolio.

The portfolio staff must also be able to manage and delegate across the organization. Cross-organizational management can be difficult because managers are usually dealing with other managers at similar levels within the organization who do not report directly to them. Depending on the linkages between portfolios within an organization, this cross-organizational management function can be critical to providing senior executives with the necessary information for a timely and correct decision.

Before looking at each of the four functional areas, notice that governance as listed in Figure 1-3, Section 1.8.2, of *The Standard for Portfolio Management* – Fourth Edition does not contain the word management. Of the six domains listed, only governance and stakeholder engagement are not explained as management domains. This result is a rather abbreviated list of activities within the four functions listed under the governance domain since only elements of that domain function that are directly related to governance are listed. We will now examine how each of the four governance domain functions are implemented within the portfolio management area.

4.2.1. Decision making

The establishment of processes within the portfolio structure sets how the portfolio is managed. These processes cover all aspects of strategic alignment to how employees are to report time billed. The establishment of processes is a direct result of the decisions concerning those processes. Who within the portfolio structure makes those decisions concerning processes is determined by the authority delegated by the portfolio manager. For example, the portfolio manager is likely not worried about a process for determining breaks within an independent and self-managing small team. However, the aforementioned process for determining employee time off may have corporate considerations, and as part of governance provided by senior management that process may be held above the portfolio at the corporate level. The above shows how governance guides and shapes the establishment of processes and where within the organization decisions about those processes are made.

4.2.2. Oversight

One of the principal roles of any staff, whether at the project or senior staff levels, is to provide leadership and direction. However, this is particularly important at upper levels of management. The portfolio staff, and specifically the portfolio manager, must bridge the gap between the senior executive staff who operate principally outside the project, program, and portfolio space and the management elements within the portfolio. The concept of leadership and direction in this context is very broad.[42] First, we are looking at leadership as a multidimensional activity as opposed to a traditional top-down relationship where the boss provides direction and the subordinates follow. Second, the term "direction" should be taken in the context of providing vision and guidance, not in terms of a superior subordinate relationship where one dictates and the other follows.

Although, it is recognized that some organizations take a traditional, hierarchical approach to management, this may be due to societal considerations, the nature of the particular program or project, or the individual corporate culture of the organization. Without knowledge of the specific project, program, or operational considerations, and an understanding of societal and cultural considerations, it cannot be said that one approach is better than another. However, it can be said that a strict hierarchical or traditional approach is not preferred. Whether dealing with PMI, IPMA, the International Organization for Standardization (ISO), or other professional or standards bodies, there is an overwhelming consensus within the management community that participative and adaptive leadership and management techniques are preferred. How a specific company structures its organization is a question of governance.

Participative and adaptive techniques also work well within the governance development arena. Although governance is promulgated in a top-down manner from senior staff to the portfolio level on down, the establishment of governance should not be dictatorial in nature. Each level of management should be free to establish governance procedures within the overall bounds set by superiors. For example, the senior executive staff may set corporate guidance, strategy, and vision for the enterprise as a whole. Looking just at the strategy and vision statements, the portfolio manager should execute portfolio functions within the supplied corporate strategy and vision, and likewise set a portfolio strategy and vision tailored to the specifics of the portfolio. Program and operations managers then formulate their management approaches based on the promulgated corporate and supporting portfolio guidance. Individual program and operations managers may also develop strategy and vision statements. However, at this level, the character of the strategy becomes narrow with respect to the corporate and portfolio guidance vision statements that usually focus on specific work-related goals and objectives. Project managers may also develop strategic and vision statements. At a minimum, each project team member should understand how their efforts fit into the project they are working on, how that project supports their parent program,[43] how that program delivers benefits to the organization and fulfills overall portfolio objectives, and finally how their efforts support senior corporate strategy and vision. The above process is governed and guided by governance procedures.

The leadership style of the organization, whether participative, dictatorial, or somewhere in between, drives the corporate climate. The corporate climate is the environment in which all actions of the enterprise take place in much the same way that the physical climate is the environment in which our lives and actions exist. To take this analogy just a bit further, we can think of the corporate climate as changeable just as climate changes between seasons. On the other hand, societal and corporate culture is taken to be more static. Cultural changes are generally measured in decades or generations, whereas corporate climate may change within a year or less. As such, a change in corporate climate precedes changes in corporate culture.

From just a governance view, the oversight function involves actions that support the establishment of an organizational leadership approach and direction that is usually in the form of a vision statement. Governance provides the overarching guidance and bounds in which the leadership approach is developed and the vision promulgated. Once established and aligned with the overall organizational governance, the leadership approach and direction set the corporate climate which, in turn, supports the overall corporate culture.

4.2.3. Control

The control function of governance is essentially what one would expect to see within any management structure. The purpose of portfolio governance control is to measure and monitor progress and to report findings as required across the project, program, and portfolio space. Key to measuring progress is the selection of proper metrics so that status may be accurately measured. As an example, when looking at product sales, a number of metrics may be appropriate as a measure of success. They include but are not limited to market penetration, profit per unit sold, return on investment, or from a nonquantitative perspective, branding considerations.[44] The selection of metrics is driven, in part, by strategic considerations and specific portfolio goals and objects. Governance is not directly linked to the selection of these parameters. However, governance does provide a guide for the formation of the organization's approach to management, and hence, indirectly shapes the selection of these metrics. For example, governance principles that emphasize a shorter midterm time frame for analysis and decision making will likely favor metrics that focus on measurements such as profit or cost per unit.

Governance is also a "product" that is delivered by the portfolio staff to elements within the portfolio structure. Governance control measures the quality of the delivered governance within the portfolio. This is easier said than done, as governance is a qualitative factor within the portfolio management structure. Although governance is seen as a distinct element separate from management and operational execution, it touches all aspects of the project, program, and portfolio space. Good governance does not exist separately from these elements as a delivered product exists separately from the management structure that delivered it. Good governance emerges from the interplay of many elements within the project, program, and portfolio space, and includes the organizational culture, the overall business environment, and internal factors, such as the organization's management structure, facilities, and personnel.

Areas to look at for metrics include measures of corporate health, such as employee turnover rate, management climate such as staff work satisfaction, or employee knowledge checks concerning portfolio vision, its connection to the enterprise vision, and the role played by individual employees at the project or operations levels to support higher level goals and objectives. The guiding principle of governance is also a guide for metric identification. The accomplishment of transparency, the assignment of responsibility and accountability, and the establishment of fairness need to be measured. Responsibility and accountability should be straightforward since individuals either are held accountable and take on assigned responsibility, or they don't. The two remaining factors are qualitative and perception-based.

As stated above, transparency and fairness are strongly linked. It is assumed that a transparent process would be perceived as fair. However, this may not be the case, as an unfair process may be completely transparent.

In any case, the assignment of fairness is highly subjective. Lack of transparency may result in a perception of unfairness in processes, which makes the determination of fairness difficult to estimate in isolation. Metrics dealing with employee perception will likely involve surveys and focus groups to gather feedback concerning information flow, perception of management taking responsibility and accountability, and the process of decision making at various levels of the organization.

Finally, transparency, or how open an organization is, would appear to be easy to measure. A given process is either well known, accurately communicated, and understood by all within an organization or it is not. However, like fairness, individual perception enters into the assessment of transparency. A statistical study of reports delivered, decisions communicated, or meetings held does not give a complete picture of how portfolio and subordinate team members perceive the management environment. A measure of employee whistleblower actions could indicate how transparent an organizational structure is. However, this metric is a trailing indicator. Use of a leading indicator is preferred. The management staff should look at the number of suggestions submitted by employees, how many are adopted, how long it takes to resolve a suggestion, and whether results of suggestions are communicated back to the management team and the individual. Another area to examine is whether a true flow of two-way communication exists between management levels or whether most communications are just top-down.

4.2.4. Integration

The integration activity is how managers perform the process of linking various levels of governance with each other. Examples of how governance is propagated have already been discussed above. Integration also involves actions across the portfolio structure and, in many cases, across the enterprise between various portfolios. This cross- or lateral channel of communications is best exemplified by the idea of no "silos" or vertical channels of information within an organization. From a governance perspective, integration chiefly involves the flow of information and the linking of processes throughout the organization. Each manager is thus responsible for their specific assigned area. Portfolio managers integrate across their portfolio and up to the senior executive level of management.

Another way of looking at integration can be found in Figure 7. In this case, we are looking at the results of the integration process, which is to have a smooth operating management structure within the portfolio. Each element of the portfolio is thought of as a system within a system. The activity of integration involves working the interface between systems, assuring that data, information, and knowledge[45] flow between systems and subsystems. As stated above, governance activities provide the means to address complexity within an organization. This is done through the propagation of clearly defined processes and constant communication throughout the organization. In this way, managers can focus on the interface between management systems and subsystems assuring the outputs of one system appropriately feed the inputs of another system. The internal operating of the system is not managed at the integration level. The parallel between the flow of governance within an organization and the focusing on system integration is noteworthy. Governance also focuses on interfaces and assuring alignment of management practices throughout the organization, but leaves, where appropriate, the development of specific management processes to the responsible managers at each level.

4.3. Tools and Techniques

This final section will deal with some of the tools and techniques related to portfolio governance. In most cases, the tools and techniques used in portfolio management are not unique to the portfolio arena. For example, *The Standard for Portfolio Management* – Third Edition or PfM Standard (3.0), Figure 5-1 lists, "Portfolio review meetings" and "Elicitation techniques" as tools and techniques for the process, "Provide Portfolio Oversight." Further, in Section 5.5.2.1 of the PfM Standard (3.0), review meetings are described as, "meetings . . . held by the portfolio governing body to review the current status of the portfolio and to determine if any decision needs to be made regarding the portfolio and it components." Similarly, in Section 5.5.2.2, examples of elicitation techniques are given as, "compiling status reporting, facilitating meetings, and conducting questionnaires and surveys." These tools and techniques are also described within the project and program management standards, although under slightly different names. Holding a meeting, whether at the portfolio, program, or project levels is still holding a meeting. This is also true of elicitation techniques. Compiling status reporting is the same function, only the topic of the report differs. As a result, the review of tools and techniques will be limited, and the reader is directed to other management text for details concerning a specific tool or technique.

4.3.1. Portfolio authorization

If a portfolio charter is used, portfolio authorization should be part of the chartering process. However, because of the long-term nature of most portfolios, actions will likely involve something akin to a reauthorization process where an existing portfolio is significantly modified in response to a change in organizational strategic objectives or some outside environmental influence. Whatever the process or action, governance considerations should include portfolio authorization and modification elements. For example, governance considerations may state that new portfolios will be initiated as deemed necessary by senior executive management using a process of engagement across the executive management suite and in consultation with projected portfolio management personnel. The actual process and procedure of portfolio authorization or modification is not part of the governance process, and would be worked out separately but within the above-mentioned governance guidance. These procedures are part of the senior board's operating procedure and may be codified in corporate policy or process documents.

4.3.2. Planning

Governance planning should ideally come before the actual implementation of a specific portfolio. The ideal is that portfolios are managed consistently across the enterprise. As such, senior executive management should have minimal governance guidance in place that will be used by the portfolio manager to develop and extend corporate governance practices to each portfolio. The portfolio charter should reference this high-level governance guidance and task the portfolio team to develop supporting portfolio governance processes as the need to supplement the overarching enterprise guidance. We will now look at a methodology for portfolio governance development.

There is an axiom in the field of project management that says, "Project managers don't do anything unless there is a plan first." Preplanning is even more critical at higher levels of management because of increased complexity. There are two approaches to planning. The first is to plan all actions ahead of time and then implement the plan, and the second is to perform some level of incremental planning that can accommodate change over time. The plan is then implemented and updated as the effort progresses. Incremental development and progressive elaboration of work had to be a part of *A Guide to the Project Management Body of Knowledge (PMBOK® Guide)* for over 21 years, and was encouraged within project processes well before the publication of the *Agile Manifesto* in February 2001.

The type of planning process used at any level of management should be related to the complexity of the effort. The more complex an undertaking, the more incremental planning should be used. Length of the effort is also a consideration because long efforts have more uncertainty associated with them. Complexity and uncertainty are related due to the difficulty in projecting future events. Uncertainty is also associated with risk, and although much of portfolio management involves dealing with risk, risk in and of itself does not imply a complex undertaking. For example, the safety certification process for a nuclear power plant may involve great risks because of legislative and public approval uncertainty. However, the actual process of certification is well-defined by statute in most countries and although complicated, does not involve the attribute of complexity as discussed here.[46] That's not to say designing a nuclear power plant and operating the interfaces between the various systems and subsystems are not complex.

In most cases, portfolio management is a complex endeavor. The grouping of multiple programs and projects along with operations portends a system of systems structure where component interrelationships are not well known nor predictable. Further portfolios tend to be long lasting, resulting in considerable uncertainty with regard to future events. As such, at the portfolio level, incremental and iterative planning is recommended.

Pictured in Figure 9 is a nonlinear planning model. The emphasis of this model is on assessments and evaluations along with critical thinking to drive an incremental planning process. It may be used for any planning activity but is particularly applicable to strategic and governance planning. Notice that there are no ordered steps in the process. One does not go from development of a portfolio management plan, to portfolio definition and optimization, to portfolio authorization and execution, with an oversight function to monitor execution throughout the life of the portfolio.[47]

Four overlapping activities of situation or problem investigation, objective determination, and alternatives generation and solution selection

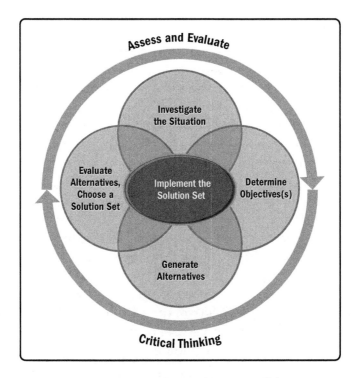

Figure 9. Nonlinear Planning Model

are shown. A traditional problem-solving methodology would picture these activities following a linear, stepwise path from investigation to solution set selection, similar to what was outlined in the PfM Standard (3.0).

However, in this model, feedback loops and parallel accomplishment of activities are accommodated through the overlapping areas of activities. As an example, during the development of the portfolio roadmap, it may be discovered that the portfolio charter needs updating. Additionally, certain items within the roadmap may need to be coordinated with subordinate elements of the portfolio. The process is not a clearly linear one in that changes to one document may impact another and coordination up and down the portfolio may have unplanned impacts on any number of documents related to the portfolio charter or roadmap. Thus, it is seen that management of the portfolio, and in particular, management of the governance aspects of the portfolio, is complex. The portfolio governance structure should accommodate this type of planning due to the uncertain environment faced by most portfolio managers and senior executive staff.

4.3.3. Change control

Change control is a well-acknowledged requirement at both the project and program levels of management. The same holds for the portfolio level of management. However, since the success of the portfolio is measured by "the aggregate investment performance and benefit realization of the portfolio"[48] and portfolio managers manage to the organization's strategic initiatives and objectives, change management processes must have a different focus than at the program and project level. The focus should not be on specific product design requirements. There also must be a methodology to include changes that might occur in the operational environment since operations may also be a sub-element of the portfolio. More than one system may be implemented within the portfolio for change control. For example, operational considerations may be sufficiently different from program and project considerations, requiring a completely different process for managing operational changes. However, from a governance perspective, the same overarching principles of a good change control system must still be in place as at the project level. In brief, a change control system should:

- Be comprehensive and include all change requests;
- Document all actions taken to include both approvals and denials;
- Have processes that are open, well-documented, and timely;
- Have all key stakeholders involved in the change control process; and
- Include full funding for all approved changes.

Finally, clear lines of authority and responsibility must be defined between the portfolio and subordinate change control board. Subordinate change control boards do not necessarily roll up to the portfolio change control board. In fact, it would be unusual for a project change control board to roll up into a portfolio change control board due to the difference in focus of the two.

## CHAPTER 5

Portfolio Resource Capacity and Capability Management

by Panos Chatzipanos

> Man often becomes what he believes himself to be.
> If I keep on saying to myself that I cannot do a certain
> thing, it is possible that I may end by really becoming
> incapable of doing it. On the contrary, if I have the
> belief that I can do it, I shall surely acquire the capac-
> ity to do it even if I may not have it at the beginning.
> — **Mahatma Gandhi**

5.1. Overview

The objective of portfolio resource capability and capacity management is to determine the optimal balance between what the organization has the potential to do, "capability," and what the organization can
do now, "capacity." Capability and capacity management focuses on the
human, financial, and other assets an organization utilizes to resource
the entire portfolio. The capacity and capability management function
plays a critical role in the organization's overall portfolio management—
from strategic planning to portfolio selection and optimization through

portfolio execution, toward realizing the envisioned added value for the organization.

All portfolio work is executed in order to implement organizational strategy through the portfolio components. If those components are not resourced properly, the portfolio will fail to accomplish its intent to fulfill organizational strategic objectives. Each organization has an ideal potential as to what it can achieve organizationally and what can be done at any given point in time. These conditions are always based on the organizational process asset restrictions at that particular point in time within the portfolio life cycle. The portfolio manager must look across the organization and establish programs and supporting projects that not only meet strategic objectives of the organization but that are realistically achievable. This is usually accomplished through the balancing of the organization's capability to achieve business goals and its capacity to accomplish the individual programs and projects toward these goals. A portfolio is balanced if there is a suitable distribution of projects on aspects such as outsourced products or services, new technologies, varying risk, project complexity, resource demand, completion time, return on investment, and so forth. If there are too many projects in the pipeline, there is a high degree of conflict over existing resources, which reflects directly on portfolio progress and success in component delivery and resulting benefits.

There are a number of ways in which portfolio balance can be attained. This requires the right mix of components (e.g., size, duration, resource requirements, etc.) versus attainable benefits, plus an overall portfolio risk profile that is suited to the organization and its environment. Balance on project size is quite important because the commitment of a high proportion of resources to a few large portfolio components may be catastrophic if a couple of components fail. And too many long-term projects, no matter how promising they are, may cause cash flow problems since expected benefits realization may take too long to materialize. In achieving portfolio balance on the risk dimension, it is well known that the greater the risks that are taken, the greater the potential rewards are. For this reason, the portfolio must be balanced to counter risks that may materialize and become serious problems. Thus, in choosing the portfolio components, risky projects should be adequately balanced with less risky projects to avoid jeopardizing the overall organizational strategic objectives, (e.g., maximizing profitability, ensuring long-term survival, and entrance in new markets).

Portfolio component selection and execution, decision making, change management, risk management, as well as the management of portfolio value and the benefits derived from successful execution of the portfolio components have a direct impact on resource capacities and capabilities. The balancing of the organization's capability and capacity is a complex endeavor. The integration of components within the portfolio to meet the organization's strategic objectives involves interrelationships between many systems and their subsystems, namely the organization, its internal and external environment, portfolio components, organizational business and supporting units, departments, divisions, and so forth. The merits of a parallel, systems thinking approach toward the above issues and the navigation of the encountered complexity are discussed in Chapters 10 and 11 of this book. Under this approach, portfolio management must be understood as a complex adaptive system rather than a system of isolated or even simply connected components. Capability and capacity management is a very important aspect of the interconnected processes that shape the portfolio and allow portfolio managers to plan, monitor, and control the execution of portfolios. This is done to meet organizational strategic goals and aggregate the organization's investment performance and benefits realization. *The Standard for Portfolio Management* – Fourth Edition[49] states that the objective for portfolio capacity and capability management is, "to ensure that the portfolio's capacity and capability demands are in alignment with portfolio objectives and can be supported or met by the organization's resource capacities and capabilities, thus enabling successful portfolio execution and expected portfolio returns."

5.2. Guiding Principles for Managing Organizational Resource Capacity and Capability

Organizations, irrespective of the size, complexity, and nature of the business environment need to define and embrace a set of guiding principles to be effective in managing capacity and capability. Capacity and capability management involves decisions under risk, with incomplete information, poorly defined boundary conditions, multiple feedback loops, and ambiguous end states. As *The Standard for Portfolio Management* underlines, "Organizations, irrespective of size, complexity, or nature of the business environment, need to define and embrace a set of guiding principles to be effective with capacity and capability management and succeed at the portfolio level." Portfolio management principles that underpin effective capacity and capability management and should be followed by the portfolio manager include:

- Under a holistic approach, exercise active and decisive leadership for the optimization of resource utilization;
- Achieve excellence in portfolio execution and actively engage all key stakeholders;
- Know at all times during the portfolio life cycle, portfolio resource capacity and capability as well as the resource flow through portfolio components, and thus, balance regularly portfolio value against overall risks; and
- Navigate complexity and plan for multiple end state solutions.

Thus, capacity and capability management's primary function is to balance resource supply with resource demand for all the components of the portfolio throughout the portfolio life cycle. The term "supply" refers to resource capacity, including funding and staffing resources as well as equipment and other physical assets shared among portfolio components. "Demand" is the resource requirement from the portfolio components and the component proposals requesting resources. The goal of managing supply and demand is to ensure resource capacity is optimally allocated against resource requirements or demand based on known organizational priorities and potential value. Resources should be allocated to minimize both unused capacity and unmet demand. Naturally, resourcing should also be based on portfolio components' prioritization and ranking—the higher the rank or importance, the more resources the component gets. The ideal outcome requires diligent, iterative resource management and optimization processes. The balancing of these resources to the output of the portfolio or the portfolio's resultant value is commonly referred to as capacity balancing. Forecasting of supply and demand at the portfolio level is key to balancing portfolio capacity over time.

Consistently and efficiently balancing resource supply and demand is paramount. Organizations worldwide are resource constrained, where resources can be available within a range of variability. Fluctuations in operational workload will have an impact on the availability of resources for work managed within the portfolio. Moreover, the capability and productivity of human resources can vary widely, even in the rare cases when training, background, organizational culture, and experience are quite similar. For example, labor rates can vary based on skill set, experience, industry, and physical location of the resources. Labor resources can be hired or contracted. Equipment and physical assets can be purchased or leased and made available locally or remotely. Every organization has scarce resources that typically create "bottlenecks." These limited resources are quite often of the human kind. Specialized equipment, certain facilities, or other physical assets can also be bottleneck resources. The demand for these resources needs to be managed continuously. It can be difficult to accurately determine the demand for resources across a portfolio of projects, programs, and operations, at any particular point in the portfolio life cycle before detailed planning has occurred and thus a performance baseline has been established. As portfolio components are selected, prioritized, and ranked and planning is conducted, new information regarding resource requirements is often learned. It is a constant iterative process throughout the portfolio life cycle.

To maximize the use of resources, organizations will commit them to authorized portfolio components, based on the expected end date of an active portfolio component (commonly referred to as "soft booking"). Unexpected delays or unrecognized dependencies between portfolio components can result in situations where a resource is not available when expected. Resource allocation must take into account the strategic intent and the expected value or benefits from the portfolio components when it is approved for funding. Portfolio components with the higher expected benefits and stronger strategic intent should have the higher priority over the resource allocations when these are approved and funded. In addition to the strategic intent and benefits for resource allocations, the risk profile needs to be considered as well to ensure that risk appetite and associated opportunities are capitalized to maximize portfolio value. Resource bottlenecks and constraints must be identified continuously and monitored during the portfolio execution, while appropriate strategies for resource leveling and resolution of "bottleneck" effects must be implemented in a timely fashion to minimize any adverse impacts on portfolio performance. The portfolio manager must strive continuously for an optimal balance between the overall demand and supply at the aggregate portfolio level and regularly confirm that expected portfolio value is preserved and maximized.

5.3. Capacity Management

Capacity management is one of the most complex and critical areas of portfolio management. It ensures that the overall resource demands of portfolios and their components are consistently and optimally met. At the organizational level, concerns such as staffing, the creation of needed new infrastructure or development of existing infrastructure, and availability of necessary funds become key in reaching organizational strategic objectives. The major purpose of capacity management is to avoid waste of organizational resources (e.g., time, financial resources, human resources, IT resources, and infrastructure resources). A fundamental goal of managing capacity is to avoid obtaining costly unused capacity. Thus, proper capacity management includes reclaiming unused resources, and these reclaimed resources can then be directed to other portfolio components.

The needs for capacity to implement portfolio management successfully, via the execution of the portfolio components, include primarily:

1. Talent availability – the availability of competent human resources capable of supporting the portfolio implementation
2. Funds availability – to support the portfolio
3. Physical assets availability
4. Intellectual capital availability (e.g., patents, copyrights, and service marks)

The ratios and relevance of the above resource categories depend on the specific industry and portfolio component mix. Resource categories have strong interdependencies that may enhance or reduce the individual potential of each resource. Awareness of such interdependencies is quite important for the practitioner.

5.4. Capacity Planning

Resources are often an organization's most valuable asset and potentially its biggest financial burden. By properly planning the management of available organizational resources and optimally utilizing these, the portfolio manager can retain and further develop available assets while simultaneously realizing business strategy. Capacity planning allows for the understanding and determination of resource needs by measuring the portfolio components' requirements against the capacity of the available organizational resources. Capacity planning affects all aspects of the portfolio. It enables the portfolio manager to obtain and create the necessary resources in order to ensure that the organization can successfully execute its business initiatives as identified in the portfolio. It may be thought of as strategic resource planning and involves the identification and measurement of the total capacity of resources needed to be utilized for the execution of all the portfolio components. Capacity planning includes analysis of what kind of capacity is needed for each portfolio component as well as the needed overall portfolio capacity, how much is needed per each of the ranked components, when each resource is needed, and for how long, and so forth. Capacity planning includes the following steps: Estimate future capacity requirement, evaluate existing overall capacity, including infrastructure capacity, organize resources into meaningful resource pools, set resource utilization percentages, and identify resource gaps by resource gap analysis. Once resource gap analysis is performed, the identification of alternatives toward meeting component requirements should be conducted, followed by the assessment of key qualitative issues for each alternative.

The portfolio manager creates the initial demand forecast for all portfolio components, which is combined with corresponding supply forecasts to create consolidated scenarios for what-if analysis. Such a conditional analysis helps the portfolio manager to determine the optimal balance of available resources and pending work at any time period within the portfolio life cycle. The selection of the most viable alternative is followed by consistent monitoring and controlling of results under a constant proactive approach. The portfolio manager can plan under a prevailing "match" or "lead" or "lag" capacity planning framework. The advantage of employing a "match" strategy is that it most effectively matches actual capacity to what's required. The "lead" strategy tries to anticipate future needed capacity and expands capacity to meet it. The "lag" strategy only develops capacity when present capacity is fully used. Both have a high risk of not providing required capacity. The portfolio manager should strive and develop a consistent process for the "match" strategy, which closely tracks capacity use throughout the portfolio life cycle and proactively adjusts capacity as needed.

Utilizing proven practices of capacity planning under an iterative and continuous process, the portfolio manager can effectively forecast requirements and allocate resources across the portfolio components efficiently. Such a process also requires the use of performance metrics as feedback for re-evaluation at regular intervals in order to determine resource gaps and inefficiencies. Capacity planning mainly involves decisions about the organization's resource demand and supply. While project managers are busy estimating resource requirements in the shorter term and for their project alone, it is imperative that portfolio management set overall utilization targets, portfolio component performance metrics, and a robust process to forecast future organizational needs and maximize resource allocation. From the portfolio perspective, overall demand and available supply should be identified and compiled as an overall supply and demand profile for resource analysis and allocations to follow as part of demand management. A portfolio supply and demand profile provides a consolidated view of forecasted resources for the whole portfolio system. It also captures the risk attitudes and thresholds specific to resources and investments, which are essential in defining resource allocations. Risk attitudes and thresholds specific to resources are also indispensable for making trade-off decisions for portfolio component selection, prioritization, and ranking, along with the consistent ongoing balancing and optimization of the overall portfolio.

An integrated review of the organizational strategic plan, risk management plans, organizational process assets, portfolio process assets, and enterprise environmental factors provides essential information in developing an aggregate and comprehensive forecast of demand and the available supply to support the portfolio. The aggregate supply and demand profile highlights the resource capacity available from the organization across the human, financial, asset, and intellectual dimensions, including boundaries and constraints, and provides valuable guidance in portfolio execution and governance to select and fund components. While accounting for the entire portfolio, capacity planning also needs to accommodate special instances when the portfolio may have mandatory or legislative initiatives that exceed the capacity or capability limits of the organization. Depending on the organization's risk profile, capacity planning may have governance or management contingency reserves for unplanned components that may come up during future business cycles. Successful capacity planning enables the portfolio manager to commit to the highest priority components with confidence, knowing that sufficient resource capacity exists within the organization.

5.5. Supply and Demand Management

Demand-side resource management must balance with supply-side resource management. At the portfolio level, alignment of overall resource supply with overall demand must be sought after on a continuous basis. This continuous balancing engagement involves the iterative analysis of resource gaps and consequently, resource allocations and monitoring to balance supply with resource demand for each portfolio component. Demand-side management, which concerns all the resources the portfolio manager needs to execute the components of the portfolio, entails resisting the desire to control the detail. Details must be examined, analyzed, assessed and validated by the component managers at a program as well as at a project level and integrated information should be submitted at the portfolio level.

A supply and demand analysis for the entire portfolio provides a critical decision framework to be utilized for resource allocation during portfolio selection, authorizing, and funding as well as for the validated information required for a capacity and capability analysis of available or obtainable resources to be allocated to the components. A study of the capability of the available resources needed to deliver projects (e.g., component team members' competencies and talent, computer systems, or software tools to cope with the demands of the portfolio, physical infrastructure, networks, office space, and real estate) should be performed next. Moreover, the results of such studies should be matched to the portfolio component's objectives and goals to meet the overall portfolio demand. At the portfolio management level, the concept of supply and demand takes on a wider meaning than at the program and project levels. The goal in managing supply and demand is to ensure that organizations optimally allocate resource capacity against resource requirements based on strategic goals of the organization and associated portfolio composition. Moreover, the goal is to minimize both capacity underutilization and overutilization.

5.5.1. Supply and demand analysis

Supply and demand analysis is performed to understand the human, financial, physical asset, and intellectual capital capacity and capability available in the organization. This is paramount to managing the portfolio and particularly to select, resource, and execute the portfolio components. From a portfolio perspective, overall portfolio demands, and available supply are identified and compiled as an over-all demand-supply profile for resource examination, inspection, and allocations to follow. The demand is mapped to existing organizational resources, such as funds, other tangible and intangible assets, and key human resources, such as program and project managers and subject matter experts. The portfolio demand and supply profile should provide a clear, consolidated view of the anticipated demand and supply of resources. It also captures the risk objectives and thresholds specific to resources, which are essential in defining the trade-off criteria for each portfolio component. Capability is a specific competency that enables an organization to execute components and deliver results. Portfolio capability is what the enterprise can do but may not be doing presently due to certain organizational or logistical limitations within the portfolio system. It differs from capacity as discussed above in that capacity is what the enterprise is doing now or doing at present. Capability can also be thought of as a characteristic of the organization that may or may not be fulfilled. The sum of all such characteristics of the organization represents the organization's capability while the sum total of currently realized characteristics are the organization's capacity, or what can be done now. Synergy also plays into this equation, as the sum of characteristics is not a simple linear mathematical equation. It may be much more due to the interdependencies between these characteristics.

Projects and programs are driven by requirements that seek to fill a capability gap relating to some product or service. Requirements are balanced via project processes to meet an optimized solution delivering a new product or service. Similarly, at the portfolio level, capability gaps are filled through a balancing of capability and capacity. A capability gap is the difference between the organization's capability and its capacity. Thus, capacity and capability analysis, which drives the decision criteria for resource allocation may include the following:

- **Scenario analysis** – Scenario analysis is necessary to determine various possibilities of resource allocations and the impact to component schedules. Analysis may be used to determine what would happen if human, financial, or equipment funding was increased or decreased, or if constrained resources were not available as scheduled. This type of analysis is important to ensure that the organization is prepared for changes in demand or changes to resource supplies.

Organizations need to position themselves to absorb these changes with minimal impact. Resource management tools are also available for modeling alternative scenarios for using resources to meet the demand of portfolio component priorities.

- **Quantitative and qualitative analysis** – Quantitative and qualitative analysis includes various approaches to studying the demand for resources against capacity and constraints to determine how to best allocate resources. When bottleneck resources or resource downtime are identified, resource leveling or project sequencing techniques can be applied. Resource leveling strives to smooth performance levels by managing bottleneck areas and communicating delayed schedules if necessary. The portfolio manager communicates recommended changes and requests for more resources, and updates the governing body when resource leveling does not produce sufficient results. The qualitative analysis, dependency analysis, review of resource schedules, and making changes to improve capacity become quantitative when working with the number of full-time equivalents required and when determining how many hours need to be allocated for each component, and so on.

- **Risk analysis** – Risk analysis includes the review of risk appetite and risk thresholds to aid with resource allocations and continued resource management. The organization's strategic plan, enterprise risk plan, and portfolio risk plans provide essential guidance on the risk appetite, risk objectives, risk tolerance, and risk thresholds for the portfolio components, their relative priorities, and perceived benefits and value propositions. The portfolio manager must consider and assess these critical elements while defining the decision criteria for resource allocations.

When demand is the primary driver, the organization needs to adjust the resource supply through temporary and permanent resources. When the resource supply is relatively fixed, the organization needs to manage the portfolio components' demand and sequence portfolio component work based on resource availability and component priority. In most cases, organizations must both adjust the resource supply and manage project demand, managing and maintaining a dynamic balance between resource supply and demand.

5.6. Monitor, Control, and Optimize Supply and Demand

The portfolio manager needs to capture critical metrics, key trends and patterns, and lessons learned on capacity and capability. These are key inputs of the measuring and monitoring process. Such information enables the organization to build a knowledge repository, an organizational asset that can be extremely valuable for future use in capacity and capability planning. With changes in the business environment and unplanned events that emerge during portfolio execution, organizations need to continuously evaluate their portfolio for needed adjustments, course corrections, and optimizations. Such inevitable changes during the portfolio life cycle necessitate continual adjustments and refinements to the resource allocations. In order to succeed with this challenge, organizations need to implement lean and robust change management processes to drive agility, effectiveness, and timeliness in response actions and associated decisions. Effective end-to-end change management—including identification, impact assessment, communication, disposition, and execution—is critical for ensuring portfolio value and associated benefits. A prioritized list of portfolio components, decision criteria, and capacity and capability analysis collectively enable effective resource allocations to balance supply against the portfolio demands. A master schedule of resource allocation is necessary to plan the consolidated demand of portfolio resources.

Changes to portfolio components, such as overruns, cancellation, rescheduling, and so on, are intended to drive resource optimization and balancing. The portfolio management team needs to identify resource impacts resulting from the components' changes. The portfolio manager must communicate with and gain concurrence on consequent schedule changes from portfolio governance and key stakeholders for optimal portfolio performance. Such changes can only be made if a robust monitoring and control system is in place, so portfolio decision makers know the current state of the portfolio, variances to plan, and the path toward fulfillment of strategic objectives and goals. Proactive and continuous engagement with portfolio stakeholders with a focus on capacity and capability is extremely important and beneficial in identifying and evaluating any potential risks or issues related to resources. Once potential risk or issues are identified and evaluated, a planned response or mitigation approach can be formulated and implemented, thus avoiding expensive stoppages or disruptions.

In addition to the strategic intent and benefits for resource allocations, the organization's risk appetite needs to be taken into account as well to ensure that threats and opportunities are balanced appropriately to optimize portfolio value. Resource bottlenecks and constraints should be continually identified and constantly monitored during portfolio execution, and appropriate strategies for resource leveling and bottlenecks should be implemented in a timely fashion to minimize any adverse impacts on portfolio performance. Changes to components such as overruns, changes to scope, termination, and rescheduling drive resource optimization and balancing. The portfolio management team needs to identify resource impacts that result from portfolio component changes. The portfolio manager needs to communicate with and gain concurrence on consequential schedule changes from portfolio stakeholders to ensure optimal portfolio performance. The expected value of components can change as program and project managers plan, develop, and execute their components. Changes in actual scope, schedule, cost, or performance can affect the portfolio's expected value. External factors such as market conditions, competitor actions, laws and regulations, and risks realized can also change the expected value at delivery of the products, services, or assets created or enhanced.

5.7. Organizational Capabilities – Assessment and Development

According to *The Standard for Portfolio Management* – Fourth Edition, a capability is the ability of an organization via its people, processes, and systems to execute an entire portfolio of initiatives for delivering goods and services for meeting customer needs. In the context of portfolio management, capabilities include not only project management processes, but also the enabling organizational capabilities, such as:

- Talent: ability to attract, motivate, and retain competent and committed people;
- Speed: ability to make important changes rapidly;
- Shared mind-set and coherent brand identity: ability to ensure that employees and customers have positive and consistent images of and experiences with the organization;

- Accountability: ability to obtain high performance from employees;
- Employee performance management: ability to align systems and processes to ensure employees effectively contribute to goal achievement;
- Collaboration: ability to work across boundaries to ensure both efficiency and leverage;
- Learning: ability to generate ideas with impact;
- Leadership: ability to embed leaders throughout the organization;
- Customer connectivity: ability to build enduring relationships of trust with targeted customers;
- Strategic unity: ability to articulate and share a strategic point of view;
- Innovation: ability to do something new in both content and process;
- Efficiency: ability to manage costs;
- Business analytics and information management: ability to use skills, technologies, applications, and practices to drive business planning;
- Middle-management effectiveness: ability of middle managers to carry strategy into the organization;
- Informal/virtual networks: ability of important but informal channels for reinforcing culture and communicating key information;
- Adaptability and flexibility: ability to leverage a flexible structure that allows adapting to external challenges;
- Culture: ability to unify the organization through a set of shared values; and
- Organizational change management: ability to manage change efforts across the organization.

Dynamic capacity is the current ability of management to make quick decisions under risk that embrace change either within corporate processes or when dealing with specific portfolio goals, objectives, or deliverables. The capacity for change is directly linked to the portfolio management team and the senior executive staff of the company. The management staff's potential to change is sometimes referred to as a company's dynamic capability. Adaptive processes are difficult to implement when dynamic capability and capacity are not present within an organization. Gaps between dynamic capacity and capability may only be filled through personnel actions that either educate, train, or replace individuals. As such, filling a company's dynamic capacity and capability gaps may be the most challenging management undertaking within the capability and capacity management area. Dynamic capacity provides the ability of companies to exercise strategic agility.

Portfolios are the primary means for the execution of strategic plans through the transformation of the enterprise from a current state to some future state as identified within senior-level corporate vision and planning documents. State change within the company is driven by capacity and capability balancing. The portfolio manager must "manage up" to support corporate vision, and strategy and must also "manage down" to execute the portfolio components. The portfolio manager links the business execution to strategy, in part through capacity and capability balancing. The goal is to affect a state change that delivers value to the enterprise. Portfolio elements are managed through an adaptive process that embraces change and drives benefit delivery through the portfolio's component parts.

Dynamic capacity also drives innovation within a company. At the portfolio level, dynamic capacity is critical to the ability to perform strategic planning and visioning. In fact, the execution of capability and capacity balancing is itself dependent on a strong dynamic capacity within the portfolio management team and senior corporate staff. There is an implied contradiction here in that to perform efficient capacity and capability balancing, an organization must possess dynamic capacity. However, if there is a dynamic capacity gap, then the implementation of change becomes difficult, thus making it hard to fulfill the gap between the company's dynamic capability and its dynamic capacity. Unlike other capacity and capability gaps where the focus is on modifications to capacity or what the enterprise can do now when filling a dynamic capacity and capability gap, one must look first to raising dynamic capability through education, training, or personnel changes.

Once the potential for change is established as part of the management approach, it is then possible to increase the capacity for change through processes that encourage dynamic planning and action. Dynamic capability and capacity are crucial to innovation; balancing dynamic capability and capacity is especially difficult because it deals primarily with human soft skills. The process of balancing capability and capacity involves the integration of organizational strategic plans, organizational process assets, portfolio process assets, and enterprise environmental factors. A proposed assessment process is discussed below:

The assessment process has four steps:

1. **Review strategic goals:** The first step is to review and/or clarify the organization's strategic goals, measurable targets, and degree of strategic alignment.

2. **Collect organizational data:** The next step is to collect data through interviews, focus groups, process reviews, and document reviews; stratify data; then quantify qualitative feedback and identify trends.

3. **Analyze the data:** After collecting, reviewing, and quantifying organizational data, the next step is to perform a gap analysis and identify the type, number, size, and impact of the gaps; determine root causes; and define key organizational issues. Part of this analysis will include identifying the key capabilities needed for success and then rating both the relative importance of each capability and the current performance of that capability. This will reveal capability surpluses (better than competitors and/or needed to accomplish goals), alignment, and gaps (worse than competitors and/or needed to achieve goals).

4. **Develop recommendations with an implementation plan:** The last step is to document organizational strengths, key organizational findings, and the impact of critical issues on the organization. This step also includes developing a set of prioritized, actionable, and measurable recommendations to address key issues and reduce or eliminate gaps, establishing a strategically aligned roadmap or implementation plan.

High-performing organizations continually assess their capabilities to develop strategies to close gaps, identify emerging requirements, and deploy resources appropriately. The challenge for any organization is to build capabilities before competitors do, or before market shifts or customers demand their existence. Moreover, capabilities may have to be built as a response to significant internal or external situation shifts.

As mentioned in the previous section, before detailed planning and recognition of resource constraints (bottlenecks) occur, it can be difficult to predict the demand for resources across a portfolio of projects, programs, and operations. As top management and the portfolio team select components and conduct detailed planning, new information regarding needed resources and capabilities is often uncovered. PMI's *The Standard for Portfolio Management* includes several capability elements that organizations should consider as they build the capabilities needed to support the implementation of their organizational strategy via portfolio management. These are:

- Mission: the purpose of the capability, how it will operate, and what it will deliver as derived from the company's strategy;
- Talent: the skills, incentives, and workforce planning that enable an optimal talent base to execute the capability;
- Process: the integrated set of processes and activities to achieve the desired outcome;
- Technology: the systems required to support capacity of the capability;
- Integration: clear roles, decision rights, and policies that inform the organizational structure; and
- Insights: the information, analytics, and decision flow that drive informed and timely decision making.

Managers often face the strategic challenge of determining how to deploy their limited resources, not only to build capabilities to achieve a competitive advantage, but also to make that advantage sustainable. It is important to understand that capabilities are generally interdependent. While organizations should target no more than three capabilities for primary attention, they can stretch limited resources to build sustainable capabilities by focusing on ones that are interconnected. For example, to build speed, the organization will likely need to target fast learning, fast innovation, or fast collaboration. As one capability improves, it may in turn improve other capabilities. Leaders build capabilities, so working on any one of them builds leadership. As the quality of leadership improves, talent and collaboration issues often surface—and in the process of resolving those problems, the organization usually strengthens its accountability and learning.

As with any change process, the portfolio team working to build or enhance a capability will accomplish the following tasks:

- Clarify the new capabilities to be delivered;
- Assess the impact of this new/enhanced capability on other existing capabilities;
- Analyze the ability of the organization to integrate the new/ enhanced capability both structurally and culturally;
- Identify structures needed to sustain the capability;
- Agree on the pace of capability implementation;
- Prepare the organization to leverage the capability (develop the talent);
- Alert stakeholders to any passive or active resistance to implementing the new/enhanced capability;
- Assess the need to decrease or accelerate the pace of implementation; and
- Finalize any residual implementation activities once the implementation project is closed to promote sustainment of the capability.

To enhance the sustainability of the competitive advantage of a capability, managers must work to embed the capabilities throughout different interconnected and hierarchical processes within the organization, (i.e., address the process, technology, and integration capability elements). By establishing the formal system of regulations and organizational hierarchies to shape deliberative decision making regarding the use of the capability, the organization can enhance the sustainability of a capability. Sustaining capability also requires gaining insight via regular checkpoints. These checkpoints include conducting capabilities audits to help gauge—and ultimately boost—the status of the organization's capabilities as well as measuring benefits realization associated with the new/enhanced capability.

5.8. Balance Capacity and Capability

At the portfolio level, capability gaps are reduced through a balancing of capacity and capability. The balancing act at the portfolio level does not involve trade-offs between requirements. Rather, it involves resource trades to balance the organization's potential, its use of its capabilities in its current operating state, and its capacity. Balancing does not necessarily mean maximization of capacity to achieve an organization's theoretical capability. The goal is not to minimize the capability gap without regard to other factors. Balancing capacity and capability is not a simple task because it is part of a complex system. Within complex systems, organizations need to consider many interrelationships. Balancing capacity and capability involves the integration of organizational strategic plans, organizational process assets, portfolio process assets, and enterprise environmental factors. Dynamic capability and capacity is crucial to innovation since it primarily deals with soft skills and human behavior.

Adopting best-practice resource management techniques, by balancing capacity and capability, helps organizations accomplish the following:

- Gain visibility and control using an enterprise resource pool: With a large number of employees and globally dispersed teams, it can be difficult to keep track of who is available, what they are capable of doing, and where they are located. Centralizing resources and standardizing metadata on the enterprise resource pool is the first step to gaining visibility and control.
- Proactively compare capacity to demand to maximize resource utilization: Resource capacity often determines whether organizations are able to complete strategic projects on a specific planning horizon. Capturing resource requirements early in the project life cycle helps analysts anticipate future demand and proactively schedule projects to maximize resource utilization.
- Finding and managing the right resources, particularly the right human capital for each portfolio component: Portfolio components may include globally dispersed teams and may need a diverse set of skills. Quickly finding the right people with availability for each portfolio component significantly increases the chance of successfully implementing organizational strategy.

5.9. Performance: Analytics and Reporting

Performance analytics and reporting, a major part of managing portfolio performance, involves identifying, capturing, and processing data, performing the associated analysis and reporting the information derived from the data analysis at regular intervals. This activity, which needs to be comprehensive, is necessary for progress updates, trends, and patterns to support and substantiate portfolio decision making. Suitability, selection, and frequency of the resource capacity- and capability-related metrics are driven by the size, complexity, and nature of the portfolio and organizational culture. For example, an important role of managing the portfolio is also to deploy resources available for executing the components in such a way that reduces the impact of environmental threats. This is an iterative process and relies on accurate resource capacity- and capability-related metrics. Although capacity- and capability-related metrics have vital importance throughout portfolio management, they are immensely valuable in building a knowledge base of historical data that can be leveraged in future strategic planning cycles or portfolio management activities.

The various performance reports are portfolio assets. The portfolio manager is generally responsible for updating and adding to the portfolio process assets as necessary. These may include: processes, guidelines, policies, and procedures (e.g., strategic alignment, governance, change management, information distribution, optimization, risk and performance management, etc.); specifications, work instructions, proposal evaluation criteria, and performance measurement criteria and templates; performance measurement databases used to collect and make available measurement data on portfolio components and track cash flow, including actual resources used and forecast of resources required; historical information and lessons learned knowledge bases (e.g., portfolio records and documents, portfolio component closure information and documentation, information about both the results of previous portfolio-selection decisions and previous portfolio-performance information, and information from the risk management effort).

Portfolio managers should also strive toward providing assessed information rather than just collected data. Directors at the execution level of the portfolio and senior leadership guiding organizational strategy are inundated with data. Information must be actionable for the level of leadership or management receiving it. This means that a critical role of the portfolio manager is to not only pass information up and down the management chain, but to also assess and tailor the provided information to provide each level of management with actionable information in an easy to comprehend format. In general, the portfolio manager should present complex management information in a "dashboard" type of format where the manager may pull additional information based on data needs. The portfolio manager can push other information within the dashboard to the decision maker or manager, but the data push must be tailored for the individual receiving the information.

Performance reporting and metrics involves identifying, capturing, and distributing data and associated analysis for progress updates, trends, and patterns to aid with portfolio decision making. Suitability and selection and frequency of the capacity- and capability-related metrics is driven by the size, complexity, and nature of the portfolio and organizational culture. While capacity- and capability-related metrics have vital importance throughout the portfolio management, they are immensely valuable in building a knowledge base of historical data, which can be leveraged in future strategic planning cycles or portfolio management activities. Some of the critical areas where key capacity- and capability-related metrics have profound impact are outlined below:

1. Portfolio selection and funding – capacity plans (available supply);
2. Portfolio governance – capacity plans (demand to supply utilization), ongoing utilization, variance analysis of planned to actual;
3. Portfolio execution – ongoing utilization, variance analysis of planned to actual;
4. Portfolio optimization – resource changes and shifts;
5. Portfolio value management – value and benefits measurements (resources spent);
6. Future portfolio planning – resource trends and analytics; and
7. Organizational strategic planning – resource trends and analytics.

Being, in reality, an adaptive complex system,[50] each organization, through its chosen strategic position, interacts and interprets its environment, responds to emergent situations, and many times adapts its strategy to the requirements of the environment. Making sure that the portfolio is constantly aligned with organizational strategy means adapting the implementation of strategy via applying change management processes to the portfolio. Validated portfolio analytics regarding capacity and capability aggregates and portfolio performance reports related to allocated resources are vital for applying such changes successfully.

Furthermore, these metrics are immensely valuable in building a knowledge base of historical data and good practices that can be leveraged in future strategic planning cycles and portfolio management activities.

In conclusion, portfolio resource capacity and capability management includes the processes that allow an organization to effectively assign the appropriate resources to successfully execute the programs and projects in the portfolio to meet the business needs. It also provides management with information for forecasting future resource requirements. Maturity in capacity and capability management is paramount for the implementation of all strategic initiatives. An organization with low maturity may recognize the need for a resource management process consisting of identifying resource requirements and "reserving" them without any disciplined processes; an organization of medium maturity may have standardized, documented, in-place and repeatable implemented resource management processes; an organization of high maturity may have all resource management processes and standards integrated with all other organizational processes and systems. Moreover, a mature organization will have established resource management improvement processes, and the lessons learned will be regularly examined and used to improve documented processes. Compliance with all documented and repeatable resource management processes will be mandated, and processes will be in place to measure capacity and capability management effectiveness and efficiency.

## CHAPTER 6

Engaging Portfolio Stakeholders

by Te Wu

> When people talk, listen completely. Most people
> never listen.
> — **Ernest Hemingway**

6.1. Defining Stakeholder Management

The concept of the stakeholder is relatively new as a major area of performance within project and portfolio management. In *Strategic Management: A Stakeholder Approach*, a pioneering work on the subject of stakeholders, Freeman (1984) formalized an emerging field called "stakeholder theory," based on strategic management.

This theory provides a new lens through which we can understand the differentiation and competitiveness of firms within the same industry. It focuses on the identification of stakeholders, setting the strategic direction, and formulating strategies for them, while also implementing and monitoring their performance to give due regard to the interests of these groups, hence creating value for them. The stakeholder theory goes beyond the traditional view of the firm, which is centered on owners and shareholders, to include all interested parties. Project management is a recent adopter of stakeholder theory.

Although the concept of stakeholder has existed since the first *A Guide to the Project Management Body of Knowledge (PMBOK® Guide)*, it was not until the fifth edition of the *PMBOK® Guide* that stakeholders were finally elevated to a Knowledge Area. This evolution in the relative importance of stakeholders in project management follows a circuitous route. Today, as organizational endeavors are becoming ever more complex, the need to involve key stakeholders at every level of planning, implementation, and operations is becoming self-evident. Thus, following this gradual but growing focus on people in *The Standard for Portfolio Management – Fourth Edition*, portfolio stakeholder management is viewed as more proactive than managing communication. In short, stakeholders play an increasingly important role in the definition, implementation, creation, and appropriation of value.

Contemporary organizations strive to achieve and maintain sustainable competitive advantages, and this requires a proactive focus on resources. In this resource-intensive view of organizations, with a focus on building core competencies, engaging portfolio stakeholders is becoming ever more important for portfolios to achieve their intended value. At a portfolio level, there is a considerable expansion of stakeholders as compared with traditional project management. The category of stakeholder can now include not only the traditional categories, such as portfolio team members, customers, partners, and executives, but also extended groups such as financiers, regulatory and government bodies, trade unions, partnerships, communities, and even competitors. In short, any group that can influence a portfolio's performance can now be incorporated into this framework.

6.2. Why Are Stakeholders so Critical?

Stakeholders have been defined as "any group or individuals who can affect or is affected by the achievement of the organization's objectives" (Freeman 1984, 46) and as individuals or organizations with "a vested interest in the outcome of the project" (Cleland 1985, cited in Littau, Jujagiri, and Adlbrecht 2010, 6). Similarly, PMI defines a project stakeholder as "an individual, group, or organization who may affect, be affected by, or perceive itself to be affected by a decision, activity, or outcome of the project" (Project Management Institute 2013a, 30).

From a portfolio perspective, internal project stakeholders are often defined as the sponsor (sometimes synonymous with the organization), top management, component manager, component team, and internal user groups. External project stakeholders include the customer or consumer, client, suppliers, competitors, regulators, and occasionally the broader community.

From an impact perspective, in an interesting study of 368 published journal sources, Davis (2014) found only one reference to an external factor listed as having an influence on project success by internal stakeholders. The remaining 367 references categorized stakeholders as internal resources; the most frequently studied stakeholders include project managers, project teams, and clients (Davis 2014). In another study by Rothaermel (2012), about 20 percent of superior performance can be explained by industry or external effects, about 30–40 percent can be explained by firm or internal effects, and about 30–50 percent are the result of other causes, such as a corporate parent and years of operation. There is considerable literature demonstrating the importance of stakeholders on projects, programs, and portfolios.

6.3. Important Activities of Portfolio Stakeholder Management

As *The Standard for Portfolio Management* – Fourth Edition indicates, there are many approaches to stakeholder management. To simplify the process, this section outlines a five-step approach to managing stakeholders. These five steps can be iterative and require re-examination whenever there are significant changes to the portfolio:

1. Identify stakeholders – Early in a portfolio life cycle, portfolio managers should determine the people and groups affected by the portfolio activities. These effects can be either real *or* perceived.
2. Prioritize stakeholders – Since portfolio managers have finite resources, it is important to evaluate and rate the portfolio stakeholders from the most important to the least.
3. Plan stakeholder engagement – Portfolio managers should develop a specific stakeholder engagement plan, taking their priorities into consideration. This way, portfolio managers can maximize their probability of achieving success.
4. Develop communication plan – Communication is extremely important, especially when there are a large number of

stakeholders in the portfolio. As such, communication planning is viewed as a distinct activity.

5. Engage stakeholders, execute communication plan, and continuously monitor and adapt – Throughout the portfolio life cycle, portfolio managers should execute the stakeholder engagement plan and communication plan to enable stakeholder support of the portfolio. Since portfolios can be long-lasting, it is important for portfolio managers to continuously monitor and control the progress of implementing the stakeholder engagement plan and communication plan. As often required throughout the long life cycle of portfolios, portfolio managers should adjust the process and adapt to the changing portfolios.

The remainder of these sections focus on the specific methods of performing these five activities.

6.4. How to Identify Stakeholders

During the initial establishment of the portfolio or when changes are made to the portfolio, managers should work with their core team and sponsors to identify and re-identify the portfolio stakeholders. There are a number of valuable inputs to jumpstart this activity: organization and portfolio strategy, portfolio and component charters, portfolio management plan, and other organizational assets. There are multiple methods of identifying portfolio stakeholders, and this chapter highlights three methods presented in the order of simple to complex.

These three methods can work together. For example, in a portfolio that is still emerging, portfolio managers can start with method one. As the portfolio complexity increases, portfolio managers can leverage the results of the first method and deepen the process using method two. Later, especially when there are considerable external entities working on the portfolio, portfolio managers can progress to method three.

Method one is the simplest of the three frameworks. Proposed by Wilson, Bunn, and Savage (2010, 80), this framework suggests the use of two categories: primary stakeholders and secondary stakeholders. Primary stakeholders are the individuals or organizations who must collaborate in order to deliver the project outcome: project sponsors, customers and owners, and project managers. Secondary stakeholders are the individuals or organizations not directly involved in the project, but who can affect or be affected by the outcome. This method is suitable for organizations that are entrepreneurial and flexible. Portfolio managers can readily apply this method or even start with this method before morphing into the next.

Method two is derived from Turner (2006), who groups project stakeholders into the following seven categories:

1. Owner – provides the resources to finance the asset and derives the benefits from its operation;
2. User – operates the asset on the owner's behalf;
3. Sponsor – channels the resources to the portfolio on the owner's behalf;
4. Resources – are assigned to the portfolio and its components and will do the work to deliver the asset;
5. Broker – works with the owner and the sponsor to define the required outcome of the portfolio and portfolio components, and the output that will achieve that;
6. Steward – works with the broker to identify the means of obtaining the output, the work, and the resources required; and
7. Manager – manages the portfolio and portfolio component teams to ensure that the right work is done to deliver the defined output, and to monitor and control progress.

While this method was originally created for project management, its robustness makes it even more suitable for portfolio management. Method two works well for more sophisticated and mature organizations, and where more in-depth categorization of stakeholders can assist with portfolio performance.

Method three is a further expansion by taking into account the internal and external resources across the portfolio life cycle. Figure 10 is illustrative, and it shows the various stakeholder groups organized by internal versus external and across the portfolio life cycle.

6.5. How to Best Organize and Prioritize Stakeholders

There are a number of useful frameworks that examine how to best organize and cluster stakeholders. A popular framework for identification of stakeholders, developed by Johnson, Whittington, and Scholes (2011) is the Power and Interest Grid. This framework maps stakeholders along

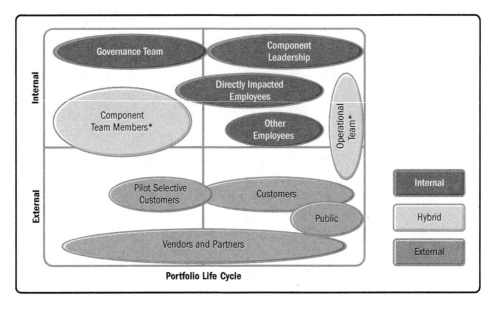

Figure 10. Example of Stakeholders[51]

the dimensions of power and interest. Figure 11 is a modified version designed for portfolio management.

The x-axis (horizontal) represents the degree of interest by the stakeholders. The higher the interest, the more likely the stakeholders will be actively involved in the portfolio. The y-axis (vertical) indicates the amount of influence that the stakeholder has over the portfolio.

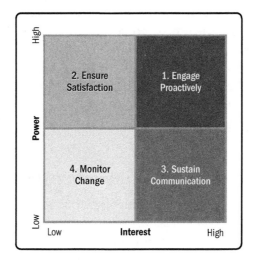

Figure 11. Power and Interest Grid[52]

Influential or powerful stakeholders can steer the direction of the portfolio. When these two dimensions are drawn in a 2x2 matrix or grid, there are four resulting groups:

1. High power, high interest – This is the most important group of stakeholders and requires proactive engagement. These stakeholders are influential and are highly interested in the portfolio. Blockers in this group can be detrimental to the success of the portfolio, and portfolio managers should work with members of this group closely, including designing specialized communication initiatives and change programs to secure their support. Members of this group typically include sponsors, steering committees, and customers.

2. High power, low interest – This group of stakeholders is highly influential, but their focus is largely elsewhere. They may become engaged, both as a supporter or a blocker, should their interest intercept with this portfolio. As such, it is important to keep them pleased throughout the portfolio life cycle. Portfolio managers should leverage the existing activities and perhaps even design special ones to ensure their satisfaction. Members of this group include organizational executives and regulators.

3. Low power, high interest – In most portfolios, this group's lower amount of power is deceptive because the sheer number of stakeholders in this group can be high. When energized with their high interest, this group can be a formidable collective. Portfolio managers should develop a sustainable communication plan to engage with this group regularly and to keep them informed at all times. Members of this group include portfolio and portfolio component team members, functional managers, and end users.

4. Low power, low interest – This group of stakeholders is the least important. It's generally composed of dispassionate end users, consumers, and stakeholders who are indirectly involved with the portfolio manager. Portfolio managers should ideally leverage an existing portfolio management activity to monitor this group and provide them with some regular updates to ensure continual support.

While graphically intuitive, the Power and Interest Grid can be difficult for portfolio managers to rank stakeholders who are nearby in the grid, either in the same quadrant or in the adjacent quadrant.

PMO Advisory, a highly specialized project management consultancy and a PMI Global Registered Education Provider, offers another powerful model. The Simplified Stakeholder Evaluation Method (SSEM) has three major benefits when compared with the Power and Interest Grid: 1) Uses a simple, five-question model; 2) Incorporates stakeholders who may have perceived impact (versus real impact); and 3) Provides a single scoring model for easy quantitative analysis and ranking. The SSEM provides the following five questions for the portfolio stakeholder analysis:

1. Does this stakeholder have any expectation of this portfolio? If yes, how high?
2. What is the magnitude of real or perceived impact of change to this stakeholder?
3. What is the extent of emotional impact of this portfolio to this stakeholder?
4. If nothing is done to manage this stakeholder, what is the extent of negative impact that this stakeholder can result?
5. How much influence does this stakeholder have on your initiative?

All questions are evaluated on a scale of zero to five, where:

0. No expectation or no impact
1. Very little expectation or low impact that is barely perceptible
2. Minor expectation or low impact that is perceived but relatively easy to tackle
3. Moderate expectation and impact that requires some planning to tackle
4. High expectation and impact that requires significant planning to properly manage
5. Very high expectation and impact that requires dedicated and intense efforts to manage

When evaluating stakeholders, the stakeholder importance score (SIS) is the sum of the ratings for Questions 1 to 4 multiplied by a rating for Question 5 or

$SIS = \Sigma Q_{(1-4)} * Q5$, where Q1, Q2, . . . Q5 are the ratings of each question per stakeholder

Table 8 is an example of applying the SSEM tool to a merger and acquisition portfolio of two construction companies. The portfolio

Table 8. Simplified Stakeholder Evaluation Method (SSEM)

Stakeholder Name	Internal or External Stakeholder	Q1: Does this stakeholder have any expectation of this portfolio? If yes, how high? Use "0" for no.	Q2: What is the magnitude of real or perceived impact of change to this stakeholder?	Q3: What is the extent of "emotional" impact to this stakeholder?	Q4: If nothing is done to manage this stakeholder, what is the extent of negative impact that this stakeholder can result?	Q5: How much influence does this stakeholder have on your initiative?	Stakeholder Importance Score (SIS)
Executives	External	5	5	5	5	5	100
Core Portfolio Team	Internal	5	4	5	5	4	76
Leaders & Managers	Internal	5	4	4	4	4	68
Shareholders	External	5	5	1	4	4	60
Regulatory Bodies	External	2	2	0	4	5	40
Employees - Directly	Internal	4	4	3	3	2	28
Employees - Peripheral	Internal	3	3	2	2	2	20
Suppliers	External	3	3	1	2	2	18
Customers	External	1	3	1	3	2	16
General Public	External	2	1	0	2	0	0

To download this and other tools and templates, please visit the book site at www.implementppm.com and register to receive access to a secured website.

Table 9. Sample Stakeholder Scoring

Score Range	Category	Relative % of Stakeholders	Description
80–100	Very Important	Very Few	Portfolio managers must proactively manage these high-stake stakeholders by creating special engagement activities for this category of stakeholders.
60–79	Important	Few	Portfolio managers should also proactively manage this category of important stakeholders. Where possible, leverage the activities created for the higher-priority stakeholders, but clearly some new activities are required for the important stakeholders.
40–59	Moderate	Moderate	Portfolio managers should leverage the existing activities whenever possible. At the minimum, make sure this group of stakeholders is included in the communication plan.
20–39	Low	High	Portfolio managers should leverage the existing activities and avoid creating additional activities unless there are compelling reasons.
0–19	Very Low	Very High	Since portfolio managers have limited resources (and attention span), portfolio managers should mostly leverage existing activities to make sure this stakeholder group is informed.

contains 55 components, of which 20 percent of the projects are human resources oriented, including alignment of compensation and titles.

As this example shows, the stakeholder importance score (SIS) has a range of zero to 100, where 100 is the highest. Based on PMO Advisory's experience, Table 9 shows the recommendations and actions. It is also important to note that as SIS falls, the sheer number of stakeholders typically increases as each category becomes broader. Before applying this matrix, portfolio managers should tailor the scoring for their portfolios.

6.6. How to Plan Stakeholder Engagement

Now with the stakeholders identified and evaluated, portfolio managers are ready for stakeholder engagement planning. While there are many ways to manage stakeholders, an easy and proven method comes from PMO Advisory's library of tools. The Simplified Stakeholder Engagement Plan (SSEP) leverages the evaluation performance using SSEM in the earlier chapter. The SSEP contains the following attributes, shown in Table 10.

Table 11 provides an illustrative analysis of six stakeholder groups from the earlier stakeholder prioritization scenario.

Table 10. Sample Stakeholder Engagement Plan

Column #	Name	Description
1	ID	This is the stakeholder ID, often ranked from the most important to the least important.
2	Stakeholder Importance Score (SIS)	This is the achieved SIS from the stakeholder evaluation using the Simplified Stakeholder Evaluation Method (SSEM).
3	Role	Describe the role that this stakeholder plays on the portfolio.
4	Status	Describe the current status of the stakeholders. Are they currently: • Blocker – Actively works against the portfolio • Pessimist – Negative perceptions of the portfolio, but does not actively engage to block this portfolio • Disinterested – Largely neutral about the portfolio • Supporter – Works actively to support the portfolio
5	Level of Support Required	What's the required level of support from these stakeholders? Are they: • Necessary, which is vitally important for the success of the portfolio • Desirable, which would be helpful but not detrimental to the portfolio • Unnecessary, which makes the support nice, but without tangible benefits
6	Stakeholder Needs/Expectations	Identify what this stakeholder wants or needs from the portfolio or the portfolio management team. For example, are they interested in achieving the desired outcome and value or are they more interested in the process and governance from the portfolio management team?
7	Portfolio Needs/Expectations	What does the portfolio and portfolio management team need from this stakeholder? Is it knowledge of the industry, executive guidance, removal of obstacles, approval of processes and standards, or something else?
8	Engagement Required	Should the portfolio management plan proactively engage this stakeholder? If yes, determine when, how frequently, and how best to engage them.
9	Responsible Parties for Engagement	Identify the party who is best equipped to manage this group of stakeholders.

6.7. How to Develop a Robust Portfolio Management Communication Plan

Even though the portfolio management communication plan is a specific activity within the stakeholder engagement plan, its importance to the overall success of the portfolio is high. Thus, to ensure the appropriate level of emphasis, the portfolio management communication plan is placed in a dedicated section.

The high-level portfolio management communication plan highlights the major communication activities required to achieve portfolio success. There are many ways to create the communication plan, and Table 12 provides one such example of a high-level plan.

To make this operational, portfolio managers are encouraged to create a detailed communication plan for each of the activities listed.

Table 11. Simplified Stakeholder Engagement Plan (SSEP)

#	Stakeholder/ Group	Score	Role (from the initiative perspective)	Status - Blocker, Pessimist/ Disinterested, Supporter	Level of Support Required (necessary, desirable, unnecessary)	Stakeholder Needs/ Expectations (What do they want from the portfolio management team?)	Portfolio Needs/ Expectations (What does the portfolio team need from the stakeholders? What level of commitment/ support is necessary?)	Engagement Required? (Timing/ Frequency)	Responsible Parties for Engagement
1	Executives	100	Serve on the portfolio steering committee	Disinterested – Supporter	Necessary	Successful outcome, both internal harmony and share price	High commitment required to remove obstacles	Yes, monthly meetings	Portfolio manager
2	Core Portfolio Team	76	Core members of the M&A Integration Team	Supporter	Necessary	This is the portfolio management team	With aggressive time-line and 55 initiatives, they need each other	Yes, daily – weekly	Portfolio manager
3	Shareholders	60	The top five shareholder groups control 52 percent of the new firm; they are very vocal	Supporter	Necessary	Successful outcome, mainly share price	Governance support	Yes, quarterly report; semian-nual meeting	Executives (e.g., CxOs)
4	Regulatory Bodies	40	The relationship is traditionally excellent, but some of the regulators are concerned about aligning construction codes across international boundaries	Pessimist – Disinterested	Necessary	Assurance of standards	Approval on standards and building codes	Yes, as needed	Engineers, portfolio manager, legal
5	Employees – Directly Impacted	28	As these employees are directly impacted by process or technological changes, they can be collectively influential. Plus, there is a large majority of employees who were against the merger and acquisition	Pessimist – Blockers	Desirable	Smooth transition and change for the better (more favorable to them personally)	Strong support, both mentally and physically	Yes, real-time updates via portal, monthly newsletter, quar-terly company-wide portfolio status report	Portfolio manager working with sales and marketing teams
6	Customers	16	Customers are less concerned with internal changes than the pricing model and quality standards	Pessimist – Disinterested	Desirable	New products and services; maintain or improve from existing processes and fees	General support of the new company with additional jobs and referrals	Yes, leverage the reports from above	Chief marketing officer; public relations

Table 12. Simplified Stakeholder Engagement Plan (SSEP)

Name	Purpose	Delivery Method/ Communication Tool	Target Stakeholders	Expected Outcome/Reaction	Primary Owner (Responsible)	Frequency
Portfolio Website	Transparency and engagement	Intranet	Mainly employees; some suppliers	Achieves a higher degree of support, especially from blockers and pessimistic stakeholders. While these groups may not fully support the portfolio in their hearts, the team hopes to win their minds	Portfolio management team	Near real time
Performance Report – Executive	Monitor, control, and escalation	Portfolio management information system (PMIS) with executive dashboard and detailed reports	Executives (e.g., governance team, sponsor, selective CxOs)	Provides timely updates on the portfolio and resolves escalated issues and risks effectively	Portfolio manager	Monthly portfolio meeting; quarterly strategic review
Performance Report – Component Manager	Monitor, control, and resource review	Portfolio management information system (PMIS) with portfolio dashboard and detailed component reports	All portfolio component managers and selective functional managers	Reviews the details of the portfolio progress, including implementation of approved components, pipeline of new ideas, stability of operations, and organizational adoption on completed components	Portfolio manager	Weekly
Performance Report – Dashboard	Communication and new idea generation (special component of #1)	Intranet	Mainly employees, also some suppliers	Actively engages employees to generate new ideas to improve the new company	Portfolio manager	Monthly (updated after review with executives)
Performance Report – Community	Community engagement	Internet	Mainly regulators, but also customers, vendors, and the general public	Provides timely updates to manage expectations of important external parties	Portfolio management team working with marketing and public relations	Quarterly
Shareholders	Shareholder engagement focusing on business value	Official company reports	Shareholders	Provides timely updates to manage expectations of shareholders	Portfolio manager working with CEO, COO, CFO, and investor relations	Quarterly report and annual report

Further analysis can include the timeline for executing the communication plan, target audience, primary messages, expected outcomes, responsible and accountable parties, and dependencies.

6.8. How to Engage Stakeholders and Manage Their Expectations Sustainably throughout the Portfolio Life Cycle

With the planning activities completed, portfolio managers must implement them, including the stakeholder engagement plan and communication plan. If the portfolio management approach is new to the organization, an excellent starting point is conducting training and information sessions. Since portfolios usually involve a significant portion of organizational resources, it is important to engage the stakeholders early in the portfolio life cycle and set the tone for transparency and inclusion.

The initial focus should be on information sharing, collaboration, invitations to contribute new ideas, process clarity, and alignment of interest so all impacted members can feel comfortable being a part of the portfolio team. At this early stage, it is especially important to align the approved components with the portfolio and organizational strategy. By creating an environment of transparency, cooperation, and strategic alignment, portfolio managers can create a virtuous momentum toward the eventual implementation of the portfolio and its components.

During the planning phase of the portfolio life cycle, there is often more friction, as decisions with regard to component approvals, resource allocations, schedule constraints, and interdependencies can be contentious and political. Portfolio managers should be viewed as a neutral and objective management body working in the interest of the organization, not specific departments or interest groups. By enabling the portfolio stakeholders through training and information sharing, portfolio managers can achieve a high degree of process legitimacy in which even the blockers can appreciate the stakeholder engagement processes and activities. Furthermore, by being objective and engaging, portfolio managers greatly enhance the likelihood of achieving portfolio success.

During implementation, portfolio managers are often the "fire fighters," coming to extinguish the latest problems and risks. Portfolio managers should champion the deliberation of difficult choices and decisions to give stakeholders a fair chance of voicing their concerns. By actively engaging stakeholders and implementing the communication plan, portfolio managers are constantly working with key stakeholders to set, manage, and reset stakeholder expectations and involvement.

In a full portfolio, there are likely projects and programs and other components in all phases of the life cycle, from initiation (e.g., new ideas still waiting for approval) to post-implementation. The portfolio itself has entered the optimization phase with some components already finished while others are still being planned, and portfolio managers now have the opportunity to conduct a thorough review of what went well and what can be improved. There can be valuable inputs from portfolio component evaluations (e.g., project and program postmortems). This feedback can serve as important methods for continuous improvements of portfolio management.

## CHAPTER 7

Portfolio Value Management

by Debbie McKee

> [Price is what you pay. Value is what you get.
> — **Warren Buffett**]

This chapter explores value management in the context of portfolio management. Value management is a key principle of portfolio management, driving organizational performance. As described within the PfM Standard,[53] all portfolios are managed to enhance and maintain the value of the organization, whether that value is tangible or intangible. An organization can only maximize the value of its portfolio if it adopts a deliberate approach built on a set of principles.

The definition of "value" from the PfM Standard sets the foundation on which this chapter builds:

> Essentially all (definitions) revolve around the idea that value is an indicator of the effect an entity or offering can deliver. That effect can be seen in a number of ways—for example, as increased revenue, increased profit, or reduced risk. Value is contextual. The effects that an organization seeks to command are driven by the purpose of the organization and its worldview, reflected in its strategy. The value

of an entity or offering increases the more impactful it is and the more relevant to the organization's strategy the impact is. An entity or offering is high in value where it has a significant impact on an organization's environment and where that impact is relevant to the organization's strategy.[54]

A portfolio's value is driven by its constituent components. These can be programs, projects, or operations. From this guide's perspective, projects produce deliverables, programs deliver benefits, and operations contribute ongoing value. The aggregate product of these components is the overall portfolio value.

Regarding "how-to" concepts, much of the detailed process work instructions apply to these lower-level component activities. At the portfolio level, we are more interested in the "command and control of the components" and making in-flight course corrections to them in order to maximize value in response to external factors and internal change. This chapter focuses on the following:

- Setting and negotiating value targets;
- Balancing value and risk; and
- Monitoring and measuring value.

7.1. Setting and Negotiating Value Targets

Portfolio value targets are set at two levels:

1. The overall value target for the portfolio; and
2. The targets for the individual components that comprise the portfolio, which are then aggregated to meet the overall target.

7.1.1. Overall portfolio value target

The overall portfolio value target is the allocated target value to be delivered by the portfolio as a whole. It is negotiated in response to part or all of the organizational strategy. This target may be defined as a composite of a number of metrics. While financial performance is usually a factor in at least maintaining organizational viability, it may not be the sole or indeed—a primary—metric. Other metrics may include:

1. Number of patents registered
2. Market share gained
3. Skills acquired

4. Regional realignment
5. Statutory certifications achieved
6. Environmental impact

Thus, each portfolio within an organization may deliver one or more of the above. To reasonably assess interportfolio performance, a weighted scoring model can be used to develop a common baseline for comparing value measures (e.g., to achieve one performance point, a portfolio might need to register 10 patents or achieve a 0.5 percent increase in market share or a 1 percent increase in annual revenue).

7.1.2. Component value target

The overall portfolio value target is further decomposed into component value targets, which may be higher or lower than the overall, depending on their particular risk, investment, and duration profiles. The approach for setting intraportfolio component targets mirrors that for the overall portfolio, albeit at a more granular level and carried out under the direction of the portfolio manager.

The portfolio components inherit the value measures from their portfolio on the basis of their strategic importance to the organization, but they may be aggregated from other measures, and components may have different targets based on their cost, risk, and duration profiles. To consider an example:

> In pursuit of the strategic value targets of financial improvement (reduced operating cost) and reducing (negative) environmental impact, an airline manufacturer might initiate a portfolio aimed at reducing fuel consumption per mile with programs investigating alternative fuels and reductions in airframe weight. This latter program might, in turn, have a project to increase the heat tolerance of certain airframe components allowing the same performance to be achieved at a lower overall weight.

So, the value, reduced operating cost, is driven by reduced fuel consumption per mile, which in turn is driven by reduced weight.

These measures are encapsulated within the component and within the portfolio. If the contribution to the overall measure is correctly understood, and the reporting chain is consistent, these factors need not be the day-to-day concern of the portfolio manager. Their focus should be on the strategic impact of the portfolio and balance of the components within it. Execution of the component activities is the responsibility of the program, project, and operations managers.

7.2. Value Management Framework

As explained in the PfM Standard, the results of the target value negotiation are encapsulated in the value management framework (VMF). The VMF is developed during portfolio initiation, referenced, and then refined during the balancing of value and risk, which occurs as part of the maximizing value activity.

The VMF defines the configuration "guard rails" for each component within a portfolio. Typically, it will include:

1. The value measures that could form part of the target for each component type within the portfolio (e.g., operational cost reduction, market share improvement);
2. A baseline reference for each item in 1. (e.g., prior year's annual report);
3. The measurement calculation for each measure, including a statement of any specific exclusions (e.g., where one particular operations category should be ignored due to acquisition/ merger plans);
4. The expected timeline of value realization. Any other particular constraints on components, including:

    - Funding delimited by financial years,
    - Dependencies between components for value realization,
    - Upcoming legislation, and
    - Known resource limits;

5. Reporting method and frequency; and
6. Key stakeholders.

7.3. Balancing Value and Risk, Strategic Prioritization

Portfolio management is an exercise in the achievement of business strategy through the conscious allocation of resources.

There are two "value management" decision points. The first occurs where the organization converts its strategy into a set of portfolios that will lead to the realization of that strategy. At that point, the allocation is between "competing" portfolios and the organization is trying to build a set of portfolios that will maximize the return on the investment to be made. As we will discuss in the next paragraph, the "return" need not be financial, although the investment usually will be.

The second decision point occurs within each portfolio and informs the negotiation of the value to be returned by each for its specific investment. At that point, the question of allocation revolves around designing and selecting components that will deliver the aims of the portfolio at the lowest safe economic cost. Essentially, the first debate is one among competing "whats" and the second is concerned with "hows." For best results, some form of tool or technique is needed to work through the allocation questions, and this chapter discusses the use of the portfolio efficient frontier, adapted for this purpose.

The concept of the efficient frontier was created by the mathematician Harry Markowitz, who documented the concept in 1952 in an article titled "Portfolio Selection" (Markowitz 1952). The basis of his theory was that given a choice between two paths equally beneficial, people would choose the path with the lowest risk. Equally, when a higher-risk path is taken, people expect a higher return. His article focused on the performance of differing financial portfolios, comparing expected return and risk (which he quantified by considering the variance in return). Figure 12 shows how the efficient frontier can be identified as the curve that represents the highest return for the particular level of risk.

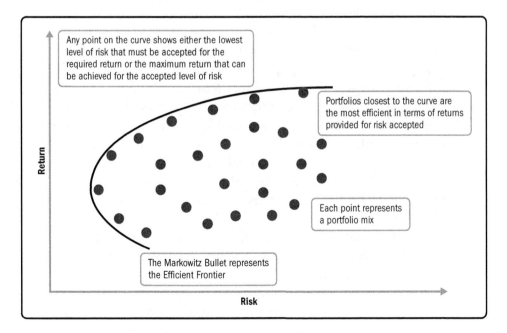

Figure 12. Markowitz's Efficient Frontier

In looking at the use of the efficient frontier in the context of portfolio management, we need to make one significant adjustment: changing the x-axis from measuring risk to measuring cost. We also need to recognize that the possible portfolio mixes are not as continuous as they might be in constructing financial portfolios. In this use of the efficient frontier, we will be mixing components that are broadly inelastic in terms of cost. Other required adjustments include:

- Finding a common metric for return. In a portfolio of financial products, monetary value is the ready measure of return. A company strategy may drive a number of portfolios each with a different primary measure of return—for example, in the case of an aid agency example in value management, increased receipts from donors (monetary), more rapid lift of supplies into a disaster area (tonnage per day, time to deliver first load), reduction in medical intervention attributable to lack of aid (reduced demand for hospital capacity), and so on. To compare portfolios, some common metrics must be found, and rules agreed upon for using them. The rules are there to force transparency in the process, not to constrain it. Therefore, there must also be a means of adjusting the rules and their working. Pursuing the case of the aid agency further, it could be that its management team decides that "malnutrition prevented" will be the common measure of return applied to every portfolio for the purposes of comparison. A key step in comparing the possible portfolio mixes will be to convert—for example, receipts from donors into "malnutrition prevented" using a documented approach. This normalization of the approach to measuring return is likely to be most straightforward in the business sector where a financial measure, typically net present value, might be calculated.
- Ensuring there is a rich set of portfolio outcomes to be measured. There are two areas to be considered here:
  - The deliberate introduction of lower cost, lower return options into a portfolio to increase the set of possible portfolios—for example, a hotel chain considering improving its contact center might consider modeling that on the basis of a 10-second average response time, a 30-second average response time, and a 60-second average response time. While pursuing the latter approach

suboptimizes the contact center responsiveness, it could be that there is a set of portfolios in which that approach delivers a higher return than anywhere the contact center has a 10-second response time. The difference in cost enables higher returns in the wider set of portfolios.

○ The modeling of risk/opportunity as it applies to return and to cost: This serves two purposes. It helps tackle the optimism bias that leads us to believe that the output of a modeling exercise creates future truth, and it serves to demonstrate the benefit of effective risk management. If every portfolio carried a cost-risk premium modeled using, for example, a triangular distribution from 5 percent to 10 percent to 25 percent, then it becomes possible to demonstrate the value of investment in risk management by showing how—where risk is tolerated, unmitigated—the organization's options become increasingly limited by the need to afford the risk.

The first use of the efficient frontier is to allocate resources between competing portfolios. This needs to be done moderately, swiftly, and pragmatically. The aim here is strategic allocation and there's likely to be too little knowledge to make a detailed model worthwhile. The following steps explained in Section 7.3.1. define the allocation between portfolios.

7.3.1. The organization updates its strategy

The updated strategy is used to confirm the set of portfolios required to meet the strategy, including defining the desired and tolerable levels of return and likely costs. The organization identifies a common measure of return and, for each portfolio, a means of transforming the natural measure of return into the common measure. The strategy can help guide this—for instance, if the outcomes for the strategy are framed in terms of finance, then a common approach based on monetary value would seem appropriate. Below are the high-level steps:

- Each portfolio leader develops and shares a high-level model, linking investment and outcome where the model accounts for the risk of requiring more budget and undershooting the target performance. The model should allow for a deliberate approach to building up the investment from a "minimum viable" approach to something that could be seen as gold-plated. The requirement to share limits the opportunity for magic modeling, and the act of sharing helps build consensus and commitment in the leadership team and among the portfolio managers.

- Each portfolio generates a spread of outcomes for the various, agreed-upon investment scenarios (e.g., by using Monte Carlo modeling).
- The organization creates/updates a set of rules that will be used to build candidate portfolios of portfolios and then uses the rules to generate those sets.
- The organization plots out the efficient frontier. Figure 13 illustrates the key points of the efficient frontier in this context.
- The organization takes a very limited number of the portfolios and hands them off to the respective portfolios for further analysis.

The results of that analysis, discussed below, drive final confirmation of the set of portfolios to support the strategy together with associated commitments to investments and returns.

The second application of the efficient frontier is to maximize the efficiency within a portfolio. The assumption is that the organization

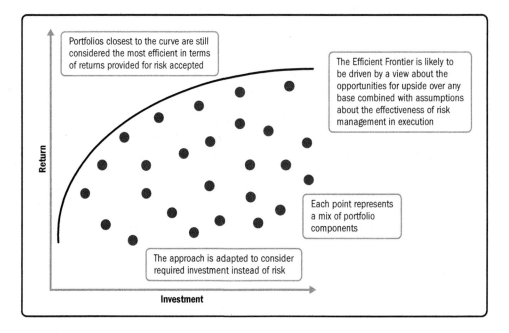

Figure 13.   Large Portfolio Mix

has used the strategic allocation approach just described as part of its strategic planning process to identify the return required from a portfolio and the investment it is prepared to make. At this point, we use the principles of the efficient frontier to examine marginal trade-offs between investment and return, based on a deeper understanding of the components within the portfolio. In considering "return," at this point, each portfolio measures return using the appropriate native measure (e.g., additional client calls handled, fatalities avoided, stores on hand, etc.). The following steps are required.

The components required to deliver the portfolio are designed. The overall aims of the portfolio, together with the scenarios for return and investment form part of the design input. Component owners should be encouraged to identify approaches to reduce cost, increase return, and manage risk.

The portfolio manager assembles a set of candidate approaches to delivering the portfolio based on the proposals offered by the component owners and models them to identify the efficient frontier. The extent of the efficient frontier will be much narrower than for the strategic allocation because the individual portfolio is already constrained in terms of available investment and required return. The much narrower extent of the of the efficient frontier is depicted in Figure 14 below.

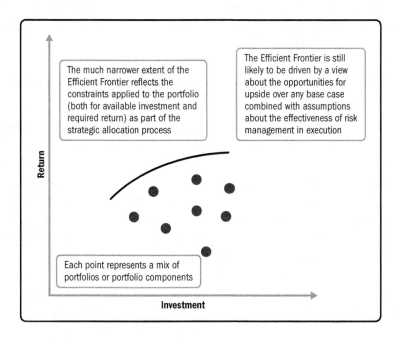

Figure 14.   Narrow Portfolio Mix

The portfolio manager offers a limited set of candidate approaches to the wider organization. The organization selects the one it believes most appropriate, striking a contract with the portfolio manager based on achieving an agreed-upon return for an agreed-upon investment with an accepted level of risk.

The use of the efficient frontier in this context provides a robust and recognized approach to considering the merits of the various options in a manner that supports transparency and testability. Overall, the approach should increase consensus and commitment and therefore the chances of successful execution.

7.4. Monitoring and Measuring Value

The continuing monitoring and measurement of value are the key tools by which the portfolio manager steers the active portfolio. There are two key questions that need to be asked and answered on a continuing basis to ensure that the portfolio is on track and still relevant:

7.4.1. Are the components delivering the value expected?

While the day-to-day delivery activities for the portfolio components are not of direct interest to the portfolio manager, it is important that an assurance framework is implemented that provides an appropriate level of feedback on component delivery performance without detracting from those delivery activities.

7.4.2. Is that component/portfolio value still relevant in the context of the organization's strategy?

Consider our earlier example of reducing airframe weight in order to reduce fuel consumption, in turn reducing operating costs. We could envisage a scenario whereby a new type of fuel is developed that is significantly cheaper, thereby rendering the return on the investment in weight reduction worthless. It is important that we have feedback loops not only validating that components are on track with delivering their expected value (including assuring that they are within their assigned risk threshold), but also that their contribution is still relevant to the organization.

In both cases, this value monitoring and assurance activity may be an "add-on" to an existing governance process for programs or projects, but it provides a direct feedback loop to the portfolio manager.

A proven approach in a number of forms is the use of "gated" assurance and feedback. The aim of a gated approach is to ensure that, at defined points in the life cycle, the outputs of all the work streams supporting a component are considered holistically with a view to answering four key questions:

- If the component work continues from this point, can we expect it to deliver its required value contribution?
- Has anything happened or been revealed that materially impacts the risk profile of the work in terms of the delivery of its outputs and the ability of the target audience to exploit them?
- Are there any opportunities to increase the value profile that this work might yield?
- Do the key stakeholders agree that, given current progress and understanding, the work will yield the intended value and should continue?

Early reviews in the model primarily ask questions about work that has been done. Later reviews are more forward-looking, interrogating preparedness, particularly in later stages—the preparedness of the wider business to assimilate, adopt, and exploit the outputs of the component. There is no fixed model that defines a perfect number of gates. Equally, relying only on the major gates and having no other reviews will likely lead to failure at the gates themselves.

Figure 15 provides an illustrative view of a development life cycle managed through a set of gates. The life cycle could be applied to many component types and is in no way constrained only to IT projects.

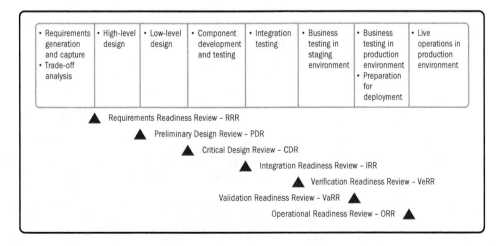

Figure 15.   Illustrative Development Life Cycle with Value Assurance Reviews

The model uses the seven gates shown, which are described in Table 13. The purpose of each gate is described in outline, but each must also address the four key questions listed earlier.

Table 13. Definitions of Assurance Gates in Illustrative Gated Approach to Value Assurance

Ser No	Name of Gate	Purpose of Gate
1	Requirements Readiness Review (RRR)	• Confirm that all the requirements have been captured, prioritized, and understood, including the approach to testing them. • Examine the results of trade-off studies into different approaches to meeting the requirements. • Endorse the overall approach to meeting the requirements.
2	Preliminary Design Review (PDR)	• Confirm that the high-level design can be traced to the agreed-upon requirements. • Demonstrate that agreed-upon design principles have been followed. • Demonstrate that there is a process for eventual validation that the solution meets the requirements.
3	Critical Design Review (CDR)	• Confirm that the design has advanced to a point at which individual components can be commissioned/built and tested. • Confirm that the more detailed designs remain aligned to the designs assured during PDR. • Demonstrate continuing adherence to agreed-upon portfolio principles. • Demonstrate the design is capable of being evaluated against the requirements.
4	Integration Readiness Review (IRR)	• Confirm that units/components built from the designs assured at CDR are at a state of maturity and compliance with the designs, and that they can be brought together for more complex testing. • Demonstrate that the capabilities required to support such testing are available.
5	Validation Readiness Review (VaRR)	• Confirm that all the components required to deliver the intended outcomes have matured to the point where they can be brought together and tested in an operational context in the production environment. • Demonstrate that the receiving organization is ready to support the testing and assurance and understands and accepts the risks related to the (limited) deployment of the capability in the production environment.
6	Operational Readiness Review (ORR)	• Confirm that all those elements of the business that are intended to "use" or "exploit" the capability are ready to receive it. There is a focus in the ORR on confirming not just that the capability to be deployed should enable the required benefits, but also that the organizations that will realize those benefits have taken all the enabling steps required for success. • Depending on the nature of the output of the component and the size of the deployment, the rollout is likely to be phased; therefore, elements of the ORR will be appropriate in each phase.

CHAPTER 8

Portfolio Risk Management
by Nick Clemens and Debbie McKee

> It seems to be a law of nature, inflexible and inexorable, that those who will not risk cannot win.
> — John Paul Jones

This chapter elaborates on topics covered in the portfolio risk management section of *The Standard for Portfolio Management* – Fourth Edition. As such, the chapter supplements and is not a replacement for the portfolio risk management section of the standard. We begin by describing the context of risk management at the portfolio level and outline the unique characteristics of risks at the portfolio level of management. Tools and techniques are not explicitly covered in this work, nor are they discussed in the PfM Standard as they are in the *PMBOK® Guide*. The tools of risk management and analysis may be used at various levels of management and the reader should look to one of many other works on risk management qualitative and quantitative assessment tools for more detail. The focus of risk management at the portfolio level is then discussed. This discussion derives from the context of risk management within the project, program, and portfolio management spaces. Product, execution, and structural risk area definitions are extended from content within the PfM Standard. Since portfolios are the extension of their component parts, risk focus areas are completely discussed within the context of the project, program, and portfolio management space.

The bulk of the chapter involves a detailed discussion of the sources of risk as these are depicted for reference in Figure 16 below. Each major element of portfolio risk management is reviewed and portions of management areas within the PfM Standard are assessed to discover possible sources of portfolio risk. A prescriptive structure of the portfolio management is not offered. However, four major areas that the plan should cover are suggested. The capacity and capability management and value management sections of the PfM Standard are shown to contribute portfolio-level risk approach, process, and policies areas. The other three areas, guidance to subordinate-level projects, programs, and operational entities, linkages to support senior-level decision processes above the portfolio level, and linkages into and support of enterprise risk management (ERM) activities are then briefly discussed in turn. Risks associated with stakeholder engagement are then covered, with potential risk sources being drawn from the PfM Standard's stakeholder engagement section.

Although tools are not explicitly covered, risk assessment techniques are briefly discussed next, demonstrating that these techniques are similar no matter at which level of management they are applied. A very short discussion on portfolio risk response follows, similarly concluding that as was found with risk assessment, the portfolio level of risk response or execution of risk plans are similar as that at other levels of management. The chapter then wraps up by emphasizing the need to consider the overhead impact of risk management and to be sure that the risk effort adds value to the portfolio and is consistent with business strategic goals and the overall expected portfolio return on investment.

8.1. Context of Portfolio Risk Management

Risk management activities span all projects, programs, and portfolios. It is part of small team management within work packages and is part of agile management practices. Risk definition and management is a fundamental action of portfolios and above management practices. In fact, business risk management may be thought of as the primary function of senior board-level executives. Whether working in the project, program, or operations spaces, risk factors play in most all business actions.

Interestingly, risk was not a separate chapter in the original edition of the PfM Standard published in 2006. However, in the second edition of the standard, published in 2008, a risk chapter was added that covered portfolio risk identification and analysis, the development of portfolio

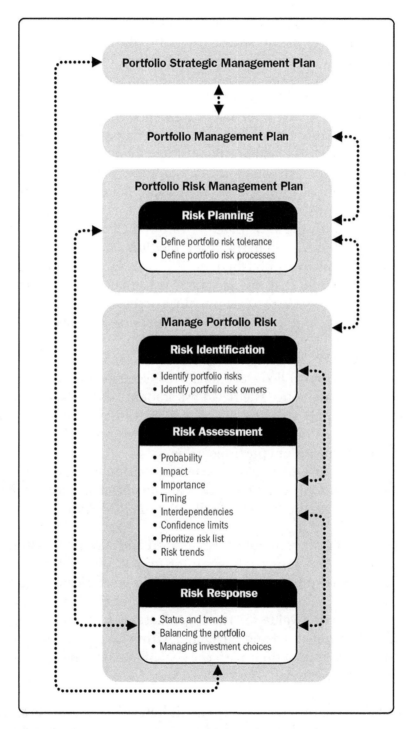

Figure 16.   Elements of Portfolio Risk Management[55]

risk responses, and monitoring and controlling of portfolio risks. The second edition of the PfM Standard states that "[t]he objectives of Portfolio Risk Management are to increase the probability and impact of positive events and to decrease the probability and impact of events adverse to the portfolio." The PfM Standard (3.0) refocused the risk discussion at the portfolio level to just three major elements, the development of the portfolio performance management plan, the management of supply and demand, and finally the management of portfolio value. The PfM Standard (3.0) departed from what essentially appears to be a project-focused risk object statement changing keywords, and states that, "[t]he objective of portfolio risk management is to accept the right amount of risk commensurate with the anticipated reward to deliver the optimum outcomes for the organization in the short, medium, and longer term."

The PfM Standard, published in 2017, states that "[t]he primary objective of Portfolio Risk Management is to make sure that portfolio components will achieve the best possible success according to the organization's strategy and business model. From a risk perspective, this is done through the balancing of risks, both positive (opportunities) and negative (threats)." The PfM Standard thus initiated a significant change in how risk at the portfolio level and above is seen by the inclusion of the concept of risk balancing. The new PfM Standard extends the approach toward risk as simply avoiding threats and maximizing benefits that the previous standards described, and includes the approach of balancing risks to achieve maximum portfolio value.

The concept of balancing as opposed to limiting is significant, as risk is now seen as a tool to achieve strategic business objectives within a company's business model. As described in the PfM Standard,

> Risk and change should be embraced and navigated within an environment of nonlinear interactions. Within this nonlinear environment, specific portfolio-level risks are addressed by the portfolio management team with the goal of optimizing value for the organization. Risk and change are thus embraced and navigated within an environment of nonlinear interactions with the goal of maximizing value for the organization.

The PfM Standard extension of not only how risk is viewed but also how the risk environment is understood is in direct response to complexity being identified as a fundamental characteristic of the portfolio space. Within the concept of complexity, we could argue as to whether risk may be "managed," as in a predetermined set of rule-based linear responses or if risk management under complexity is, at best, limited to "fuzzy" approaches within a "decision under risk" process defined by but not bounded[56] by incomplete data. The realization of complexity as a fundamental characteristic of portfolios leads us away from linear responses and the traditional idea of "checklist" management. Hence, in the PfM Standard, there is a movement away from describing risk regarding a management process that may imply a rule-based linear process as opposed to a balancing process of some type that embraces complexity and all its implications. See our section on complexity in this book and the appendix on complexity within the PfM Standard.

In this chapter, we look at risk as expressed in the PfM Standard. The focus is on explaining how risk may be used as a tool that will help portfolio management teams achieve maximum value for their organizations. According to the PfM Standard, the following three guiding principles are central to risk management processes at the portfolio level:

- Maximize portfolio value while balancing risks;
- Foster a culture that embraces change and risk, and
- Navigate complexity to enable successful outcomes.

These principles, along with the concept of complexity as a fundamental characteristic of the portfolio space, form the underpinning of the approach to risk management within the PfM Standard.

8.2. Tools and Techniques

There are many books available[57] that describe various tools and techniques for risk management. One such book, *Risk Analysis: A Quantitative Guide* by David Vose, provides over 100 models and examples of quantitative risk analysis tools spread over 22 chapters and some 735 pages. Books like this usually deal with project-based risk or discussions concerning either data types and quality or some mathematical technique for data analysis. Books that deal specifically with strategic management or portfolio management usually do not discuss risk as a separate element but provide a cross-section of management techniques that seek to reduce uncertainty or support senior executive decision processes, thus addressing risk through either management or technical processes. A third type of book, particularly popular during the late 1990s, involved "Six Sigma" approaches and their application at various levels of management. Six Sigma approaches use technical or process-oriented analysis that supports decision processes.

Popular now are books dealing with extensions to agile processes that seek to apply agile management philosophy to project, program, and portfolio levels and above. The agile community has yet to standardize approaches above the small team level. However, much experimentation is underway, with the primary impediment being the use of standard terminology. A significant step forward has been made with the publication of the PMI and Agile Alliance *Agile Practice Guide* and the current publication of the *PMBOK® Guide* – Sixth Edition. Agile extensions above the small team seek to support both decision processes and the management of workflow at and above the project level. (See the chapter in this book on agile at the portfolio level.) From the portfolio level, the project life cycle selected is a management decision that is most appropriately made by the program or project manager. The selection of predictive, iterative, incremental, or agile management approaches as described in the *Agile Practice Guide* is seen as a risk response action. However, it is not seen as primarily a portfolio management function, at least not in a large enterprise composed of multiple portfolios and a robust and layered management structure. With the above said, it is certainly appropriate for agile approaches to be incorporated into the program and portfolio levels through the application of various small team agile extensions and an individual portfolio manager may decide to structure the management of a portfolio along agile or lean approaches. However, above the portfolio, this should be a governance decision decided by senior management.

The intent for the remainder of this chapter is not to replicate the already outstanding and exhaustive work of cataloging and to explain various risk tools and management approaches outlined above and completed by others. Nor will we reinvent the already available survey of management techniques or software tools to support executive decision processes. Our goal is to explain how the concept of risk as a tool may be used within the context of risk management as introduced by the PfM Standard. Our focus will be on dealing with complexity and embracing risk as a means of achieving strategic goals and delivering value to our organizations through the management of portfolios. As such, we assume that all portfolios are by nature complex and that it's the role of the portfolio manager to manage complexity and, where possible, avoid a descent into chaotic environments.

8.3. Risk Focus

The PfM Standard asserts that risk management at the portfolio level is fundamentally different from risk management found at the project level. As written in the PfM Standard, Section 8.2.1, "Portfolio risk management differs from project risk management in that the goal of risk management at the project level is to minimize threats and maximize opportunities;" in Section 8.4.1, "At the portfolio level, risks are usually not 'controlled'—they are managed within a comprehensive risk strategy;" and finally in Section 8.5.1, "Differences are expected between the portfolio, program, project, and operations risk management areas." The role of complexity in shaping the risk environment at the portfolio level has been discussed above. The risk focus area also contributes to the uniqueness of risk at the portfolio level. In Section 8.4.1, structural and execution risks are briefly discussed in relation to their being driven predominantly by individual risk perceptions.[58] A third but unmentioned risk category is product risks. These risk categories define the risk focus at each level of management, and they are pictured in the following illustration. Notice that since programs contain both projects and ongoing operations, they may contain all three risk focus areas. However, the primary purpose of a project is to deliver a product or service. Hence, the product focus risk area is associated with the project. Similarly, portfolios manage efforts through their subordinate programs and projects, so the primary risk focus area within the portfolio is the structural risk area. By focus area, we mean the primary driver for risk concerns. Other drivers may be present. For example, the product risk focus area is primarily restricted to schedule, cost, scope, and quality risks directly associated with the product or service deliverable.

The risk focus areas at each level of management within and adjacent to the project, program, and portfolio management space are shown in Table 14 and defined as follows. Product risks are focused on the project and program levels of management. The structural risk focus area includes a wide range of risks from personnel management, to cross-organizational coordination, to general strategic management concerns. Strategic management concerns include business risks. Operational or execution risks are considered separately due to the unique characteristics

Table 14.   Types of Risks across Project, Program, and Portfolio

Management Level	Major Risk Concerns	Risk Focus
Work Package (Small Team)	Short-term feature or item delivery	Product and Structural (Execution DevOps only and small team management)
Project	Midterm product delivery or incremental upgrade	Product
Program	Mid- and long-term benefit delivery through program projects and operations	Product, Structural, Execution (cross-project and program management)
Portfolio	Mid- and long-term delivery in support of strategic objectives and integration of program activities across the portfolio and coordination between enterprise portfolios	Structural (inter- and intra-portfolio management and senior-level coordination and support)
Above Portfolio	Corporate visioning, establishment of goal and business objectives, and coordination of portfolio actives across the enterprise	Structural (strategic and cross-portfolio management)

of ongoing operations. Execution risks in this context do not include programmatic management actions associated with the execution of projects, programs, or portfolios that are usually seen as internal to the portfolio staff, or program or project management offices. However, there is a conflation of operations and project execution in the agile environment where a DevOps[59] delivery approach is used.

Table 14 illustrates each level of the project, program, and portfolio management space along with the adjacent above-portfolio management level. The above-portfolio management level consists of the senior executive management organization or governance-management level tasked with cross-portfolio management. The small team management level is part of the project management level, but is included as a separate level of management to illustrate how small teams or working-level management actions fit into the overall risk-focus structure. It is at the small team level where the agile process takes place.[60] Looking at the project level, only product risks are seen as the focus. This does not exclude structural or execution risks from playing in the project space. The intent is only to identify the driving focus in relation to the primary functions at each level of management.

From a project management perspective, management actions within the small team are accomplished either through work package managers or, in the case of an agile effort, via self-governing teams facilitated by a scrum master when Scrum-related management processes are used. The project's purpose is to deliver a unique product, service, or capability. As such, risk considerations are focused on the product deliverable. Programs may be ongoing and deliver benefits to their organizations through the delivery of products and services. Program risk may involve execution (operations), product delivery, and structural considerations dealing with management across projects and between programs. At the program level, risk analysis primarily deals with management processes and secondarily with deliverables. These deliverables are managed within the program's subordinate projects. Since programs may also contain operations, operational risks are also included at the program level.

At the portfolio level, all product delivery and operational considerations are carried out through the portfolio's subordinate program, project, or operational entities, and thus the handling of product, operational, and some structural risk actions are properly addressed through the portfolio's subordinate organizations. Therefore, the activities within the portfolio primarily involve management considerations such as establishing strategic goals, coordinating actions between portfolio elements and other portfolios, coordinating portfolio actions, and aligning benefit delivery to strategic business objectives. Risks associated with these activities involve the structural focus area. Further, a key function of the portfolio management staff is facilitation of senior executive decisions. This is also a structural function and involves cross-program and portfolio risk considerations. The primary focus of risk activities at the portfolio therefore involves supporting senior staff decisions and coordinating actions, not fixing product or operational-related issues. Operational or product risks are addressed through the portfolio's subordinate projects and operational organization. Figure 17 is a graphic representation of the aforementioned relationship between project, program, and portfolio risk focus areas showing the overlapping risk areas and their associated level of management within the project, program, and portfolio space.

Figure 18 shows how risk response actions are implemented through the three management levels. The solid lines represent direct action paths. For example, at the project level of management, product risk responses are implemented directly, as pictured by the solid arrow extending from the project box to the product risk response. Similar responses at the program level of management are implemented through the program's subordinate projects, and thus the action line is shown as dashed. Similarly, at the portfolio level, risk actions are implemented

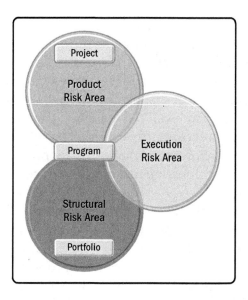

Figure 17. Primary Risk Focus Areas for Projects, Programs, and Portfolios

through the portfolio's subordinate projects or programs, as shown by the arrows above the project, program, and portfolio boxes. Portfolio managers and their staff interact directly with their subordinate organizations, but risk-related activities are executed indirectly through those subordinate organizations. In summary, at the portfolio level, structural

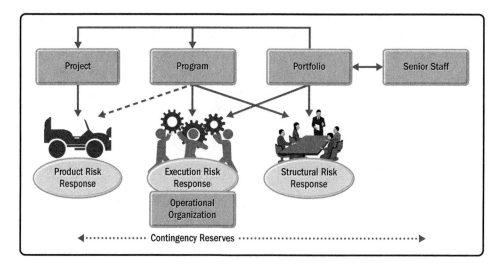

Figure 18. Risk Response Action Paths by Project, Program, and Portfolio Management Levels

risk responses may be implemented directly while execution responses may be implemented through the portfolio's operational organizations. Risk response actions are usually funded through contingency reserves, as shown by the dotted arrow extending across the management levels. The establishment of reserves will be discussed further on in more detail.

In Figure 18, we see that the risk focus area at the portfolio level is primarily structural. However, structural risk at the portfolio level involves strategic business concerns, which is the primary contributor to complexity at the portfolio level. In addition to these strategic concerns, there is also the management interrelationships between portfolios, between subordinate entities within each portfolio, and coordination with senior management. These risk concerns below the portfolio level tend to be "stove-piped" within their respective projects, programs, or operational entities. A further function of the portfolio management team is to break down the stovepipes so that enterprise risk management issues may be addressed at and above the portfolio level. At best, unknowns associated with even a simple organizational structure may have emergent complexities involved with coordinating actions at senior levels of the organization. The lack of control of external factors on the organization is also a constant contributor and acts as a catalyst for the emergence of complexities. The position of the portfolio within the organization structure, its focus on structural risk, and presence of complexity combine to make risk management at the portfolio level unique and challenging.

8.4. Portfolio Risk Management Plan and Risk Identification

The portfolio risk management plan is an extension of the portfolio management plan. Its purpose is to describe how portfolio risks will be handled in support of portfolio objectives. This relationship is shown in Figure 16. The double arrows between the portfolio strategic management plan and portfolio management plan boxes illustrate a two-way channel of communication or relationship between the portfolio strategic management plan writing process and the portfolio management plan writing process. Dotted feedback loops are also shown, indicating that both plans are living documents that should be updated on a continuous basis.

Risk context is defined within the portfolio risk management plan. A brief description of the portfolio risk management plan is given in

Section 8.5.2 of the PfM Standard and further outlined as part of the strategic portfolio management plan outlined in the strategy section of this work. As outlined in the standard, "The portfolio risk management plan extends the vision articulated within the risk management framework (see Figure 8-1 in the PfM Standard). However, the portfolio risk management plan should not be prescriptive down to the project level . . . " As such, each element of the portfolio should have its separate risk management approach. Each subordinate element's plan should be aligned with and supportive of the overall portfolio risk management plan. Although not explicitly articulated in the PfM Standard, the following four items are implied requirements of the portfolio risk management plan. The portfolio risk management plan thus:

- Provides guidance for risk handling to subordinate levels of the portfolio;
- Establishes contingency reserve processes at the portfolio level;
- Supports decision processes at and above the portfolio level of management; and
- Facilitates enterprise risk management activities at and above the portfolio level of management.

A prescriptive outline of what could form a portfolio risk management plan will not be provided. Numerous suggestions may be found from a simple internet search. From the four items listed above, the portfolio risk management plans should, in broad terms, cover the following four areas:

1. Portfolio-level risk approach, processes, and policies;
2. Guidance to subordinate-level projects, programs, and operational entities;
3. Linkages to support senior-level decision processes above the portfolio level; and
4. Linkages into and support of enterprise risk management (ERM) activities.

Sources of risks for each of these four areas, which form a general outline for a portfolio management plan, will be covered in the following sections. When considering the portfolio risk management plan, realize that most plan outlines found in other books are from a project-level perspective in which the focus is on product risks. The exception to this is where enterprise risk management (ERM) is explicitly covered. At the portfolio level, the plan must cover a broader perspective to include cross-portfolio management considerations and the breaking down of silos between projects, programs, and operations to facilitate ERM actions at and above the portfolio level. However, the portfolio risk management plan does not perform the function of planning for the ERM. This is a separate activity that is usually done as part of a senior staff function above the portfolio level or at the organization's governance or enterprise levels.

Finally, under risk planning, two sub-elements are listed, defining risk tolerance and defining portfolio risk processes. Risk tolerance may be discussed from either an individual or an organizational perspective. Generally, the organizational risk tolerance is thought of as an average risk tolerance of the individuals who make up the organization. However, under a strong leader, the organizational risk tolerance may be set by the leadership. Risk tolerance is a function of personal perception and by nature hard to quantify.

However, a less qualitative approach to looking at an individual's or organization's approach to risk would be to establish the risk appetite of individuals or the organization. This is done through writing risk appetite statements that illustrate the approach of the individual or organization, along with feelings about risk. From a portfolio risk perspective, the approach is usually to focus on the organization as opposed to the individual. Nevertheless, it is the culmination of individual responses that make up the data that defines the organization's response. Based on the risk appetite statements, risk thresholds are set, which serve as metrics for the qualitative risk appetite statements. The risk appetite is measured through setting risk thresholds. This analysis technique goes beyond the more general qualitative risk assessment process that ends with the development of a risk matrix categorizing risks into usually three areas of high, medium, or low. Risk appetite data feeds into the quantitative risk analysis process. However, it may also be used to supplement a qualitative risk assessment.

8.5. Portfolio-Level Risk Approach, Processes, and Policies

With the above in mind, let's look closer at item one, portfolio-level risk approach, processes, and policies. Remember, "[t]he primary objective of Portfolio Risk Management is to make sure that portfolio components will achieve the best possible success according to the organization's strategy and business model."[61] Portfolio management involves the processes of screening, selection, balancing, implementation, and close-out of projects, programs, and operational actions to achieve strategic business goals. Portfolio-level risks will involve structural and execution risk areas associated with the above processes. From a risk perspective, the processes of screening and selection of portfolio activities to achieve business goals requires business and environmental-related risk analysis. A wide definition of environmental risk should be adopted, encompassing political, social, and governance concerns. Balancing and implementation concerns and their associated risks are addressed under the function of portfolio capability and capacity management. This topic is covered in both this book and the PfM Standard in Section 5. The following outline made of major headings from the portfolio capacity and capability management chapter of the PfM Standard provides a good starting point for portfolio-level risk sources:

> **PfM Standard 5.3 Capacity Management** (Structural Risk Area) – The management of capacity involves human, financial, and intellectual capital, and other assets. Each of these resource categories is important to the ongoing health of the enterprise and may be a source of risks either independently or collectively. At lower levels of management, planning risks may be overcome by quick response actions, but at the portfolio level, impacts may be so significant as to make recovery difficult. Additionally, these risks generally impact enterprise-level functions and may require ERM actions. The coordination of ERM processes may result in the realization of benefits to the portfolio through the realization of positive risks. Figure 5-1, Capacity and Capability Management Components of Portfolio Management,[62] shows how various components of capacity and capability management are connected. An expansion of this diagram into a causal loop diagram tailored to your organization would help identify areas of risk (both benefits and threats) that are not readily apparent.
>
> **PfM Standard 5.4 Capacity Planning** (Structural Risk Area) – The overall portfolio supply and demand profile results from the capacity planning effort. The supply and demand profile

is the basis for supply and demand management. Uncertain factors such as regulatory or other government measures may impact the overall portfolio supply and demand profile. The success of supply and demand management will be closely tied to the quality of the capacity planning activities. Planning risks at the portfolio level are similar to planning risks found at any level of management. A primary concern at the portfolio level is proper alignment of plans both up and down the organization.

PfM Standard 5.5 Supply and Demand Management – Risks associated with supply and demand management may be in the area of execution or structural risk depending on the organization deriving the risk. If this function is implemented under an operations organization, it would be considered in the execution risk area. However, if the analysis is a staff or non-operations function then the risk would be in the structural risk area. The key to managing supply and demand is balancing the sometimes-conflicting requirements of both supply and demand. Failure in management may result from either poor planning, errors in analysis, or a simple failure to decide properly (Structural Risk Area). Risk associated with poor decision processes usually results from personal styles of executive leadership (Structural Risk Area). Risks of this type are difficult to quantify and do not lend themselves to quantitative analysis. Benefit analysis may be critical in the balancing of supply and demand as creative ways are sought to increase supply to meet demand or control demand to align it with the supply side of the equation.

PfM Standard 5.6 Supply and Demand Optimization (Structural Risk Area) – These risks involve a mistake in either the input data or the analysis itself. Usually analysis risks may be minimized by using well-known and approved analytic techniques and validated data. Generally, benefit analysis would be limited to a redefinition of the problem that may lead to a unique perspective, which allows a better way to optimize the relationship between supply and demand.

PfM Standard 5.7 Organizational Capabilities – Risks associated with organizational capabilities may be in the area of execution or structural risk depending on the organization deriving the risk. If the organization is an operational entity, then the risk would be characterized as in the execution risk area. For staff-related or non-operational functions, the risk area would be structural. The key risk factor is: Can the organization or staff deliver on its assigned mission or tasking?

PfM Standard 5.8 Capability Assessment – Risks associated with capability assessment may be in the area of execution or structural risk, depending on the organization deriving the risk. If the organization is an operational entity, then the risk would be characterized as in the execution risk area. For staff-related or non-operational functions, the risk area would be structural. The key risk factor is concerned with potential analysis issues. These issues fall into two major categories: the reliability of data and the correctness of the analytic process. Generally, benefit analysis would be limited to a redefinition of the problem that may lead to a unique perspective that allows a better way to optimize the relationship between supply and demand. The risk of poor decisions resulting from the analysis is considered separately as an executive leadership issue.

PfM Standard 5.9 Capability Development – This is essentially an assessment function. Risks associated with capability development may occur in the area of execution or structural risk depending on the organization deriving the risk. See discussion under Subsection 5.7 on capability assessment.

PfM Standard 5.10 Performance Reporting and Analytics – Risks associated with performance reporting and analytics may be in the area of execution or structural risk depending on the organization deriving the risk. See discussion under Subsection 5.7 on capability assessment. Communications risks also come into play. See the following section on stakeholder-related risks.

PfM Standard 5.11 Balancing Capacity and Capability (Execution Risk Area) – Balancing capacity and capability is a dynamic activity related to the balancing of capacity and demand discussed above. Both activities involve complexity and the need to trade positive and negative risks to maximize the probability of achieving strategic business objectives.

Similarly, Sections 7.3 through 7.10 of the PfM Standard also provide a good starting point for considering additional sources of risk that are related to the portfolio value proposition. The outline of the referenced sections from the PfM Standard section is provided below.

PfM Standard 7.3 What Is Value Management? (Structural Risk Area) – It is stated in this section that the measurement of value is not necessarily straightforward. Whenever there is uncertainty in a process, risks come into play. Sources or risks of particular concern include impacts on, or effects of, brand awareness, organizational reputation, regulatory compliance, and value to society. With the exception of regulatory compliance, the other three items are perception-based and hard to quantify. Benefit analysis can be particularly fruitful with regard to those factors driven by perception.

PfM Standard 7.4 Components of Value Management – Figure 7.1, Key Activities in Portfolio Value Management, shows the first-level interrelationships between various elements of portfolio management. From a risk perspective, a causal loop diagram analysis of this diagram tailored to your organization would help identify otherwise hidden risk areas. The causal loop diagram may lead to the discovery of both positive and negative risks as interrelationships are explored.

PfM Standard 7.5 Negotiating Expected Value (Structural Risk Area) – Any negotiation process involves risk. From the perspective of portfolio management, the primary concern is negotiating an unachievable value proposition. Errors in the negotiation process may stem from poor analysis that could result from incorrect data or improper analytical techniques; uncontrollable environmental considerations that include but are not limited to economic, weather, or business changes; and poor decisions.

The ability to achieve benefits from a negotiation process is largely dependent on the negotiation process selected. For example, an "integrative" negotiation strategy based on a win-win focus generally results in a compromised position that is less than either side's initial best value position. Although this negotiation approach encourages people to work together and avoids the pitfalls of other negotiating strategies based on either a political or adversary model, it does result in less-than-optimal solutions. The common saying that a camel is a horse designed by committee applies here. Again, risks must be balanced. In this case, the risks are of pressing for an optimal solution, thereby achieving some type of positive risk or benefit against the negative risk or threat of harming the work environment due to alienation of competing teams or groups within an organization.

> **PfM Standard 7.6 Maximizing Value** (Structural Risk Area) – Maximizing value should be seen in the overall context of balancing to achieve portfolio strategic business goals. Balancing occurs in the capacity and capability assessment, when dealing with supply and demand, and when making risk-related trades concerning maximizing value. In all cases when risks come into play, both positive and negative risks should be balanced to maximize value consistent with other considerations within the often-complex portfolio management environment.

> **PfM Standard 7.7 Assuring Value** (Structural Risk Area) – Assuring value deals with making sure the portfolio deliverables support the overall strategic business goals of the portfolio. In short, do the portfolio deliverables meet the agreed-upon portfolio value proposition? Risks associated with assuring value at the portfolio level should not involve product quality issues that are handled at the project level. Program managers should address this issue at the program level by assuring project deliverables support and are aligned with the overall program benefit delivery goals. At the portfolio level, the portfolio manager should ensure that there is a strong linkage between the portfolio value proposition and the benefit delivery goals of subordinate programs. Defining and monitoring value risks is thus primarily related to communication and coordination actions between the portfolio level of management and the subordinate program and project management teams. Operations within the portfolio should be run by the portfolio's subordinate programs. If this is not the case, then the portfolio manager must take responsibility to directly work operational risks associated with

value delivery. The above is pictorially described in Figure 7-2, The Link Between Strategy and Portfolio Performance via Component Deliverable.[63] From a risk perspective, a causal loop diagram analysis of this diagram tailored to your organization would help identify otherwise hidden risk areas.

PfM Standard 7.8 Realizing Value (Structural Risk Area) – Figure 7-3, Value Realization Chain,[64] shows the path leading to improved value. As shown by the chart, various outcomes resulting from investments are known only contingently. In fact, as projections are projected into the future, the chart shows widening error bars concerning the expected value outcome. These error bars are not driven by the availability of data but rather by the inherent uncertainty of the input data. This means that additional data taken at the same time as other data may not significantly reduce errors projecting into the future. Risks fall into two major categories, data and process.

PfM Standard 7.9 Measuring Value and 7.10 Reporting Value (Structural Risk Area) – Measuring and reporting value are taken together. Measuring value is dependent on data and the process used. Risks center around a choosing of the correct metric, which will properly measure value in relation to the overall portfolio objectives and strategic business goals to achieve. There must be a strong correlation between changes in the measured value metric and the meeting of portfolio objectives that support strategic business goals. Measuring risks are thus associated with the selection of proper metrics that accurately measure progress to achieving strategic business goals. Reporting value is essentially a communications function and reporting risks are handled below, under the heading of stakeholder engagement.

8.6. Guidance to Subordinate-Level Projects, Programs, and Operational Entities

The following discussion focuses primarily on negative risks. This is because the portfolio manager generally has control over the management vision, goals, and objectives within the portfolio. The portfolio governance, risk strategy, and management practices are for the most part controlled by the portfolio manager. Given the above, why would the portfolio manager settle for a suboptimal governance and management structure within their portfolio? If there is the possibility for enhancement, then the portfolio manager should implement practices that maximize the multiple directional flows of information and knowledge.

That said, there are cases in which impediments may block the establishment of optimal management practices. We will look at two examples. The first example, if the organization does not have a robust program and project data management system that integrates cost, schedule, and performance data, then the portfolio management support personnel will be unable to provide timely and accurate project, program, and operational progress reports to senior management. However, this is a classical negative risk statement and, as explained, the enterprise already lacks the integrated reporting system. This is simply an issue that needs to be worked on by the portfolio management staff. The opportunity of enhancement is merely the result of an issue with a resulting negative consequence.

Other benefits may arise from better training. For the second example, if SAFe® Agile[65] training is provided, then portfolio actions will be better integrated, resulting in the achievement of 80 percent of the portfolio's strategic goals. This is a good example of a positive risk. However, the same question must be asked. Why doesn't the portfolio staff find a way to provide the necessary training? There is a place for positive risks. However, in this area, where either the portfolio management staff or the senior staff managing across portfolios chooses to accept less-than-optimal management practices, risk is not the issue. The problem is the acceptance of less-than-optimal practices by management, which is again an issue, not a risk. We will now look at the portfolio guidance and management chain from a traditional perspective, where optimal management practices are assumed, and the focus is on threats or negative risks associated with poor practices or degraded communications.

Figure 1-2, The Organizational Context of Portfolio Management of the PfM Standard, provides a high-level picture of how major elements are organized within the portfolio management area. Linkages are shown, for example, between organizational strategy and objectives and the portfolio management strategic planning and management of programs, projects, and operations. Other links are shown between management of ongoing operations and the management of programs and projects. A distinction is made between projectized management activities (project and program management) and recurring management activities (operations management). Linkages are also shown between the management of projectized and recurring activities. Links are always a potential source of risk should they be broken or degraded. Usually this break or degradation is the result of specific policies, management practices, or just poor communication.

Another way to look at this problem may be found through Figure 19, which is copied from Figure 4-1, Governance Hierarchy, Including Principles and Objectives, from Section 4 of the PfM Standard.

Each management linkage represents a channel of communication that may be degraded or broken. From a governance perspective, this would be particularly troublesome, as the governance structure may be considered the management "glue" that holds the organization together. A breakdown of the governance structure, for whatever reason, leads to a disintegration of the management chain and disconnects

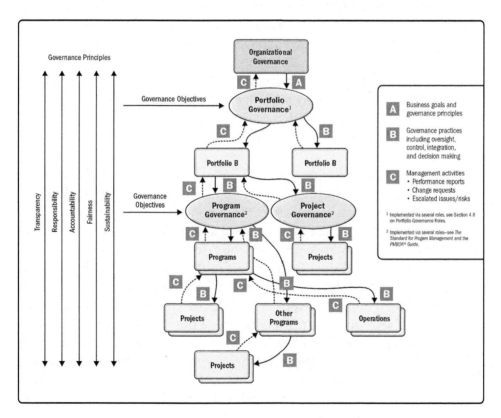

Figure 19.   Governance Hierarchy, Including Principles and Objectives[66]

mid- to senior-level leadership from the working level of the organization and from each other. In short, vertical and horizontal channels of communication are blocked. Additional risk sources will be examined through the related area of stakeholder engagement covered after the next section.

8.6.1. Linkages to support senior-level decision processes above the portfolio level and support of enterprise risk management (ERM) activities

This area is unique to the portfolio level of management. From the governance model pictured in Figure 19, the entire process of strategic alignment starts with a close and well-developed communication channel between senior management (organizational governance) and the portfolio management team. See our chapter on strategic portfolio management. Alternately, one could also look at Figure 1-2 of the PfM Standard, Section 1.8.1, and focus on the linkages at the top of the pictured pyramid that show the chain from vision to mission to organizational strategy and then to portfolio management and strategic planning. The key to alignment up, down, and across the enterprise is strong ties between the portfolio level of management, and levels above the portfolio. If the portfolio management team "gets it right," then alignment down to the working level is assured, assuming that the governance and management chain is well-established completely down and across the organization.

Management of cross-portfolio elements within an enterprise is incompletely explained within the PfM Standard. This is partially because this function rests with management or governance levels above the portfolio, program, and project management space. As such, cross-portfolio management occurs above the portfolio level and is partially out of scope of this work and the PfM Standard, although much can be inferred through a close reading of complexity within both the PfM Standard and this work. The required strong links to strategic guidance, planning, and management mentioned in the PfM Standard and this book assumes a robust senior governance and leadership capability. Although ERM is strictly not part of the portfolio risk management effort, a strong ERM effort at the senior management level is a natural outgrowth of a well-functioning senior staff and a critical necessity for a complete portfolio risk management effort.

8.7. Risks Associated with Stakeholder Engagement

Risks associated with stakeholder engagement permeate all aspects of risk throughout the portfolio, program, and project management space. At the portfolio level, the engagement with stakeholders, both internal and external, is critical since most of what occurs in terms of management and activity at the portfolio level is people related. The portfolio proper does not produce products or operational work per se. Effort dealing with product delivery or operations execution is conducted through the portfolio's subordinate projects, programs, or operational entities. Stakeholder or personnel-related concerns thus impact all four of the aforementioned risk management plan areas. As was done above with portfolio capability and capacity and value management, sources of risks will be examined by looking at major elements of the stakeholder engagement section of the PfM Standard.

> **PfM Standard 6.1 Introduction** (Stakeholder Interest Table) – Table 6.1, Stakeholder Interest Table, PfM Standard, Section 6.1 contains a list of stakeholder groups, roles, interests, and expectations. Sources of positive risk or potential opportunities may be derived from the list of stakeholder interests. For example, external stakeholders are interested in the effect of portfolio and component execution on their requirements and interests. Any actions taken to enhance or exploit opportunities to better communicate with stakeholders to meet their interests should result in benefits to the portfolio. On the other hand, failure to meet minimal stakeholder expectations as outlined in the fourth column of Table 6.1 may result in degraded communications or cooperation from these stakeholders. The entire table presents a good starting point for the categorization by stakeholder group of potential sources of risk.
>
> **PfM Standard 6.2 Guiding Principles** – "Fostering a culture that embraces change," and "risk navigating complexity to enable successful outcomes" are principles in the stakeholder section of the PfM Standard that are shared with the portfolio risk management area. Below the portfolio level of management, risks and resulting issues tend to be stovepiped. A chief role of the portfolio manager is to break down these stovepipes

to allow risks and issues to be known both across and up and down the organization. The breaking down of stovepipes is uniquely a leadership issue. At all levels, most organizations have governance procedures that encourage transparency. However, it is very difficult to achieve transparency in the area of risk management because of the potential negative consequences of failure. Only a corporate climate and management philosophy that encourage openness and do not penalize the "messenger" will succeed in establishing true openness across teams, projects, programs, and portfolios. Leadership concerns are included in the structural risk area.

PfM Standard 6.3 Definition and Identification of Portfolio Stakeholders (Structural Risk Area) – The risks associated with definition and identification of portfolio stakeholders deal with process. The primary danger is that the definition and identification of stakeholders will be incomplete. Usually, the issue is time constraints, or the desire to proceed to another task shortens the analysis.

PfM Standard 6.4 Analysis of Portfolio Stakeholders (Structural Risk Area) – Table 6-2, Example of Key Stakeholder Context, Section 6.4 of the PfM Standard provides a good start at analyzing stakeholders. This chart is related to the aforementioned Table 6-1. As with Table 6-1, the listed concerns and context provide a great starting point for developing a comprehensive list of stakeholder-related risks. As this is also an analysis function, the risks associated with it are primarily process related, as listed above in paragraph 6.3. However, data integrity may also be a risk area as stakeholders' concerns and their context are defined. In most cases, this data will be subjective. Care must be taken to assure that the inputted data are based on authoritative sources and not just opinion.

PfM Standard 6.5 Stakeholder Engagement Planning (Structural Risk Area) – Planning risks at the portfolio level are similar to planning risks found at any level of management. A primary concern at the portfolio level is proper alignment of plans both up and down the organization.

PfM Standard 6.6 Identifying Communications Management Approaches – A wide range of topics are covered in this section. Alignment with governance has already been covered above under the linkages section (8.6.1). Communications infrastructure is important because it supports all other areas of portfolio management. The effects of a poor communications infrastructure have been briefly covered above in Section 8.6. Communications requirements are summarized in Table 6-3, Example Communications Matrix found in Section 6.6 of the PfM Standard. As with other tables listing similar data previously discussed, the primary risks are incomplete or inaccurate data. This is a process-related structural risk. The table itself provides a good starting point to access required communications. The vehicle used and the adequacy of the communications infrastructure are paramount for effective and efficient communications. From the analysis found in Table 6-3, both positive (opportunities) and negative (threats) risks may be discovered.

PfM Standard 6.7 Manage Portfolio Communications (Structural Risk) – As with all of the portfolio management areas, agility and adaptability are key to being successful. Any possible impediment to making quick and correct decisions, or executing those decisions, may result in management failures and could be a source of negative risks or threats. On the contrary, opportunities that enhance agility and adaptability should result in benefits to the portfolio through better and quicker decisions and decision execution. As is seen above, the enhancement of management techniques is not a technical risk alone, but rather a personnel risk that involves all the complexity of dealing with individuals and groups of people. Good technical data and reporting processes may look impressive, but unless executives can make reasonable decisions that are quickly implemented, then the reporting and fancy charts are just that, nice pictures.

8.8. Portfolio Risk Assessment

The assessment of risk, whether conducted at the portfolio level of management or another level of management, is essentially a similar process. But there are significant contextual differences, as is discussed at the beginning of this section. The *PMBOK® Guide* – Sixth Edition[67] lists the following processes as making up risk management at the project level:

- Plan risk management
- Identify risks
- Perform qualitative risk analysis
- Perform quantitative risk analysis
- Plan risk responses
- Implement risk responses
- Monitor risks

Assuming risks are identified, assessment then involves the processes of qualitative and quantitative risk analysis and planning of risk responses. These processes are highly iterative in nature.

Risk assessment at the program level, according to *The Standard for Program Management* – Fourth Edition, focuses on program alignment and providing a risk strategy under which subordinate projects and operational entities may operate. Risks that are either project or operations related will be handled by the program's subordinate projects or operational organization. However, risks that are escalated to the program level or taken on at the program level are assessed using an iterative risk identification, qualitative and quantitative analysis process, and a response identification or planning process of some type. Similarly, risks may also be elevated to the portfolio level or to an ERM effort where a similar risk analysis process takes place. The wider the scope of concern for a particular entity, the more important the definition of context to the overall risk assessment process. For example, the U.S. Department of Homeland Security in its department-level risk management guide has "definition of context" as the first step in its enterprise-focused risk management process. Additionally, quantitative risk assessments will be less important as risks are less defined or subject less to analytic mathematical approaches.

Figure 16 lists the following sub-elements of the risk assessment process:

- Probability
- Impact
- Importance
- Timing

- Interdependencies
- Confidence limits
- Prioritized risk list
- Risk trends

The above is not an ordered or exhaustive list but aligns with the general process of risk assessment as outlined above. As implied from the above list, a qualitative assessment of risks at the portfolio level would involve more than just an assessment of probability and impact and the ranking of risks within a risk impact matrix. Although similar tools are used, the input data may be different. Other items come into play, such as interdependencies, confidence limits, and timing considerations like speed of onset. The quantitative assessment follows a similar pattern as that of the qualitative assessment. Standard tools for quantitative assessment include Monte Carlo, genetic, neural network, and decision tree modeling.

8.9. Portfolio Risk Response

The element of risk response, also from Figure 16, contains the following three sub-elements: status and trends, balancing the portfolio, and managing investment choices. Common risk response strategies for either positive or negative risks as listed in the *PMBOK® Guide* and elsewhere may be used in connection with the listed sub-elements. As above, the list is "notional."[68] The status and trends sub-element may be thought of as a "catch-all" element. Each of the potential risk areas discussed could come under one of the three sub-elements listed or additional risk sub-elements may be created.

8.10. Risk Management Overhead and the Value Proposition

All management processes have an overhead associated with their implementation. In the area of risk management, as opposed to other management areas, the amount of funds spent on the management of risk is variable based on the risk appetite and tolerance of the organization. Part of the risk management process is to determine how much is spent or kept in reserve on various risk response strategies in an effort to control risk. The amount spent on risk control measures must be weighed against strategic goals. This process is also a balancing effort between expected positive returns and costs. A return on investment calculation should be done that incorporates the overall strategic benefit of the risk management processes that includes portfolio goals and enterprise business objectives. However, when risks do materialize, the organization may not have the ability to choose whether to spend funds on an issue. Under drastic business conditions such as the U.S. subprime mortgage collapse of 2007, the Dutch tulip collapse of 1636,[69] or the result of catastrophic natural events, businesses may be driven to bankruptcy. The portfolio level of management is particularly exposed to such risk extremes because of the wide area of operations covered by most portfolios and the inability of portfolios to screen themselves from outside risks.

Reserves are pictured in Figure 17. Contingency reserves are usually held at one or more management levels within the portfolio, program, and project management space with management reserves held at the portfolio level and above. Reserves are calculated in response to known risks or set aside for general unspecified risks. There are processes for calculating contingency reserves for known risks that involve either qualitative or quantitative risk analysis techniques. Generally, reserves of any type are never enough to cover any and all possible risk events.[70] Thus, trades must be made based on the value to the portfolio or enterprise organization. The opportunity costs also come into play, as funds held in reserve cannot be used on other efforts, which may bring value into the organization.

8.11. Summary

The PfM Standard was written from a principle-based perspective. This was a significant change from previously written PMI standards, which were primarily directive in tone and prescriptive in nature. The prescriptive approach may make sense for documents such as the *PMBOK® Guide*. However, even the *PMBOK® Guide* has moved away from its formally perceived directive tone. In this chapter, we have extended the foundation for portfolio risk management as outlined in the PfM Standard, but we have still kept the principle-based approach. Because of the variability of how companies organize and execute their portfolios, a prescriptive approach would likely not address most of the management possibilities implemented by companies around the world. Portfolio risk management has been explained as a unique form of risk management due to its position between the completely strategic concerns of ERM and the more focused risk concerns of project, program, and operations management. The role of complexity in management and execution considerations below the portfolio level may be argued. However, at the portfolio level and above, we take complexity as a given and its effects must be accounted for as part of any portfolio risk management process. Finally, risk response is seen as a balancing act at the portfolio level. The key concern, whether dealing with capacity and capability, supply and demand, benefit and investment, or the overall value proposition, is the balancing of both positive and negative risks, opportunities, and threats to achieve the strategic business goals and objectives of the enterprise.

In closing, according to the PfM Standard, Section 8.2:

> [T]he following principles [of risk management] are central to risk management processes at the portfolio level:
>
> - Maximize portfolio value while balancing risks;
> - Foster a culture that embraces change and risk; and
> - Navigate complexity to enable successful outcomes.
>
> The result of the combination of these three principles, from a holistic perspective, allows a balancing of portfolio components through an organized risk assessment process. This process should be proactively implemented by portfolio management to prevent or minimize loss and encourage opportunity exploitation.

Part III
A Strategist's Guide to Advance Portfolio Management

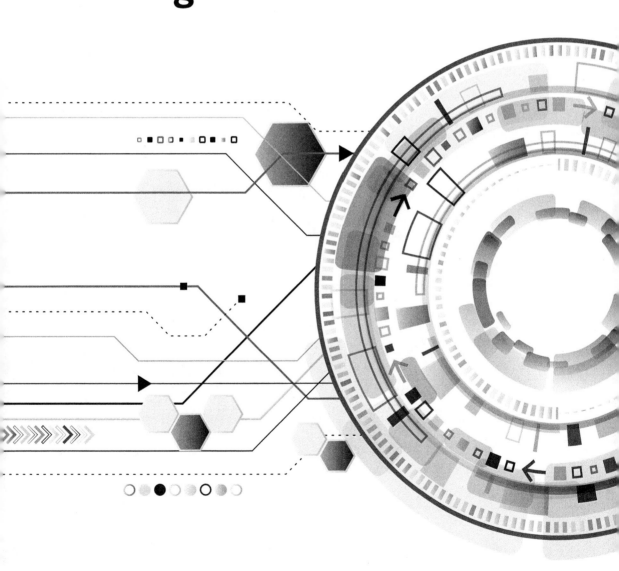

CHAPTER 9

Achieving and Sustaining Execution Excellence through Strategic Business Execution

by Te Wu

> Above all, success in business requires two things: a winning competitive strategy, and superb organizational execution. Distrust is the enemy of both. I submit that while high trust won't necessarily rescue a poor strategy, low trust will almost always derail a good one.
>
> — Stephen Covey

9.1. Introduction

With the rapid pace of globalization, technological advancements, and the ever-increasing complexity of organizations, an organization's ability to execute strategic plans and implement projects must rise to meet the demands of today's fast-paced and competitive business environment. While the results are rather mixed, organizational project management, including project, program, and portfolio management, is commonly accepted as the best mechanism to achieve strategic change and deliver value.

But there are significant obstacles to overcome. Studies show consistently that the project success rate is subpar. For example, in the Standish Chaos Report,[71] the project success rate has been consistently less than 30 percent for much of the past twenty years. In a special report by the Economist Intelligence Unit in 2013 titled "Why Good Strategies Fail," a majority of senior executives admit that they fall short of their organizations' ability to successfully execute their strategies. The Project Management Institute's study in 2016 revealed the magnitude of the problem—over 12 percent of expenses are wasted on megaprojects of US$1 billion. As the adoption of project management accelerates, to the point of "projectification of our society," the stakes are becoming even greater. Mishaps that once were painful can now severely and sometimes fatally harm the sponsoring organizations.

While conceptual and analytical models of strategy formulation have advanced rapidly since the 1960s, advancements in strategy execution have failed to keep pace. Without a successful implementation program that consistently delivers desired organizational goals, even the best strategies are hollow. After examining over two hundred pieces of academic literature and reviewing the results of a large-scale study by PMO Advisory,[72] one reason stood out: We need a new framework to examine the problem of business execution, in which project management is just one major—and perhaps dominant—mechanism of "getting things done." We need a more comprehensive and integrated viewpoint at a higher level of analysis to succeed not only for a select few projects, but a more fundamental paradigm shift that enables sustainable execution excellence. Such change will necessitate a comprehensive rethinking of how organizations plan and execute their endeavors. Strategic business execution (SBE) is an emerging field of strategy implementation that provides an integrated framework of a multidisciplinary approach to achieve sustainable execution excellence.

9.2. Some Limitations of Today's Project Environment

Undoubtedly, project management has greatly enhanced organizations' ability to deliver results, even though the rate of success has been stuck at a rather unsatisfactory level. This lack of positive momentum is surprising considering the rapid increase in both knowledge and number of certified project professionals. Examining the problems more closely, there are many reasons for the slow pace of progress. The top five reasons based on our experience are as follows:

1. Manager myopia: Many project managers are tactically focused, viewing projects as distinct trees rather than a strategic forest or a portfolio of trees. This limits the potential benefits of projects. Furthermore, by their narrow views, organizations fail to align projects with the broader strategies.
2. Process heavy: There is an overemphasis on processes and less focus on delivering solutions. The traditional waterfall methodology has been blamed with heavy and bureaucratic processes and templates. Project professionals often fail to tailor the process to the project conditions. Even the newer agile approaches suffer from a lack of tailoring.
3. Poor capacity and capability management: Some organizations undertake an unreasonable number of projects simultaneously with the hope that they have adequate resources. This is especially devastating in organizations that poorly evaluate the sheer amount of resources required to undertake projects. Without this important control, organizations then experience intense but poorly controlled environments with an extraordinarily high number of projects creating a chaotic environment where projects run rampantly.
4. Cultural misfit: The gap between the organizational culture and the portfolio team culture is significant, creating tensions and conflicts at every major juncture in the portfolio life cycle. These cultural misfits can cause unnecessary inefficiencies in the best cases and can doom controversial but important projects and portfolios.
5. Limited competencies: Organizations often unintentionally create artificial divisions within their organizations. As problems are becoming more complex, organizations can no longer rely on one or a few dominant competencies and tools to solve these problems. Organizations need to embrace a more interdisciplinary approach to tackling the sticky challenges and developing more complex solutions.

The net result of these and other challenges is a turbulent environment for projects, programs, and portfolios. Worse, large organizations often adopt very different ways of performing projects. In one Fortune 500 company, for example, there are well over 30 internal PMOs, each with its unique flavor and processes. This lack of consistency yields very mixed results—some projects are well-executed, while others are not. The remainder of this chapter presents a new framework to address these challenges and create a more consistent environment in which projects, programs, and portfolios can excel on a consistent basis.

9.3. Understanding the Strategic Business Execution Framework

As a multidisciplinary approach, strategic business execution (SBE) weaves together a wide range of disciplines, including organizational project management (e.g., project management, program management, portfolio management), organization change and development, process improvement, and performance management to solve complex strategic challenges and deliver meaningful value. Furthermore, through systematic development of an organization, the goal is to create an ecosystem in which the organization can achieve execution success continually and consistently over time.

The emergence of this field came from the recognition that strategy implementation is too broad to examine systematically, while organizational project management is too narrow. As organizations strive to achieve their strategies, the dissonance between aspiration and actualization of attaining the planned value remains significant. This dichotomy between "thinking" and "doing" has deep historical roots, and while the latest thinking on strategy attempts to view these as a continuum, in practice, the gap remains and is possibly even growing. Furthermore, the limit of the current understanding of strategy implementation is on full display, as studies show that many if not most strategies fail to achieve their value. On the other side of the spectrum and at a more specific level of execution, project management is now solidly rooted in both academia and organizations, as the discipline of choice for managing temporary endeavors. In conjunction with project, program, and portfolio management, a new broader construct, Organizational Project Management (OPM), is gaining traction as a more holistic mechanism of implementing strategic initiatives by providing a management framework for all project-based work. In today's complex organizations, however, OPM itself is insufficient to solve the larger challenges that require a multidisciplinary approach. SBE serves to close this fissure between the broader strategy implementation and the narrower, classic project management discipline through integration and synthesis of multiple disciplines suitable for that organization, its situation, and its environment.

The quest for superior business execution has deep roots in organizations. Executives inherently understand that even the best ideas require diligent execution to bring forth their true value. The dust bin of history is full of great ideas, for example AT&T's quest for "the last mile" in the late 1990s that destroyed billions of dollars in value, or the infamous AOL and Time Warner merger that produced little synergy and wasted at least US$200 billion of shareholder value by some accounts. Even when large initiatives achieve strategic success, for example, Boston's famous "Big Dig" project, the actual cost can exceed the budget by multiple times. In information technology, one of the most challenging endeavors is enterprise resource planning implementation, such as SAP and Oracle, where product success and project success are poorly aligned, costing companies such as the American chocolatier Hershey to lose US$100 million in 1999 from the inability to fulfill customer orders during their busiest season. These are just a few, but important, examples where the strategies were sound, implementation was thorough, program and project managers worked diligently, but success was elusive and poorly sustained.

To achieve sustainable execution excellence, organizations must strengthen multiple aspects, including culture, enabling competencies, core disciplines, and integrating processes:

- Culture is the invisible force that underpins how decisions are made and how people work. High-performing organizations adopt an execution-readiness attitude toward embracing change, solving problems, taking ownership, and creating high-performance teams. Each organization has its history and uniqueness, and leaders must find the optimal mix of characteristics and behaviors for their organization to excel.
- People are one of the most valuable (if not *the* most valuable) asset of most organizations. People's capabilities and skills directly contribute to the well-being of organizations. Leading companies invest to develop enabling competencies of their people and teams, such as managerial competencies, leadership, problem solving, analytical thinking, critical thinking,

and so on, to develop and maintain their competitive edge that leads to stronger execution.

- Core disciplines, such as organizational project management, process improvement, PMOs, and more, are vital for organizations to consistently and repeatedly implement change successfully. By adopting the right set of disciplines, members of the organization can communicate using the same language, apply common sets of tools and techniques, understand limitations and strengths, and execute efficiently to achieve their goals.

- But perhaps most important, it is the integrating processes that bind the organization together and provide the most strategic and lasting value. Managing performance, and continually aligning strategy with execution through effective communication and knowledge sharing, as well as issue, dependency, change, and risk management, enables a stronger cohesion of people, processes, technology, and strategy to achieve true and lasting competitiveness.

While the implementation of each of these dimensions can achieve significant value, the incredible amount of synergy that can be attained through integrating them into a common framework is the power of SBE. With the rapid pace of technology, globalization, and associated regulatory and social changes, the challenges of tomorrow are likely to be more daunting than the problems of today. In the foreseeable future, organizations will always strive to achieve more with diminishing resources. Thus, without improving the ability to deliver results and achieve strategies, organizations may languish at best and fail at worst. There also will be new opportunities for organizations to exploit, and new ideas abound. Organizations have little option other than achieving strategic business execution by investing in the right ideas, executing them in the right way sustainably, and maximizing created additional value.

9.4. Creating an Execution Excellence Culture

Culture is a system of shared values, beliefs, assumptions, and behaviors. For the most part, a culture is invisible, but everywhere. An effective culture is like an invisible hand that guides people toward achieving common goals in an agreeable set of implicit processes. Members of a common culture also tacitly acknowledge behavioral norms, such as being frank with opposing views but in a constructive manner; understanding the "rules of the game," such as the importance of collaboration; and practice of dominant values, such as always starting meetings on time. By developing a common understanding of what is important to the organization, how things work (including confronting difficult issues and decisions), and how things are done, organizations and teams can achieve extraordinary performance levels. At a portfolio level, portfolio managers are often the senior-most executives, and it is important that they set the tone at the top. This way, the core team members and the component managers can serve as role models for the rest of the portfolio team members.

To achieve a high-performing execution excellence culture, portfolio managers should encourage a culture of execution readiness. Execution readiness is a culture of getting the right things done effectively and efficiently, and it contains the attributes shown in Table 15.

Developing a culture of execution readiness will require dedication and time. Portfolio managers should first tailor the attributes for their organization and specific endeavor. For example, as discussed in a later chapter on cross-cultural management and trends in portfolio management, different styles may be required when working with people from other cultures, especially in a virtual environment. Next, portfolio managers train and work with core team members to both obtain their support and enable them to be role models for the broader portfolio teams.

Table 15. Attributes of an Execution-Readiness Culture

Category	Attribute	Description
Value – principles and beliefs	Industrious	Work hard and play hard
	Resolution	Make decisions and avoid analysis paralysis
	Integrity	Engender trust through consistent honesty and follow through on commitments
	Results Oriented	Focus on results, not just activities
Behavior – observable activities	Lead by Example	Demonstrate leadership by example; set the tone at the top
	Respect	Value diverse viewpoints even when disagreeing
	Teamwork	Appreciate the contribution of others and understand that "we" is more powerful than "I"
	Organization	Plan and coordinate work
Attitudes and Traits – implicit mind-set	"Can do"	Willingness to try, take risks, and make mistakes
	Optimism	Basic belief that problems have solutions
	Resiliency	Recover quickly from failures; get up and start again
	Empathy	Think from the other person's perspective

Finally, as portfolios often involve a large number of resources, create an onboarding program that includes training, mentoring, and coaching to instruct new members of the portfolio management team.

9.5. Enhancing Individual Competencies

A high-performance portfolio team requires highly competent individuals, not only versed in the technical skills, but also the business and soft skills required to work effectively with others in the team. According to the latest *Career Architect, 5th Edition* by Korn Ferry (originally Lominger), there are 103 areas of consideration, including 67 competencies, 10 performance dimensions, 19 career stallers and stoppers, and seven global focus areas.[73] While all these areas are important for business professionals, the top ten competencies for portfolio managers that we believe to be the most important are shown in Table 16.

Table 16. Individual Competencies for Business Execution

#	Competencies	Description
1	Action Oriented	Taking the necessary action, even under uncertain situations; Bias toward action over analysis paralysis
2	Balancing	Maintaining a healthy balance of strategic considerations, such as competing interests, capacity and capability (internal versus external), and strategic alignment; Tactical considerations can be process intensity versus solutioning
3	Conflict Management	Encouraging low to moderate levels of conflicts to bring out the best ideas, but also effectively manage conflicts so they do not spiral out of control
4	Decision Quality	Applying sound judgment most of the time that results in quality decisions; May utilize different approaches to involve core team members
5	Diversity Management	Embracing diversity of ideas, cultures, disciplines, and even behaviors to create greater value than the sum of the individual contributors
6	Innovation Management	Facilitating discussions and brainstorming sessions to generate new ideas, solving difficult challenges creatively, finding new ways of tackling project implementation, and creating better methods of working with people, especially senior executives
7	Interpersonal Savvy	Achieving superior soft skills to effectively work with people, especially challenging individuals and blockers
8	Managerial Courage	Confronting challenging situations and making the best of situations; Willingness to make difficult decisions, especially decisions that are not popular
9	Motivating Others	Bringing out the best in the portfolio team members by creating an environment conducive to learning, sharing ideas, deliberating options, finding solutions, and growing together
10	Strategic Agility	Adapting to the changing organization and its environment by constantly seeking ways to improve strategic alignment; Discover new ways to create more benefits, along with finding better tools and processes to improve portfolio planning and execution

9.6. Building and Strengthening Core Disciplines

Core disciplines are a collection of related competencies focusing on a particular management area. Core disciplines differ from individual competencies, as they largely exist at a team or an organizational level that is required for consistent implementation. By adopting the right set of core disciplines, members of the organization can communicate using the same language, apply common sets of tools and techniques, understand limitations and strengths, and execute efficiently to achieve their goals. In business execution, there are many core disciplines. Table 17 contains the most relevant ones for business execution and portfolio management.

Table 17. Core Disciplines for Business Execution

#	Competencies	Description
1	Portfolio Management	Management of a group of related projects, programs, operational initiatives, and other portfolio components. When performed well, portfolio management enables an organization to invest wisely and achieve superior business value and competitive advantage.
2	Program Management	Management of a group of highly related projects and other program components. When performed well, program management enables an organization to tackle large endeavors effectively and efficiently, achieving business benefits that exceed industry norms.
3	Project Management	Management of a temporary and unique endeavor with specific outcomes, deliverables, or results. When performed well, project management enables a company to deliver meaningful results.
4	Project Management Office (PMO)	PMOs are created to tackle the many challenges of intense project environments. PMO capabilities vary greatly but can be broadly categorized into three strategic groups: 1) Essential capabilities mainly designed around monitoring and controlling; 2) Advanced capabilities focusing on enhancing implementation capabilities; and 3) Strategic capabilities of integrating project, program, portfolio, and risk management with the rest of the organization.
5	Risk Management	Management of uncertain events, which can be either beneficial or harmful (or both) to the portfolio. At a portfolio level, risk management should be conducted in concert with organizational planning. Portfolio risks can also be escalated from the component level.
6	Strategic Planning	Organizations must plan even if directionally at first with the specific plans emerging from the actual situation. Without planning, organizations would have few meaningful ways of understanding their purpose and vision and allocating resources toward achieving goals and objectives.
7	Operational and Service Management	Business values are often *not* achieved during project and program implementation. For example, new products only achieve their value after the customers buy the new products. Savvy organizations recognize the imperative of operational and service management by incorporating their planning early in the project, program, and portfolio life cycles. At a portfolio level, operations of components after implementation can be included for a specified duration.
8	Organizational Change Management (OCM)	As organizations perform strategic business execution, whether by projects for new products or portfolios of internal improvements, the organizations and all the people will inevitably change. Change can be uncomfortable and often face resistance. OCPM is an important discipline that helps organizations and its members navigate the change obstacles and achieve higher adoption of the reality.

9.7. Achieving Integration throughout the Organization

Based on PMO Advisory studies, perhaps the most important aspect of strategic business execution is the enablement of "handshakes" across the organization through integrating processes, which are the basic unifying, workflow, and preprogrammed steps that facilitate execution. The driving paradigm is to apply the right balance between system and flexibility that routinizes otherwise complex operations. Competitive and successful organizations are more than the sum of their business units, departments, teams, and people. These organizations can tap into a mysterious force called synergy, in which the company value is significantly more than its member contribution. The integrating processes are a collection of business processes that are deeply intertwined within the organizational culture, and these processes bind the organization together by enabling the flow of right information up and down and throughout the organization. By leveraging these integrating processes, portfolio managers can manage portfolio performance and continually align strategy with execution through effective communication and knowledge sharing, solving problems and challenges, managing dependencies across the portfolio endeavors, and applying effective change and risk management. In short, the integrating processes enable stronger cohesion of people, processes, technology, and strategy to achieve true and lasting competitiveness.

There are many examples of integrating processes. The eight examples shown in Table 18 are the most important to achieve superior business execution.

9.8. Final Words on Strategic Business Execution (SBE)

The strategic business execution framework outlined in this chapter is a conceptual model designed to achieve fundamental change. It provides a new way of examining organizations' activities and proposes a comprehensive set of changes across the multiple levels of organizations. At the most ethereal unit, culture is the invisible force that permeates every corner and every activity of organizations. At a team level, the core disciplines are the backbone of how organizations carry out activities and implement projects, programs, and portfolios. At a more individual level, there are over 100 areas of considerations, of which this chapter mentioned the top 10 for portfolio management. Lastly and perhaps, most importantly, are the integrating processes that bind the organization together.

Table 18.   Examples of Integrating Processes

#	Competencies	Description
1	Planning, Organizing, and Controlling	Planning, organizing, and controlling are the three primary management processes responsible for identifying and determining organizational direction and objectives, allocating resources, coordinating actions and endeavors, and monitoring and controlling to achieve the desirable outcomes. Organizations with clear processes for these primary management processes achieve synergy through the alignment of people.
2	Governance	To achieve execution excellence, proper governance should exist at all levels of the organization, including (from top to bottom): enterprise, business unit, departmental, portfolio, program, project, operational, and sometimes even at a task level. Clear governance addresses the question of what and why, who, and how decisions are made. Governance is especially important in politically intense organizations where the legitimacy of process is more important than the decisions themselves.
3	Issue and Risk Management	Issues and risks are common occurrences that are an inevitable part of conducting business. How well organizations put out fires (e.g., issues and challenges) and manage unknowns (e.g., risks) can directly affect their overall health. As an integrating process, issue and risk management should involve the required employees and encourage a culture of collaboration to tackle the challenges, leverage the opportunities, and mitigate the threats.
4	Conflict Management	Conflicts inevitably arise, as there are always competing interests across multiple organizational units. In some cultures, conflicts are avoided and pushed aside for the sake of perceived harmony. In highly effective organizations, a moderate amount of conflict is encouraged to create more energy and excitement. More importantly, studies show that an optimal amount of conflict can reduce or avoid group think and result in better outcomes than otherwise. However, too much conflict should be avoided, as it can be detrimental to organizations.
5	Change Management	Change is all around, both internal and external to organizations. External changes can be new competitors, a worsening or improving economy, or tougher regulations. Internal changes can be executive turnover, newly acquired capabilities, or ineffective tools. As an integrating process, how well an organization manages these changes and communicates with its people can greatly affect how well employees work together.
6	Information and Knowledge Management	Organizations create new data all the time. As these data are analyzed, new information is created. When applied and synthesized, new knowledge can be gained. Often, these data, information, and knowledge are tacit, living in the minds of people. Effective organizations find ways to convert this tacit knowledge to explicit, in which the knowledge can be shared among employees and outlives any one individual.
7	Dependency Management	Dependency management is an elusive function that is casually distributed among all employees. In theory, every employee should find ways to avoid overlaps, work efficiently, and know their dependencies. In reality, when such work is farmed out to nearly everyone, no one is truly in charge. Organizations should consider creating a dedicated team with the sole job of managing dependencies across the organization. By effectively managing dependencies, organizations can reduce duplication of efforts, create synergies by solving problems better and faster, and encourage collaboration at the same time.
8	Communication Management	Perhaps the most important of the integrating processes, according to world-class organizations often on Fortune's Best Companies to Work list, is the achievement of highly effective communication to ensure employees are well-informed and engaged through multiple channels. Communication is perhaps the most fundamental glue to unite the organization.

There is no shortcut to achieving sustainable execution excellence, as the changes must be at all these levels. Organizations can start to embark on this journey at any single point, for example, encouraging timely meeting times to begin the process of creating an execution-readiness culture or applying portfolio management principles to a new set of projects and programs. The specific activities within the SBE framework are rarely isolated and alone. For example, learning to motivate others can be a part of an individual competency of motivation, a part of a project manager's improvement journey to work with team members, a part of the integrating process in communication management to excite and elevate employees with words of praise and recognition, and a core part of an execution-readiness culture as the portfolio manager attempts to lead by example.

PMO Advisory started a survey study in 2014 on the topic of strategic business execution, and it is still ongoing. If you are interested in participating in the study, please visit www.pmoadvisory.com/research.

## CHAPTER 10

Applying Systems Thinking to Portfolio Management

by Panos Chatzipanos

> Managers are not confronted with problems that are independent of each other, but with dynamic situations that consist of complex systems of changing problems that interact with each other. I call such situations messes . . .
>
> — **Russell Ackoff**[74]

The core message of this book has been that portfolio management is the domain of the project management discipline that enables executive management to implement organizational strategy and achieve strategic objectives. Portfolio management aims to provide a holistic framework for strategic management. Portfolio management requires vigilant alignment to strategic objectives and the ability to envision alternative future consequences to support and enhance strategic project portfolio decision making. As discussed, this is accomplished through efficient portfolio governance. Portfolio management is performed in an environment broader than the portfolio itself.[75] The organizational environment plays a major role in successful portfolio management, particularly today in an everchanging external environment with increased complexity.

Until recently, the prevailing approach to dealing with increasing complexity has been to try to divide the issue or the problem into smaller parts and deal with each part separately. This method, employed for most management work, is derived from the education and training that managers undergo—the scientific analytical method. Most managers analyze a complex situation by trying to break it down into elemental pieces and considering solutions for each, usually in isolation from the others. Thus, they, consciously or subconsciously, accept in the mental model they create for their analysis that the whole is the sum of the parts.

The underpinning assumption for this approach is that all the parts are virtually independent of each other. But although this approach has an excellent application to simple objects or simple situations, it often fails when applied to dynamic, organic, or cybernetic systems—which generally include all those systems where humans participate and have a role—for example, change initiatives and associated project-based work. In such cases, systems thinking approaches taken in parallel to the prevailing linear analytical approach has in many cases proven to be very important.

10.1. Understanding Systems – Frame of Reference

Systems thinking is a way of describing anything holistically. Holism puts the study of the whole before that of its parts. Holism is based on a mental model of a system of interconnected parts or components, all serving a common purpose. The system model contains the components of the system and their relations, in other words, the connections between the components. Systems are not sets of components. The main difference between sets of components and systems is the interrelationships and interactions between the components of a system. Components belonging to sets neither interact with nor interdepend upon each other. Thus, the whole set is the sum of its parts, whereas, for a system, the whole system is considerably more than the sum of its parts due to components' interdependencies. When dealing with sets, one needs to consider only each part and its properties. This approach is known as reductionism or component analysis. When analyzing a system, one needs to comprehend the set of relationships that determine the functioning of each component of the system in addition to the properties of each component. Since the components are defined by their connections, attributes, and functionality within the system, to properly understand the components, one needs first to understand the purpose of the system and how the whole system works. This approach of describing things and/or situations that are best described by understanding their place within the functioning of the whole, within which they are a part, is called synthesis. Synthesis is the foundation of systems thinking.

The systems approach represents a synthesis under an integrated perspective of the whole organization and its environment. Before one can synthesize, one must first analyze. In other words, the system is taken apart conceptually to understand the functions of each component. Once the components are separated and understood in isolation, the interactions among the components are studied. Thus, if the portfolio and its environment are not comprehended as a system of interdependent components, the imbalances and changes created by the dependencies of the components cannot be understood and proactively dealt with. The same applies for portfolio resources and particularly for portfolio human resources. If the portfolio manager does not understand the psychology (culture, objectives, perceptions, biases, etc.) that drive the people, who are usually the most important subsystem within the portfolio system, chances of successful management of the whole portfolio may be considerably hindered.

In this subsection, before we further explore systems thinking, we will briefly discuss some terms commonly used by systems thinkers. The boundary of a system is the scope of interest and analysis of the system and can change as the scope of interest changes. The components of the system inside the boundary interact with each other, creating interdependencies, but also with components of the environment outside the boundary. A portfolio may have a boundary based on its initial components, but this boundary could change as the components change. A system usually takes inputs from its environment and transforms them into desired outputs. For a portfolio component, the requirements could be considered as inputs that are transformed by the team as outputs.

The portfolio system has a structure that defines its parts and their relationships and uses principles, processes, and proven practices to perform a function. Most of the time, portfolio component implementation employs principles, structures, roles, processes, and activities. Systems are generally open, that is, they interact with the environment. They are organized by a hierarchy and exhibit emergence. Hierarchy in systems thinking relates more with vitality, sustainability, and purpose rather than the concept of command and control.[76] Managers working on complex programs or projects often report situations wherein everything seems to be going out of control; after a certain period, the project finally settles down into a new state of equilibrium.[77,78] Complex adaptive systems have the ability, if certain conditions are met, to self-organize. Portfolio managers today are expected to perform successfully under increasing complexity, change, and diversity. Under these circumstances, linear, "simple" solutions often fail because they are not holistic or creative enough. They are not holistic because they concentrate on parts of the situation, and usually over-resource these parts, rather than the whole. They also fail to acknowledge that this whole consists of its parts, and the interdependencies of its parts need to be treated accordingly. Concentrating on certain parts may lead toward pushing the capacity of certain components to their limit, thus transforming an asset into a weakness.

The prevailing concept—proven valid and effective in many cases—is that the portfolio is a mechanistic system that has no intrinsic purpose of its own. It is a tool with functions defined by management, an instrument for management to effectively plan and implement change initiatives by mainly executing programs and projects. The principle that portfolio components should not deviate from the set constraints is at the core of the required efficiency, controllability, and predictability of managing the portfolio. Components of a linear mechanical system, like the whole system, do not have transformational capabilities. Their structure is designed into them, leaving them with no ability to restructure themselves. The system functions reactively and can operate effectively only if its environment remains stable and/or does not affect the system. Of course, portfolios are commonly described by the preceding sentences. But don't portfolios also transform and restructure due to environmental changes, human (individual and group) behaviors, and environmental systemic interactions? For these reasons, the portfolio manager should concurrently understand and navigate the portfolio as an open, adaptive system, consistently applying critical thinking.

A systems approach to any risk, issue, or problem begins by understanding the situation one needs to address. Then, the construction of a hypothesis or a model can be performed to analyze the situation. It is advisable to create a number of models, testing each one by simulation. If the model can depict the situation fairly accurately, a conceivable, sustainable hypothesis has most likely been created. This should be communicated and tested by the team; feedback will fine tune the model. The model may then be applied to implement the desired planned change. Adequate skills in both analytical and critical thinking play a major role during the above process.

Complexity creates issues and problems, which rarely present themselves individually; they usually present themselves in entangled, interconnected batches that have been appropriately described by Ackoff as "messes." Portfolio practitioners are under pressure to digest an increasing amount of data in shorter periods of time. At any time in the portfolio life cycle, the available information used to support project portfolio decisions is usually extensive, everchanging, ambiguous, and characterized by uncertainties and interdependencies between various decision parameters. Many portfolios exhibit a degree of complexity that exceeds the human ability to achieve optimal decisions through mere intuition. Making sense of this complexity requires an awareness of the causes of complexity as well as flexibility, adaptability, competence in navigating complexity, and the capability to wisely utilize large quantities of data.[79]

It should be noted here that the use of large amounts of data may be associated with an increase in confidence. Research has demonstrated that in many cases such use does not create an improved understanding of the situation. As people search for data that confirm their expectations, a human characteristic known as confirmation bias emerges. This entails people choosing only the data that confirm their expectations or position. For this reason, engagement with more data does not necessarily lead to an engagement with alternative perspectives on the same problem. The consequence is that more data does not guarantee better decisions and can lead to overconfidence. Moreover, as discussed above, the need for engagement with alternative perspectives involves a holistic approach, which inevitably leads to considering the whole portfolio as a system within a larger system, the organization. Since the mid-1990s, the project management discipline has had a close relationship with systems approaches, in particular, systems engineering (SE). This close relationship, still under development, was initiated when systems engineering, operations research, and project management were used simultaneously to manage major development projects for the U.S. Department of Defense. Project-based work evolved during that period to serve engineers who employed technologies that were both complicated and innovative to successfully develop and deliver new weapons systems. This fusion also resulted in parallel systems thinking approaches to start moving away from "hard systems" (product- and technology-centric) to "soft systems" (people and process) approaches.[80] Increased awareness of the complexity always inherent in these "soft systems" was a significant result of this move.

More and more practitioners work in complex environments with overlapping and often conflicting interests. Under such conditions, practitioners are challenged by too much unfiltered information and not enough, specifically, relevant communication. This parallel approach is necessary to enhance understanding, to develop awareness of the interactions and dependencies between the various parts of the system, to grasp the characteristics of the players internal and external to the system, and to comprehend how their beliefs and actions affect the system. Such an approach also leverages natural perception skills and improves the ability of the portfolio manager to better process the available data, to proactively deal with emergent risks and problems, and to navigate the emergence of complexity. Moreover, it helps overcome human cognitive limitations and provide improved insight into decision problems.

10.2. Systems Thinking in a Portfolio Management Context

For the intent of this book, it is adequate to think of a system as an organized, purposeful structure consisting of interrelated entities that interact with each other to achieve a common objective. In portfolio management, when the practitioner thinks about a strategy they must think about the whole: the organization *and* its environment. Moreover, any system of interest, such as the portfolio system, is an interrelated entity of a larger system, having within it groups of entities or components that can be viewed as subsystems. Systems thinking is described by many as a process of blowing the problem up to its largest dimensions and then redefining issues, analyzing, synthesizing, improving through feedback, and finally verifying the alternative courses of action in the decision process. It enables a view of our ecosystem, and of the ever-present issues associated with it, as "everything" being related to "everything else."

For purposes of clarity, in this book, portfolio system elements are called portfolio components, and interconnected elements from other systems within the portfolio environment are called entities. Entities, which interact with portfolio components may include:

- Goals: enterprise goals, the organization's cultural goals;
- Inputs: physical, human, information, knowledge, external constraints;
- Processes: service operations, customer relations, knowledge management;
- Human enablers: service providers from other functional units of the organization, functional managers, consultants, contractors, suppliers;
- Physical enablers: physical assets, equipment, facilities, land, and rights of way;
- Information enablers: policies, repositories, intellectual property, tools; and
- Environment: political and economic factors, culture, legal factors, social factors.

The portfolio system (from subsystem to the whole system of the organization) should be managed as an integrated whole relative to the other systems of the organization. When portfolio management is viewed in its systemic context, it is a system that inherently contains a set of subsystems that make up the larger system. Thus, the effectiveness of the portfolio system depends on the effectiveness of the supporting subsystems, as well as the way in which these subsystems are synergized into the larger system. It is the way in which a project portfolio management system operates as a whole within its environment that ultimately determines the success or failure of the strategic objectives of the organization. Developing a concept of portfolio management in systems terms requires that the system be understood in its widest context. Kim[81] defined a system as "any group of interacting, interrelated, or interdependent parts that form a complex and unified whole that has a specific purpose." As previously discussed, each portfolio component is best considered as a separate subsystem to the portfolio system.

Another reason a portfolio should be understood as a system is that even though many of the parameters influencing the portfolio can be anticipated, one must focus on the interconnections between the portfolio components and the flow of changes related to them. Examples include strategies, interactions with key stakeholders, limits to resourcing portfolio components, and changing environmental conditions. A parallel systems approach to the prevailing standard deterministic approach involves analysis on how the whole portfolio interacts with its environment, as well as how the portfolio components interact with each other and the analysis of the effects that these interactions have on the whole portfolio system as well as its components. Additionally, the portfolio manager should focus on the other constituents of the larger system, the organization. For effective portfolio management, it is paramount to study dependencies in order to predict the behavior of the whole portfolio. More explicitly, a systems approach requires a synthesis, which is the reverse of analysis (i.e., breaking the system into constituent parts). Such a study may result in quite different conclusions than those generated by customary forms of analysis; this is particularly true with a complex portfolio or one strongly linked to subsystems that substantively influence the portfolio system.

The idea that different approaches are necessary to manage portfolios and their components has been a concern of project management scholars and practitioners for more than two decades.[82] Moreover, research has been carried out by PMI to categorize projects—portfolio components—and recommend ways to manage them based on their characteristics.[83] In the general management field, the publication of *The Fifth Discipline*[84] helped managers appreciate how their actions are influenced by dependencies, interactions, and the effects of amplifying or dampening feedback between system components. Papers are regularly published in project management journals urging project managers to use systems thinking approaches. To name a few: Pollack;[85] Winter and Checkland;[86] Cicmil et al.;[87] Morris;[88] Maani and Cavana;[89] Remington and Pollack 2008;[90] Williams;[91] PMI;[92] Geraldi et al.;[93] and Sankaran, Haslett, and Sheffield.[94] This advice is even more important for portfolio managers.

10.3. Applying Systems Thinking to Portfolio Management

A primary aim of systems thinking for project portfolios is to understand the functioning of the portfolio as a whole and the interaction with its environment (the organization system). Interdependencies may create many unanticipated evolving situations, issues, and additional, interrelated risks, as described in detail in the next chapter. Portfolio management may be best viewed as a vital subsystem to the organization's management system and in parallel as a vital subsystem of the portfolio system itself. Portfolio management practitioners should know: 1) the basic "building blocks" of the system; 2) the basic "steps" of systems thinking; and 3) the two primary system properties present in all systems. These fundamental system characteristics, applicable to the portfolio system, are presented very briefly below:

1. **Portfolio system fundamental "building blocks"** – Investigate and understand portfolio components, component interconnections and dependencies, flows between components, subcomponents and the portfolio environment (resources, information, influence, etc.), feedback loops, and portfolio system stability in time.

2. **Critical "steps" for portfolio management under systems thinking** – Select and prioritize resources based on management priorities to support portfolio components accomplishing strategic objectives. Plan the system's functionality to these objectives and create the structure to implement actions. Build several hypotheses, accounting for interactions between system entities. Prioritize and test each hypothesis, optimize the chosen hypothesis model, and act to implement the changes. Continuously direct/report/ decide/apply controls. The practitioner should note that all the above actions must be applied in parallel to the application of technical portfolio management (framework, principles, and processes), as these are referred to in the portfolio standard and described in a more "how to" basis in this book.

3. **Portfolio system properties:**

   • **System hierarchy:** Systems are parts of other systems, which are often expressed by system hierarchies to create a multilevel hierarchy. The portfolio system is composed of components that interact through rules, principles, and processes defined by portfolio management and approved by portfolio governance to create different types of outcomes, all aligned to organizational strategic objectives.

   • **System attributes:** The fundamental attributes of a project portfolio system are: alignment to organizational strategy, togetherness (structure and behavior), and emergence. The portfolio system must constantly have adequate controls throughout its life cycle (Law of Requisite Variety).[95]

Depending on the reference hierarchy and level of detail of the systems analysis, portfolio components are the subsidiary portfolios, programs, projects, and the related operations of the portfolio. A more detailed analysis will increase the levels of hierarchy, treat the above as subsystems having their own components, and so on. Depending on the viewpoint and the required detail for the analysis, system components include groups of people, individuals, principles, practices, processes, tools, techniques, rules, resources, technologies, environments, information, and concepts. Systems thinking is the way of becoming aware of the ubiquitous complexity in portfolio systems, understanding some of its causes and characteristics, and navigating the portfolio within its environment. Systems thinking as a parallel approach usually enables reduction of the encountered complexity. Complexity in portfolio management is discussed in the following chapter of this book. Literature also indicates that a systems approach helps reduce suboptimization (i.e., finding the best way to do something that should not be done at all). An example of suboptimization is pushing for priorities of certain portfolio components to the detriment of the organization or adopting a false solution due to a partial understanding of the problem. In conclusion, systems thinking may appreciably help in answering the "why" questions for the whole portfolio, that is, help understand interconnected portfolio components' structures and behaviors and thus aid portfolio management practitioners in developing hypotheses about possible emergent issues and problems.

10.4. The Portfolio System and Its Environment – A Holistic Approach

In the previous section, a systems approach to portfolio management accepts that the portfolio's "health" is related to the performance of all components within the portfolio, as well as by their interdependencies and available resources. Portfolio managers should make decisions that lead to overall portfolio success, even if these conflict with the best interests of a specific portfolio component. Thus, a project portfolio can be viewed as an open, human-made system, existing in an environment described by related systems with which it may react and respond to stimuli from any component or subsystem. Human-made systems are usually referred to as engineered systems. An engineered system, such as a project portfolio, is an open, complex system of sociotechnical components, conceptualized and planned to exist, for a defined, specific purpose. Within the project portfolio management domain, under a systems view, the basic concepts of reference are:

- Wholeness
- Component interactions
- System state (stability/instability) – change over time
- System structure, subsystems' structure – roles, behaviors, and characteristics
- Complexity (ambiguity, emergence, adaptation, nonproportionality, self-organization)

Pattern identification should leave component details out. Otherwise, clarity of patterns is almost impossible to achieve. Actions and reactions need not be necessarily closely linked (in time, in space, in strength, etc.). Based on existing patterns, the portfolio manager may reflect and determine possible small changes that may lead to big effects in the future and thus may formulate and test various hypotheses, and by following this path, create, agree upon, and utilize regularly appropriate metrics. These actions lead toward understanding of the forces and interrelationships that shape the behavior of the whole portfolio system, enabling the portfolio manager to identify needed change much more effectively. Based on the above principles, the fundamental steps in applying a systems approach to the management of project portfolios include:

- To find the cause of an issue or a problem, start by understanding the structure of its subsystems and the underlying dynamic structures and interdependencies before developing an action plan;
- Major insights emerge when the feedback loop structure of the subsystems becomes visible;
- Restructure, if necessary, or if this is not possible, develop proactive alternatives;
- Try to overcome the dominant influence of the current situation by creating dampening interacting loops from other subsystems or components;
- Expanded perception: seeing both the trees and the forest;

- Find loops of causal relationships (feedback loops: either reinforcing or balancing);
- Act upon, but do not overestimate events (try to perceive impacts of small changes); and
- Think in continuous terms, searching for recurrent patterns of behavior over time.

Today, primarily due to ever-increasing complexity, we seldom encounter a portfolio environment characterized by stability and predictability, an environment that makes it easy to deploy the organizational strategy through directive and rapid processes. The portfolio manager should endeavor to holistically and concurrently discover and understand stakeholder needs, explore opportunities, document requirements, synthesize, verify, validate, deploy, sustain, and evolve solutions. Moreover, the portfolio manager should constantly strive to proactively influence the portfolio environment. For this, they need to possess competencies such as resilience, flexibility, and adaptability.

10.5. The Simple, the Complicated, and the Complex Components of a Portfolio System

In a simple system, a method, or a "recipe," can be followed and repeated with relatively little expertise and be expected to produce roughly uniform results. In complicated systems, following a tried-and-true formula may prove insufficient. Expertise is often required, and a variety of skills and knowledge areas may need to be gathered in order to produce a successful result. Once that result is achieved, however, it is replicable. An example of a very complicated problem is developing an airplane. There are numerous inputs needed to achieve the end objectives, but once it is done, it can be successfully repeated. The manufacture of subsequent airplanes requires far less analysis and expertise than was the case during the initial phase. In short, a complicated problem, once solved, remains solved. For portfolio management, systems according to context can be thought of as:

- **Simple:** following a recipe – Recipes are essential; expertise is helpful but not essential; a deliverable is a standardized product; proven recipes give good results every time.
- **Complicated:** developing an airplane – Formulae are critical; manufacturing one airplane increases assurance that the next

airplane will be okay; high levels of expertise in multiple levels are needed; airplanes are the same in critical ways; there is a high degree of certainty in the outcome once the original issues are solved.

- **Complex:** raising a child – Formulae quite useful but may have limited use; raising one child gives experience but no assurance of success with another child; expertise can contribute but is neither necessary nor sufficient for success; each child is unique and must be approached individually; uncertainty of outcome remains.

The differences between simple, complicated, and complex systems are adeptly explained by Glouberman and Zimmerman.[96]

Portfolio components contain various subsystems; each subsystem may belong to any of the three contexts: simple, complicated, complex. Each state requires different tools and techniques to be successfully managed. Sensemaking has been proven very helpful toward understanding the characteristics of each subsystem of the portfolio. Sensemaking tools are discussed in the next chapter. A very popular sensemaking framework today is the Cynefin framework.[97] The Cynefin framework places the above concepts into a visual context that can be applied across any number of fields. In simple contexts, cause equals effect. This is the domain of the known. Situations can be clearly defined and appropriate responses precisely determined. The manager's role is to delegate, use best practices, and communicate the standard processes and operating procedures to be followed clearly and directly. Complicated contexts are the realm of expertise. Cause and effect are not self-evident but can be understood through analysis. The manager's role here is to assemble the needed expertise and encourage differing opinions. Once cause and effect are understood, actions can be undertaken to address the problem. Once the solution is obtained and implemented successfully, the solution is replicable. The complex is the realm of the unknown. It is a space of constant flux and unpredictability. There are no right answers, only emergent behaviors. The manager's role in this domain is to create spaces for patterns to emerge, which is best done by increasing levels of interaction and communication within the system to its largest manageable level. Expertise is useful but not sufficient to solve complex problems—great patience and a sharp eye for new behavioral patterns are paramount.[98]

10.6. Improving Portfolio Systems

Creating and improving systems is at the heart of successful portfolio management. The major purpose of understanding the portfolio system and its numerous subsystems is to be able to proactively respond to situational challenges, and to be able to make performance and quality improvements throughout the portfolio life cycle. Improvement initiatives should be carefully thought out and planned because sometimes such actions have proven tricky. Before making a change that affects teams and other stakeholders, it is important for the portfolio manager to understand that people are predisposed to not remain idle. This predisposition of team members, when combined with two important cognitive biases that all humans have, the "absence blindness" and the "intervention bias," if not accounted for by the portfolio manager, may hinder or distort any needed changes to the system.

Absence blindness leads us to value things we can see over things we can't. This predisposition affects how we work on systems. That is why a thorough understanding of causes of issues or problems, as discussed in the next chapter, is very important for the practitioner. The intervention bias makes people likely to introduce changes that aren't necessary to feel in control of an emergent situation. When something bad happens, it feels tempting to fix the situation by introducing additional layers of limitations and by assigning more resources. Usually the result is not an improvement in throughput or efficiency.[99] Awareness of this mental state helps us avoid unnecessary or incorrect actions. The best way for the practitioner to correct for intervention bias is to examine what would happen if nothing is done (the concept is known as the null hypothesis). Examining the null hypothesis before intervening helps toward avoiding the intervention bias and thus toward making the best possible decision.

People's mind-sets (also known as worldviews or mental models) integrate knowledge, culture, and experience. Mind-sets considerably influence the way individuals will frame and approach risks, issues, and problems. The demand to change one's prevailing mind-set for any situation arises when the individual is unable to fit the facts, observations, information, issues, or problems into their existing mental model. Under such conditions, a dilemma is created. Ackoff[100] explains a dilemma as "a problem, which cannot be solved within the current worldview." The demand to change one's mind-set—the initial mind-set in most cases is the causal approach—usually leads practitioners to a paradigm shift toward a parallel systemic approach. It has been proven that in many situations within a complex environment, only a causal approach, which is people's initial natural reaction, may lead to erroneous actions.

Systems thinking is evolving as a parallel approach to causal thinking. According to Ackoff, [26] "Analysis is paramount for revealing how a system works but synthesis reveals why a system works the way it does." When new information develops, and that information does not fit properly into the currently understood model, the first activity to be performed is to wonder on the what, the why, and the how. Wondering as opposed to observing, is key to abductive reasoning. It is the act of critically thinking about what can be done with the new information in order to orient it to the environment. This thinking process sets abductive reasoning apart from deductive or intuitive reasoning—a logical leap of the mind to make sense of the new information that does not fit in our current worldview. Critical thinking utilizes all three kinds of logic to understand the world (deductive, inductive, and abductive thinking). Portfolio managers should focus on learning critical thinking skills in practice. This can take place via the application of principles, processes, and good practices, rather than learning in theory only. Action plans are most successful when founded on authentic engagement of the stakeholders. A good practice for engaging portfolio stakeholders is the structured dialogue and deliberation process.[101] Under systems thinking, there is usually a willingness to waive the interest of the part for the interest of the whole. Thus, importance is given toward maximizing the performance of the whole.

Portfolio managers must have specific abilities to produce novel, unexpected solutions, tolerate uncertainty, work with sometimes incomplete information, and apply forethought and adaptability to practical problems. Portfolio managers must also be able to work out ill-defined problems and adopt solution-focusing strategies. Further to the "why" and the "how," the "who" is hugely important. Based on experience on the "who," some brief advice follows:

- When possible, promote from within, after benchmarking to the best external potentials. There are vast differences between the best and the rest.

- Talent management is paramount for structuring the roles of the entire portfolio management function. Talent management also encompasses managers and team members of all portfolio components. Focusing on developing talent, and consequently using the correctly talented people, is very important.
- Research shows[102] that executives make decisions 70 percent of the time based on only one alternative and make errors 52 percent of the time.
- Executives often experience choice overload.
- People are better at selecting from six offerings than from 24. Too few or too many alternatives enhance uncertainty considerably.
- Emotional intelligence (managing one's self as well as properly managing others) is a critical factor in predicting the success of executive management.
- In an uncertain world, adaptability—especially in nonlinear environments—is as important as performance.
- When selecting future colleagues/team members for managing the portfolio, one should not compromise on potential, particularly on values, cultural fit, and talent.

In conclusion, portfolio management practitioners need to understand how the components of the portfolio interrelate and how the portfolio system works over time within the whole organization system. This perspective creates awareness of the need to prepare and plan for multiple potential paths should emergent circumstances demand this. Identifying patterns of emergent issues and resulting consequences within the portfolio system and focusing on these patterns helps to understand both the structure and behavior of the whole system. It also forges recognition of the influence of component interconnections. The epitome of systems thinking is that the ever-present complexity of the real world can best be harnessed by seeing things as a whole while understanding the causes of complexity and establishing a proactive way to navigate it. As already discussed, programs and projects managed effectively and efficiently as a portfolio are the transient vehicles that successfully deliver the change initiatives for the whole organization. A systems perspective allows for better understanding of the strategic objectives of the change initiatives and of the vehicles delivering these objectives—the components of the project portfolio.

Encountering, Harnessing, and Navigating Complexity

by Panos Chatzipanos

> Nature has established patterns originating in the return of events, but only for the most part.
> — **Leibniz in a letter to Bernoulli, 1703 A.D.**

Managing an organization today is very different than it was a few decades ago. A fundamental difference is the level of complexity management that must be handled successfully. Complexity has always existed. People, groups, organizations, and societies during their lifetimes invariably had to deal with the ambiguous and the unexpected. New technologies, instant communications, fragmented supply chains, scarcer resources, and globalization have considerably increased the encountered complexity people are asked to understand and embrace. In recent times, the phenomenon has transformed from an influential characteristic of rather large systems (e.g., social systems, organizations with numerous subsystems) to something that affects almost every system. Complexity affects our daily work, the projects we plan, the products we design, the organizations and social groups that people belong to, markets, and societies.

Many systems that once existed without extensive interdependencies are now entirely interdependent, thus considerably more complex. Complexity is present in almost all portfolio systems. As discussed in the previous chapter, these systems are much more difficult to manage than merely complicated ones. It is harder to make predictions since complex systems often interact in unpredictable ways; it is harder to plan because the past behavior of a complex system often does not indicate its future behavior; it is harder to understand behaviors because complexity often overpasses our cognitive capabilities. Quite often for a complex system, the deviation is considerably more important than the normal behavior. The PfM Standard[103] says,

> Portfolios are human-made, socio-technical systems consisting of interconnected components exhibiting related and often unexpected behaviors, which fulfill a critical organizational function. Portfolios have the properties of non-linear, dynamic, complex, and sometimes complex adaptive systems.

Portfolio systems are transformational and adaptive to environmental change; they may self-organize to adapt to emergent situations and certain parts of the system usually exhibit nonproportionality. Small changes can create disproportionally large consequences. Portfolios often exhibit characteristics of a complex adaptive system.

These characteristics include:

- The interconnected portfolio components' behavior is not explainable only by the properties of the components, but behavior also emerges from the interaction of the components. These behaviors may change over time.
- Changes in initial conditions may create disproportional effects.
- Specific subsystems, if allowed, may self-organize.
- The portfolio system is nonlinear and relies on feedback to evolve and reshape.
- The portfolio system operates on multiple timescales and levels simultaneously.

Complexity theory postulates that complex adaptive systems begin as collections of individual active parts of the system (usually named "actors"), which may organize themselves and create relationships. Cause and effect relationships from the interconnected parts usually establish responses. These responses are commonly referred to as amplifying or dampening feedback loops. A degree of randomness is involved as well. New structures and behaviors emerge as the actors; dynamic parts of the system act and react to each other and with their environment. What primarily interests the portfolio manager are the new conditions that are created as a result of individual interactions. Usually, the emergent result is greater than, and qualitatively different from, the sum of the results from the individual actions. Feedback loops serve as the drivers for complexity as well as for the evolution of the system. Positive feedback moves individual actors or groups of actors closer to the desired condition perceived to be important, while negative feedback serves to suppress change.

As described in the PfM Standard, complexity is a principal characteristic of the portfolio system and its component subsystems (programs, projects, operations, portfolio stakeholders, various teams, portfolio organizational environment, etc.). The attributes of this characteristic are primarily the result of the interactions between the components and other subsystems of the portfolio system. Complexity, as it relates to the project management discipline, is discussed in detail in PMI's *Navigating Complexity: A Practice Guide*.[104]

11.1. Complexity Awareness within the Portfolio Environment

Complex portfolio systems often contain nondeterministic, and thus mostly unpredictable, subsystems. Their existence creates ambiguity. Dealing with ambiguity demands patience, agility, adaptability, and diligence in order to deal successfully with emergent risks, issues, and problems. Depending solely on tool sets and skill sets that may have been proven adequate for simple or complicated portfolio components and subcomponents may lead to failures when dealing with such components in a complex environment. The available literature contains ample proof of such failures.[105]

The required skill sets for the portfolio manager often encompass aspects of behavior as well as of competence in the areas of systems thinking, emotional intelligence, relationship and trust building, the ability to take a holistic view, and above all, excel at flexible leadership. To an extent, any portfolio component has its share of complexity since we live in a continually changing world. For simple portfolio components, such change probably won't have severe effects on the outcomes, expected benefits, and value creation. But for portfolio components that are engulfed by complexity (and these are usually the most important ones), specific causes of complexity as well as contextual change may significantly enhance the complexity that the portfolio manager must navigate.

Complexity causes and drivers for the portfolio include particular attributes of the key stakeholders, such as leadership and behavioral traits; team structure and experience; team flexibility and creativity; risk aversion; understanding the interconnectedness of each planned outcome to the portfolio component's subsystem; and so forth. Complexity causes also depend on the actual number of the portfolio component's interconnected subsystems and elements specific to each component, which include duration, cost, scope, safety, regulations, governance, intricacy, requirements stability, and maturity, among others.

It is significant to be able to reduce the effects of complexity since the presence of complexity may considerably enhance the difficulty to manage the portfolio. The presence and emergence of further complexity during the portfolio life cycle creates new emergent risks, issues, and problems. Thus, assessing complexity by the understanding of its causes is very important. Moreover, the presence of complexity necessitates the capability of adapting and evolving in an often-changing environment.

In such an environment, even minor decisions can have substantial effects. A minor decision can result in an interaction of events that snowball into additional problems. A minor decision may create conditions for evolving, self-organizing situations that may prove difficult to manage once developed. Literature confirms that it is difficult for decision makers to fully comprehend the functions of an entire complex system. Cognitive limits further hamper individuals in their understanding of other people's actions. For these reasons, complexity awareness, understanding of the causes of complexity within the portfolio environment, and the application of critical thinking toward prompt decision making are very important for successful portfolio management.

The effects of complexity may be encountered in any dimension, function, or part of a portfolio subsystem. Awareness of complexity primarily requires consistent leadership, proper organizational structures, transparent and efficient communications, cooperative teams, talent management, resilience, adaptability, and attention to early signs of emergent issues. Moreover, the presence of complexity leads to focus much more on the desired outcomes via agreed-upon and followed principles, and less on blind following of normative processes that the applicable methodology prescribes. The component's desired outcomes should be the primary portfolio component driver. The desired outcome should be constantly revalidated against current organizational contextual conditions and possible changes within certain strategic objectives.

Even if the portfolio component is delivered on time, to cost and specifications, a wrong outcome will always be a wrong outcome.

Knowledge management is also important in reducing the effects of complexity. Specifically, the means by which the organization can capture, integrate, and disseminate institutional knowledge to its whole management structure are crucial to an organization's efforts to learn from past mistakes. Disciplined knowledge management processes in an organization usually act as catalysts for the shared vision. Literature[106] indicates that shared vision[107] acting not only as a guide for all change initiatives but also as a motivating common factor for all portfolio component team members, can reduce complexity within the portfolio and its environment. Furthermore, when outsourcing and utilizing supply chains, management should recognize that because of uncertainty it is paramount for all parties to share risk according to their corresponding capacity and capability. Thus, portfolio governance should provide guidance to make the necessary provisions for contract-based outsourced work. Otherwise, contractual "zero-sum games"[108] will be created— where one contractual party must lose for the other one to gain. It has been proven beyond any doubt that such situations enhance complexity considerably and usually lead to conflict.

11.2. Causes of Complexity – Portfolio System Characteristics

The important actions toward developing complexity awareness in portfolio management include:

- Recognize and understand causes and effects of complexity and the nonlinearity/nonproportionality of such relationships;
- Expect dynamic interactions between components of the portfolio and within the portfolio ecosystem; and
- Appreciate emergent behavior and plan to mitigate its effects: build resiliency in the portfolio system and simultaneously develop agility—flexibility and adaptability.

The practitioner should be aware that complexity will pose challenges in at least three areas of managerial activity: 1) forecasting and proactivity; 2) portfolio risk mitigation; and 3) difficulty in developing an optimal balance for the portfolio, particularly, resourcing components based on prioritization and making successful trade-offs.

Practitioners also need to be aware that many aspects of portfolio complexity will not be known at any given time frame but may subsequently emerge during the portfolio life cycle (e.g., due to managerial practices, environmental change, or human behavior). Managerial practices and human behavior may result in being the principal causes of complexity within the portfolio. Hence, awareness of existing conditions and their understanding is important—for example, recognition of the system domain of each subsystem or understanding of the contextual characteristics of the portfolio system. For each portfolio subsystem, assessment of the subsystem domain is quite important (i.e., simple, complicated, complex, or chaotic). As discussed in the previous chapter, complicated systems are like machines; primarily one needs to minimize friction. A different set of competencies and tools are needed than the one needed to navigate a complex system, which usually behaves like a living organism. For navigating the complex system, critical thinking skills are very important in order to deal with the changes and variations bound to occur. System domains and sensemaking tools will be further discussed later in this chapter.

Portfolio systems are governed by technical and organizational complexity, the social intricacy of human behavior, and uncertainty of long life cycles. Evidently, portfolio complexity is enhanced by the linear increase of portfolio components. This results in an exponential increase of interactions between the components.[109] Such an increase also increases the competition between portfolio components for limited resources. Portfolio managers, whenever possible, must anticipate and administer emergent phenomena, which may arise in the absence of any central controlling mechanism, once the number of interdependencies reaches a certain threshold. These conditions primarily determine the structural complexity of the system.[110]

As briefly mentioned, our cognition imposes limits on our ability to make sense of the data we are confronted with. Research shows[111, 112] that the assumption of humans as rationally behaving decision makers is valid only up to a point. Human behavior toward decision making can be best described as bounded rationality since we all have a wide range of cognitive biases which influence our decisions considerably.[113] Our limited short-term memory makes us feel quickly overwhelmed.[114] We usually seek "satisfying solutions, and not optimal ones." Moreover, "we actively seek out evidence that confirms our expectations and avoid evidence that disconfirms them."[115] The use of massive amounts of data may be rightly correlated with an increase in confidence, but this does not necessarily lead to an improved understanding of the situation. Understanding such phenomena, as the ones briefly mentioned above, may prove crucial for successful portfolio management.

Proactive procedures to reduce complexity may be designed once at least partial understanding of the causes of complexity is achieved. Portfolio components involve people, and people's behavior is central to portfolio complexity; subsystems involving people are the most difficult to understand, let alone predict behavior. For example, any slight differences that may occur at the project "front end" of each portfolio component regarding stakeholder desires and alignment can significantly influence the outcome of the particular solution. Another example, managing a group of stakeholders having different priorities and perhaps hidden agendas can, by itself, be a very complex and daunting task.

The anticipation of the effects of complexity and the action plan to meet the emergent challenges starts from the understanding of its causes. These causes are, almost always, both intrinsic and extrinsic to the project portfolio system. Once practitioners can appreciate and understand the causes of complexity for the portfolio system, they can mitigate, or at least be prepared to administer, its emergence. A complexity navigation framework such as the one described in *Navigating Complexity: A Practice Guide* provides valuable insight. Such a framework includes regular iterations toward awareness of the causes of portfolio complexity, portfolio complexity assessment, and scenarios for navigating the encountered portfolio complexity.

Navigating Complexity suggests that practitioners must deal with three overarching causes of complexity—complexity that is due to system behavior, human behavior, and ambiguity. Complexity encountered within the portfolio system emerges as a consequence of one or more of these three overarching causes, which are summarily presented below.[116]

- **System behavior** – Complexity occurs as a result of dynamic component interdependencies—any action within a portfolio component may cause a change to the whole portfolio system.
  - **Dynamics of the portfolio system** – As constant changes occur in the portfolio system and its environment, interactions amplify, balance, or dampen such changes. Interdependencies may cause unclear and disproportional cause-effect relationships over time and unexpected

emergent dynamic situations and issues. This may lead to adaptive behavior of certain components, which creates unforeseeable issues, dragging resources that are not accounted for. Having specified objectives means having expressed the intention, having designed for a possible future. Thus, navigating complexity encompasses taking frequent corrective action so that, at regular intervals, the deviations between the designed objectives and the reached objectives are reduced as much as possible.

○ **Interconnections and interdependencies** – Portfolio components are interconnected by miscellaneous flows and feedback loops, each having unique characteristics. The nature of these connections is quite important. Depending on the situation, both the connections themselves and any missing connections between components can enhance complexity. Portfolio managers examine and understand dependencies between components; they should not overlook possible hidden dependencies within the portfolio hierarchy or within the organizational system, which may create unexpected behavior of the system. Understanding of the structure and behavior of the system as well as its hierarchy is quite important for this endeavor. Hierarchy analysis reveals hidden—sometimes called "nested"—components within the portfolio system. Such an analysis also reveals further constraints. The portfolio manager may adjust the hierarchy of constraints in the portfolio but mostly must effectively accommodate the weight of the constraints to be complied with.

- **Human behavior** – The central issue for emergent complexity has to do with people; we are the most important cause of complexity in project-based work. Humans are impeded by our cognitive limits, which are often unacknowledged. For example, most managers think they can digest more information than research proves they actually can. This leads to premature actions, executed without comprehension of the system dynamics. Complexity resulting from human behavior stems from the interplay of behaviors, demeanors, and attitudes of people. These behaviors may be the result of factors such as changing power, political influence, an individual's experiences, culture, and perspectives. Moreover, these factors may hinder the clear identification of goals and objectives. Such behaviors[117] primarily include:

- o **Individual behavior** – Examples of individual behavior that enhance complexity are human biases (optimism bias and planning fallacy, anchoring, framing effect, loss aversion, resistance to change, etc.). These cognitive biases inadvertently introduce the element of irrationality. Human behavior also includes complexity enhancers, such as hidden agendas, pet projects, and so on.
- o **Social behavior (group, organizational, political)** – Examples include: a tribal mind-set, group think, group shift, chain reaction, self-organization, and so on.
- o **Communications-related** – Examples include: lack of continuous stakeholder commitment, conflicting stakeholder commitment, varying legal perspectives, different cultural mind-sets, hiding behind the concept of "on a need-to-know basis" for noncommunicating essential information, and so on.
- o **Organizational structures-related** – Examples include: alignment processes, secondary governance issues, misalignment, transparency, and too many advisory committees.
- o **Organizational capacity** – Examples include: related talent management, leadership issues, capacity building, and capability enhancement.

Such conditions may be challenging for the portfolio manager, particularly regarding relationships with key stakeholders. Divergent expectations may create openings for disagreements and tacit agreements. For portfolios with a large number of stakeholders, obtaining consensus may be difficult. Usually stakeholders possess limited knowledge of the existing issues, problems, and risks at any given time. In such cases, further to properly structured communications, the portfolio manager should be prepared to address group think and group shift phenomena. Group shift is often encountered by portfolio practitioners since usually a dominant figure exists in any portfolio stakeholder group. Most people who have limited knowledge of an issue side with that dominant figure. For the portfolio manager, fundamental awareness of the existence of idiosyncrasies that determine human individual and group behavior is quite important. Thus, recognition of biases, identification of too many portfolio components too closely connected without any redundancy in the system (i.e., a nonresilient and thus unsustainable system), the establishment of a critically thought plan for mitigating emergent phenomena due to human behavior, and focusing on extensive communications as well as on stakeholder and risk management are key.

- **Project portfolio complexity as a result of ambiguity** – Ambiguity can be described "as a state of being unclear and not knowing what to expect or how to comprehend a situation. Unclear or misleading events, cause-and-effect confusion, emergent issues, or situations open to more than one interpretation in programs and projects lead to ambiguity." (PMI 2014). Ambiguity is a common characteristic of portfolio components and is also a common aspect of the whole portfolio. Ambiguity may produce high complexity. Causes of ambiguity in portfolio management that contribute alone or combined toward a higher level of complexity, include:
  - **Emergence** – This is an unexpected change that occurs within the context of the portfolio, driven by component interactions. Interdependencies usually have feedback characteristics, which determine new behaviors thereby creating new system or subsystem dynamics. Emergence may be concealed and then become visible. Causes of emergence include self-organization and nonproportionality. An example of self-organization is when the performance of the portfolio management team cannot be predicted only from knowledge of the performance of the individual team members, and this obviously also applies for the management teams of every portfolio component. High-performing teamwork is a characteristic that emerges when the conditions are just right and the team really is behaving as a team. This is one example of emergence, whereby the whole team performance becomes greater than the sum of its parts.
  - **Uncertainty** – Uncertainty is a result of imperfect and unknown information creating a state of being unsure and of not knowing issues, events, paths to follow, or solutions to pursue. As the number of interdependent actions increases, so usually does uncertainty. Coping with

uncertainty requires understanding and resolution of issues before they escalate and impact pursued solutions.
At the portfolio level, the resulting complexity influences
resource constraints; the constant monitoring, control,
and resource allocation decisions to ensure that portfolio
is kept in line with organizational objectives, value maximization, portfolio balance, strategic direction, and so on.

At the portfolio level, as a result of the combined influence of the above
two causes, there exists a much greater level of unknown-unknowns
(i.e., unidentifiable, unthinkable emergent risks or situations). Such
risks are in addition to the known risks, prevalent in the portfolio ecosystem, which usually interacts with the known risks, creating more
uncertainty. The practice of iterative risk management is paramount in
a complex portfolio environment. Moreover, highly complex portfolio
ecosystems require quick adaptability to changes in strategic priorities and full engagement with key stakeholders. As mentioned above, a
properly structured portfolio communication management plan, as previously described in this book, is crucial.

11.3. Classification and Characteristics of Complexity in a Portfolio Environment

In addition to the causes of complexity, there exist many classifications
of complexity associated with the project management discipline. These
are most notably manifested by:

- A methodological framework based on structural complexity,
  time-related complexity, technology-/industry-related complexity and directional/managerial complexity; and
- Associating complexity to its causes and assigning domains
  of responsibility facilitating its navigation. Suggested domains include operational complexity, objectives/outcome
  complexity, environmental complexity, stakeholder complexity, and organizational complexity.

Summarily, the above classifications refer to:

- **Structural complexity** – Significant complexity is added to
  the portfolio as the number of components increases. Complexity stems from the difficulty in coordinating and keeping

track of the large number of different interconnected tasks and activities and the consequential emergence of unanticipated issues, problems, and risks.

- **Temporal complexity** – This is primarily due to major components of the portfolio having very long planning and execution durations. The portfolio may also contain major components that are characterized by shifting environmental and strategic directions, which are generally outside the direct control of the management team. This kind of complexity stems from uncertainty regarding future constraints. Further, temporal complexity can be found in portfolios having major components that are subjected to unanticipated environmental impacts significant enough to seriously destabilize the portfolio, such as rapid and unexpected legislative changes, civil unrest and catastrophes, or the development of new technologies.
- **Technology-/industry-related complexity** – This type of complexity may be found in portfolios that have many components with technical or design issues associated with products that have never been produced before, or with techniques that are unknown and for which there are no precedents. Here the complexity stems from interconnections between multiple interdependent solution options.
- **Directional/managerial complexity** – This is encountered in portfolios that have key components characterized by unshared goals and goal paths, unclear meanings, or hidden agendas. This kind of complexity stems from ambiguity related to multiple potential interpretations of goals and objectives and has a lot to do with proper portfolio governance and stakeholder management.
- **Operational complexity** – Operational complexity is associated with not applying a standardized, established project, program, and portfolio management framework. The existence of an organizational project management framework in the organization has been proven quite beneficial toward navigating the inherent complexity in portfolios. Operational complexity may increase with the number of the portfolio components and nonbalanced resource allocation.
- **Complexity due to objectives/outcomes** – This occurs when strategic objectives are not clearly defined or entirely

known, and portfolio components do not have known pre-dictable deliverables. Outcome complexity usually increases when portfolio components must follow unprecedented activities in pursuit of novel or innovative deliverables.

- **Contextual (environmental) complexity** – This arises from an unstable portfolio ecosystem. Since it usually cannot be controlled by the portfolio manager, it must be mitigated by top management and portfolio governance. The portfolio manager must be aware and diligently report its emergence to portfolio governance to develop proactive response scenarios.

- **Stakeholder complexity** – This arises when key stakeholders do not actively support project portfolio management or key components of the portfolio. Again, this may not be under the full control of the portfolio manager, but most times proper stakeholder management is the mitigating key. On slight signs of its emergence, the portfolio manager must report and work with portfolio governance toward its mitigation.

- **Organizational complexity** – This type of complexity is associated with trying to align the views and secure the endorsements of organizational committees with distinct roles, responsibilities, perspectives, and priorities. The role of secondary governance is very important. The way secondary governance, sometimes a favorite of many executives, is structured and the authority secondary governance has on the portfolio and its key components can increase the complexity of the portfolio ecosystem considerably.

11.4. Evaluating the Effects of Complexity during the Portfolio Life Cycle

As already discussed, it is very important how the portfolio manager perceives and embraces complexity. This is a significant competence for the portfolio manager and is independent of the actual complexity of the portfolio itself. Human ability to make sound decisions when encountering complexity is constrained by three factors:

- Criticality of decision time;
- The portfolio manager's cognitive limitations, competencies, and experience; and

- Availability of reliable information or when this is missing, and the intuition capacity (i.e., nonuse of subconscious decision-making models and rules) of the portfolio manager and team. Decisions on complex, problematic situations based on human heuristics are often wrong.

Uncertainty may be a cause but also an effect of complexity. The way one approaches uncertainty is very important, since perception of uncertainty plays a critical role in how practitioners prioritize issues from a complex network of factors.

As briefly discussed in the previous chapter, a fact associated with uncertainty that merits constant attention by the portfolio manager is that people often make wrong decisions when dealing with uncertainty. Practitioners also need to consider that:

- Different people reach different conclusions when presented with uncertainty-related data;
- People instinctively avoid and distort perceptions of uncertainty; and
- People, being educated within a scientific framework (i.e., in reductionist-linear thinking), usually try to approach the issue in probabilistic, quantitative terms.

The portfolio manager may follow the steps suggested below toward navigating complexity within the portfolio and its environment. This is an iterative procedure that may need to be followed many times during the portfolio life cycle. The following steps are advised:

- Understand the causes of complexity – Apply reflective thinking; challenge assumptions; and harness emotional intelligence. Harnessing emotional intelligence helps portfolio managers learn about themselves, their team members, and their key stakeholders, reducing portfolio complexity in the process.
- Look diligently for interrelationships (reinforcing, dampening, or balancing loops) among causes and effects within the portfolio system. Consider that not only portfolio components but also the interrelationships between portfolio components may have both function and purpose.
- Understand portfolio structure. This enhances sensing of changes within the project portfolio as well as other changes

with impacts on the portfolio. The causes and effects of complexity change through the life cycle of the portfolio. Therefore, actions and approaches will need to change appropriately. A flexible leadership style may have to be adopted.

- Prepare a portfolio system diagram containing at least all top priority components (with causal flows and intercomponent feedback loops), including feedback loops from key stakeholders, primary communications, and top portfolio risks.
- Produce a complexity assessment plan (*Navigating Complexity: A Practice Guide* provides guidance).
- Review the assessment.
- Anticipate emergent issues and risks.
- Know when to give special importance to specific processes.
- Determine how complexity is manifested in portfolio components and on managing the portfolio itself.
- Design monitoring and controlling mechanisms and metrics— improve resource utilization.
- Define proactive moves—try to "envelope" effects of known-unknowns (i.e., prepare a contingency plan) for unknown-unknowns.[118,119]
- Apply critical thinking—"Black Swans" may be extremely rare events but they do happen.
- Honor constraints imposed by key stakeholders, organization resources, strategic objectives, or external situational factors.
- Prepare a contingency plan for the entire portfolio toward fulfilling at least the primary strategic objectives.
- Prepare a list of possible proactive response initiatives— discuss and get approval from portfolio governance.

The portfolio manager is primarily concerned with navigating two types of complexity:

1. The organizational complexity of the portfolio (mainly caused by system and human behavior); and
2. The complexity introduced by the strategic objectives of the portfolio (mainly due to complexity caused by the portfolio external environment and ambiguity).

The portfolio manager should be able to appreciate the importance of social interactions between people. They must develop competencies toward becoming a reflective practitioner who can learn, apply critical thinking, operate, and adapt in complex environments through knowledge, experience, talent, intuition, and consequently toward the pragmatic application of theory into practice.

Recent PMI research[120] has demonstrated that properly established portfolio governance can considerably reduce complexity within the entire organization system. Figure 20 illustrates this.

Integrating complexity awareness as defined in PMI's *Navigating Complexity: A Practice Guide* with the two complexity-valuation frameworks briefly presented above, plus the use of sensemaking techniques and tools as described below, will greatly enhance the capability of the portfolio manager to understand the origins and growth of complexity within the portfolio ecosystem; become aware of its effects; and develop mitigation, resilience, and adaptability plans to successfully navigate the portfolio through it. The bibliography of this book contains the

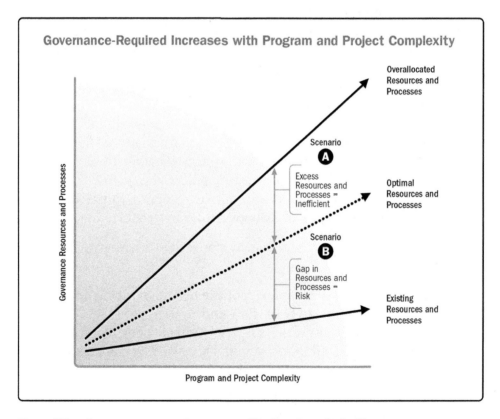

Figure 20. Governance versus Program and Project Complexity[121]

appropriate references for those portfolio management practitioners who are interested in further study of the influence of complexity on portfolio-/program-/project management-related work.

The premise of this chapter is to convey to the practitioner that the multitude of variables existing in complex systems such as portfolios become causally related to feedback loops interacting with each other. The interrelationships between feedback loops constitute the structure of the portfolio system. This is the overarching determinant of the entire portfolio system behavior and of the resulting complexity. The aim of the practitioner is to seek awareness of complexity causes and effects in a proactive way to be prepared to navigate through it. Literature provides ample evidence that complexity affects all portfolio performance domains and needs to be accounted for when applying standardized processes and good practices. Comprehension of its causes, categories, and effects allows mitigation strategies and the planning of appropriate future interventions to ensure behavior that fits the principles and purpose of portfolio management.

11.5. Navigating Portfolio Complexity

The overall architecture of the strategic objectives defines the portfolio components. If this architecture is flawed by the asymmetric complexity it creates, the integration of portfolio components toward successful implementation of the organizational strategic initiatives will be difficult to impossible. People are usually better at managing the technical subsystem, which is usually a deterministic, process-based simple system, than governing the corresponding organizational subsystem of the portfolio where complexity usually abounds. Awareness of such cognitive tendencies leads to proactive response plans in order to mitigate phenomena such as the above.

Emergent complexity can affect outcomes, resulting in notable deviations from the original plan. Examples include the removal of critical resources, changes in enterprise and component organizational structures, ineffective change management, among others. Moreover, ambiguous and untimely decisions usually increase complexity—for example, complications due to technical issues within portfolio components or a lack of clarity of objectives. Understanding the architecture and structure of the portfolio system is very important for a successful attempt to predict its behavior. Predictions are based on hypothetical scenarios.[122,123] Let's take, for example, emergent behavior. Scenarios- and action- plans are based on the tell-tale signs. Portfolio profession- als must therefore proactively plan their responses by asking these questions:

- How will the stakeholders' requirements develop?
- Will they change?
- How can the portfolio manager respond proactively?
- Will there be organizational resistance to the change initiative?
- What will be the effect of decreasing or increasing staffing levels in a primary portfolio component while balancing port- folio resources?

In order to understand and appreciate portfolio complexity, the prac- titioner may also use sensemaking models. A frame of reference (a mental model) is designed to give meaning to experiences by bringing together knowledge and proven practices from system, complexity, and cogni- tive sciences, as well as management science, organizational studies, psychology, anthropology, and cybernetics. Such a framework may give meaning to a not-well-defined problem, and thereby adequately guide decisions and actions. Sensemaking is primarily about how people make sense of the world, so they can act in it.[124] People need to comprehend enough to make a contextually appropriate decision and a sensemaking framework has been proved, in many cases, beneficial.

People use frames of reference that help explain the world around them. People also regularly refine their frames as they interact with their environment and receive inputs. Inputs include an extensive range of indications or information, such as charts and data in project reports, a conversation with stakeholders, or even a strange gesture or look. When people receive inputs that are inconsistent with their current frames, they can either discard the data and keep their existing frame or question their frame.

The sensemaking process is activated as current frames are ques- tioned. Therefore, sensemaking is an active process, where people con- sciously seek explanations toward encountered issues and problems.[125] Developing a frame is also a periodic process of fitting inputs from the environment into frames and the frames encompassing the input. If the frame cannot encompass the input and the input is not disregarded, a new frame that encompasses the input must evolve. Sensemaking is also a communication process through which groups make sense of events and circumstances, particularly of the ones that affect them. It is also a social process of making sense, through communication, of the circumstances in which people collectively find themselves.

Frames are influenced by personal preferences, experiences, and expert knowledge—they are thus idiosyncratic. They also embed a system of rules, principles, and so on, used in organizing and guiding individual behavior.[126] As the new frame leads to actions, they also shape the context and change the situation. That is why the sensemaking process not only responds to, but also constructs the context around us.[127] A 2014 review of the available literature on sensemaking in organizations identified different categories of sensemaking and numerous sensemaking-related concepts.[128]

For project-based work, particularly when complexity is encountered, a well-known and frequently used sensemaking model is Cynefin, proposed by D. Snowden. Cynefin, briefly presented in the previous chapter, is a sensemaking framework.[129] Its value, according to Snowden, is not so much in logical arguments or empirical verifications as in its effect on people's understanding through the creation of powerful constructs that help make sense of ambiguous phenomena. Cynefin suggests five decision-making domains: simple, complicated, complex, chaotic, and the "state of disorder." To work in a complex world, the Cynefin framework suggests shifting people's approaches from "seeing and categorizing," to "sensing multiple perspectives." People must become aware that these mental filters are active and affect what people see. People also need to be aware of the effects that cognitive biases can impose upon one's perceptions and decisions.

The use of effective visual representations to aid complexity perception and awareness has proven to be very beneficial. Visual representations[130] function as anchoring frames as well as inputs in the sensemaking process. Visuals can encourage the development of a more elaborate frame for three main reasons:

1.   They're an effective means for understanding large and complex quantities of data;
2.   Visuals embed more data in a particular space than text; and
3.   Visuals function as "memory milestones, and so extend our short-term memory, which in turn helps us process more data through many perspectives."

Therefore, the use of multiple visuals enables cognition of even higher quantities of data, and potentially distinct perspectives of the portfolio problem.

11.6. The Impact of Portfolio Complexity to the Organization – Organizational Management Framework Considerations

One of the most important constituents for the successful navigation of complexity within the organization is leadership. The navigation of complexity focuses attention on those aspects of organizational life that trouble portfolio managers most: disorder, irregularity, and randomness. Navigating complexity means achieving portfolio objectives while accepting instability, change, and unpredictability. This helps in avoiding the trap, in times of crisis, to try only to stabilize the crisis without eliminating its causes. Navigating complexity and portfolio management have an important bilateral relationship; available literature from conducted research demonstrates that the establishment and implementation of portfolio management in an organization considerably reduces and harnesses complexity.

Within the portfolio, external environment complexity primarily affects strategic planning, portfolio sponsorship, and portfolio governance. For strategic planning, practitioners need to consider the following factors as complexity enhancers:

- Duration of portfolio components;
- Dynamics of the portfolio ecosystem;
- Effects of many small changes during initial conditions that may transform the portfolio and its environment; and
- Changes associated with competitive situations and different goals among key stakeholders.

For portfolio sponsorship and portfolio governance, the following considerations are very important:

- As complexity increases, entropy (lack of predictability) also increases. Thus, as complexity increases, portfolio governance must adapt to exhibit anticipatory, change-oriented behavior and situational response (or more plainly, clear, swift decision making). Governance must also embrace proactivity so the portfolio system does not jump into a non-anticipated state. It is the responsibility of the portfolio manager to ensure that the processes used to accumulate the status of all components and convey the status of the whole portfolio-to-portfolio governance and executive management must be well-documented, tested, and validated.

- Long-term planning has its limits, particularly in such a complex environment. That is why experienced portfolio managers look for patterns in the whole and seek small changes in strategic objectives that can have the largest possible impact on unfavorable patterns. Complexity awareness invites looking for patterns. Such an approach enhances the development of flexible and adaptable alternate plans. Project portfolios represent what the organization will be in the future. Project portfolios co-evolve with changes in strategy and strategic objectives within complexity. Analyzing and planning the portfolio path, plus deviations to be enacted when necessary, proactive behavior, resilience, but also flexibility and adaptability under certain circumstances, are essential. If executive management cannot see their strategy continuously reflected in the portfolio, they will not champion portfolio management regardless of the fact that by adopting such behavior, they will have little chance of eventually achieving that strategy.

- A complex adaptive system approach (applied in parallel and enhancing the technical portfolio management principles described in the PfM Standard and this companion guide) has been proven to help portfolio management and governance considerably. This approach is also necessary to develop a birds-eye view for the whole portfolio and concentrate on the portfolio main objectives, which are the most beneficial to the organization. Moreover, such an approach leads to a deeper understanding of project work throughout the organization, an understanding that many executives lack. A parallel complex adaptive systems approach toward portfolio management constantly reminds both portfolio governance and executive management that the long-term future is inherently unknowable, and that strategic planning needs to account for this.

Another important issue the portfolio manager should steer toward proper implementation is portfolio component front-end management. The front-end management of key portfolio components is crucial, since large issues and problems, particularly during execution, naturally affect the performance of the portfolio. Practitioners should note that in certain cases it is not feasible to establish clear requirements at the project front end because:

- People cannot usually articulate requirements until they experience prototype solutions;
- Many times, people have a false impression of their true needs;
- Technical and organizational performance and the "solution envelope" are unknown; and
- Linear-reductionist thinking (i.e., simplification) usually does not work (see Figure 21).

Consequently, it is important to provide guidance toward eliminating the above factors as much as possible that have an adverse influence

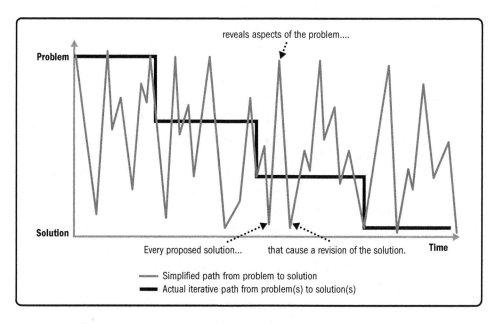

Figure 21.   The Actual Iterative Process from Problem to Solution versus Simplified Models[131]

toward portfolio component front-end management. Another issue for periodic consideration is the reconfirmation of applicable policies and processes. It is relatively common for organizations to encounter situations where policies and processes are followed long after the reason for their creation and existence becomes obsolete. Such situations may enhance complexity.

It is also imperative for executives and portfolio management practitioners to appreciate that successful portfolio management is a primary driver in navigating the complexity of the whole organization system. Executive management must support those efforts through communication, investment, dedicated resources, knowledge management, and education. Disciplined, standardized portfolio management practices can considerably reduce complexity. The proposed perspective unites a holistic approach, systems thinking, and recognition of complexity. It helps the portfolio practitioner to be aware of what is not known and investigate this. Complexity awareness is paramount in order to balance the need for innovation with the organization's risk appetite and set of constraints. One of the key benefits of a systems approach and portfolio complexity awareness is the ability to deal more effectively with change and to compensate for the ineffectiveness of immediately apparent solutions, particularly to emergent issues and risks.

Complexity means increased uncertainty regarding items outside of our control and uncertainty in the results of implementing strategies. Complexity thinking is best considered as a form of perspectives, continually generating multiple perspectives on issues. There are five capabilities that form the pillars of a development bridge that can close the gap from a current mind-set to the complexity mind-set: dynamic attention, synthetic understanding, integrated capacity, strategic clarity, and cohesive collaboration. These capabilities expand system thinking, improve performance, understand complexity systematically, and support high-impact relationships.

## CHAPTER 12

Agile Portfolio Management

by Gary Sikma and Nick Clemens

> Quality is never an accident. It is always the result of intelligent effort.
>
> — **John Ruskin**

To formulate a discussion about a portfolio that is agile, some background information is important. Agile is a philosophy for managing projects and teams that centers around the *Agile Manifesto*. The manifesto was created as an approach to consolidate a number of the best practices that were espoused by some practitioners of extreme programming (EP), Scrum, Kanban, or other adaptive software development techniques. Since the inception, the *Agile Manifesto* programming teams have continued to adopt what has become known as agile practices at an increasing rate. These techniques have been shown to significantly increase team productivity, enhance the speed of product delivery, and to increase overall product quality as measured by product owner or user satisfaction. However, agile practices at the project and the portfolio level are not without limitations.

Although the *Agile Manifesto* is applicable across a broad range of management levels, from team management to senior board-level governance, agile practice implementations each have their own set of limitations. In general, since most agile techniques have their roots in small team efforts, many agile techniques have scaling issues beyond the small team environment of just six to 10 individuals, the ideal small team size recommended for Scrum or extreme programming development efforts.

It is noteworthy to mention that PMI has described the use of adaptive life cycles and processes such as agile. According to PMI in their recently released update, *A Guide to the Project Management Body of Knowledge (PMBOK® Guide) – Sixth Edition*,[132] agile is trending for a number of organizations.

This chapter will be divided into three major sections. First, a review of agile practices will be given starting with the *Agile Manifesto*. Then the application of agile practices within the project, program, and portfolio management space will be discussed. As part of this discussion, a way ahead for portfolio management that integrates the portfolio management requirements with agile practices will be reviewed. Specifically, scaling techniques, decision cycles, requirements, and funds management will be addressed as they relate to agile practices within the project, program, and portfolio management space. Lean practices with an additional emphasis on nonhierarchical management processes will be seen as the driver for the application of agile at the portfolio level.

12.1. *Agile Manifesto*

The *Agile Manifesto* is a summary of values that 17 expert software developers, leveraging lightweight development methods, came to espouse through their experience of developing software and coaching others. This manifesto has gone relatively unchanged since they wrote it in Utah in 2001.

The manifesto reads:

> We are uncovering better ways of developing software by doing it and helping others do it. Through this work, we have come to value:
>
> - Individuals and interactions over processes and tools
> - Working software over comprehensive documentation
> - Customer collaboration over contract negotiation
> - Responding to change over following a plan

That is, while there is value in the items on the right, we value the items on the left more. [133]

While, as the *Agile Manifesto* concludes, the primary items are the preference, which does not mean that the secondary concerns were not important. The primary concerns were believed to be more critical to success.

- Individuals and interactions: Self-organization and motivation are important, as are interactions like colocation and pair programming.
- Working software: Working software is more useful and welcome than just presenting documents to clients in meetings.
- Customer collaboration: Requirements cannot be fully collected at the beginning of the software development cycle, therefore continuous customer or stakeholder involvement is very important.
- Responding to change: Agile software development methods are focused on quick responses to change and continuous development.

12.2. Difference between Agile and Traditional Project and Task Management

The agile community espouses a number of differences between agile approaches and traditional project and task management, but these differences, it must be noted, are not necessarily from the best-case scenario of both perspectives. It must also be noted that the differences are typically less stark than one might assume based on a bias toward one methodology or another.

Management style in agile should be highly collaborative as opposed to that of traditional approaches. This, of course, depends on the cultural personality of the organization. It must be noted that there are several organizations that leverage the more traditional project and task management and have also been more collaborative while those organizations attempting to embrace agile methods can get trapped into mandating certain styles of management. Similarly, control is typically more process-centric in traditional processes while agile attempts to be far more people-centric.

Within the agile community, the waterfall methodology description is usually presented as a caricature of the actual process as explained in the *PMBOK® Guide* since the mid-1990s. Just as in the agile community, where various agile techniques are practiced, so too in the project management community various management techniques are also practiced. For example, the concept of iterative or incremental development is part of the waterfall methodology and has been a *PMBOK® Guide* best practice, called progressive elaboration, since the first edition of the *PMBOK® Guide* was published in 1996. Additionally, progressive elaboration has been part of a standard earned value management system through the use of planning packages and unallocated budget as a planning tool since the system's inception in the 1960s.

Project, program, and portfolio techniques as codified within industry standards, such as PMI's *PMBOK® Guide*, have been used for decades to successfully run such programs as putting a man on the moon. Most recently, the Agile Alliance®, in partnership with the Project Management Institute, published the *Agile Practice Guide*.[134]

This guide broke with many previous agile publications, which simply trumpeted the benefits of agile as a silver bullet to fix all project management problems. Unique to this guide is the establishment of groupings of characteristics that define four project life cycle types. These groupings are summarized as predictive, where requirements are fixed and there is a single delivery; iterative where requirements are dynamic and there is a single delivery; incremental where requirements are dynamic but delivery is frequent and in smaller elements; and finally, agile where requirements are dynamic and delivery is frequent with small deliveries.[135] These groupings are seen as forming a continuum between each other where the best project life cycle may be chosen based on the position of the particular effort within the continuum and certain other management parameters unique to the effort. This structure provides project and program managers with a means for assessing the application of agile and lean process within a particular effort.

Further distinctions must also be made between the levels of management considered as project management, which has significant differences from program management, which also differs significantly from portfolio management. Additionally, depending on the project size, small team management below the project level may not be a core task of the project manager as it is for the scrum master and others working in small, self-governing teams. One weakness of the *Agile Practice Guide* is its lack of specific coverage of agile at various levels of management. Although extensions to small team agile are mentioned, the application of these extensions is not completely discussed. This chapter will fill in some of the missing information as agile at the project, program, and portfolio levels is discussed. Moving forward, lean and agile techniques will continue to be embraced by project and program managers as appropriate techniques, and with the publication of PMI's *Agile Practice Guide*, a renewed emphasis on iterative and incremental development processes will be seen. These processes have already been incorporated within PMI's *PMBOK® Guide* – Sixth Edition.

The issues concerning the application of the waterfall methodology within the software industry are well-documented. However, these problems may have been the result of a failure to embrace certain project management techniques, such as progressive elaboration, incremental development, and a collaborative management philosophy as recommended in PMI's foundational standards. Additionally, as software development transitioned from a primarily research and development effort to a production effort, programmers were increasingly seen as a commodity within their own management communities. Metrics for productivity were defined by lines of code written, and a robust system's engineering process did not become part of many software development methodologies. As such, in some cases, the caricature of the project management process as applied to the entire project management community by some agilists became the reality for those working in the programming field.

The Agile Manifesto brought these issues to the fore, resulting in the following three key approaches being emphasized within the software industry management practices. These approaches are continuous customer involvement, self-managing teams, and quick incremental development. Although these practices were being used within the general project management community as part of lean and customer-focused practices, the agile community was the first to combine and mandate them into a single management approach now known as agile.

12.3. Some Benefits of Agile

The agile philosophy was the product of the real-life project experience of 17 representatives from extreme programming, Scrum, adaptive software development, crystal, feature-driven development, pragmatic programming, and others sympathetic to the need for an alternative to documentation-driven, heavyweight software development processes. Because of the challenges and limitations of traditional development, they discarded what was, to them, a very documentation-centric rather than customer-centric mind-set.

Eventually, this philosophy of agile was accepted by the software industry as a better solution to project development. Nearly every software developer has used an agile approach in some form. It offers a light framework for assisting small teams consisting of about six or so individuals and helps them function and maintain focus on rapid delivery and customer integration through the involvement of a product owner. Ultimately, this focus aids adept organizations in reducing software development risks.

Agile strives to optimize value. The use of iterative planning coupled with frequent and direct feedback from the product owner results in teams that can continuously align a delivered product increment that reflects a client's needs. Changing design requirements can be addressed more readily and seamlessly throughout the process. The measuring and evaluating of a minimally marketable product at the end of each sprint or group of sprints, as Scrum is used, allows accurate and early visibility into the progress of each feature deliverable.

While it is often said that a solid project management methodology helps teams do things right, the agile approach is touted as an approach that helps companies build the right product. One reason for this is the involvement of the product owner as an integral part of the development team. The agile approach empowers teams, in consultation with their product owners, to define deliverables within a prescribed period and to optimize the release of incremental capabilities that drive the early delivery of value to customers. This often allows a product to be as competitive as quickly as possible as minimal marketable capabilities are incrementally delivered. The product thus remains relevant and is functional, since each increment's design requirements are championed by the product owner.

It must also be said that there are a number of naysayers and critics of the agile approach. But evidence shows that when the method is effectively leveraged, it produces results that customers appreciate and end users are pleased with.

12.4. Why Is There a Need for Agile Portfolios?

In earlier chapters, it was argued that traditional portfolios are a vital tool for organizational leadership to establish and align the work in the most effective ways in order to meet the strategic objectives of the organization. As organizational needs and requirements are relatively static, it makes sense to perform portfolio management in a more typical or traditional way. There are, however, a number of sectors, organizations, or even business verticals that have a much more significant propensity for change. For them, organizing their strategic work in the domain of well-defined projects and programs puts them in a challenging position.

Many types of organizations must learn to adapt more quickly within the environment in which they exist. Rapidly changing technology or economic conditions demand a more responsive and adaptive culture for a business's survival. It does not matter how smart, strong, or experienced organizational leadership is. The company doesn't have to be technology-specific either. Extinction may be imminent, particularly for companies dependent on creating or updating technology-based goods or services including healthcare, professional and financial services, and government agencies.

When we talk about natural selection, survival of the fittest, and other concepts within Darwinian evolution, some mistakenly assume the biggest, strongest, or possibly the richest will survive. But it is really a matter of which can adapt to the rapid environmental changes in which it exists and hopefully thrive. Successful companies have learned to adapt. In fact, they have done more than adapt. They have leveraged their changing environment and paved the way. They are rarely, if ever, caught playing "catch up."

Companies such as Amazon, Uber, Netflix, or Apple, to name a few, understand the urgency to move faster and adapt more quickly. Companies such as Kodak, Palm Computing, Blockbuster, Radio Shack, and others that don't manage to adapt to their rapidly changing environments will struggle and possibly just die on the vine. Some of those mentioned were all giants in their markets at one time. They knew how to grow and prosper in an environment, but they were all slow to change. But given the rapidly changing demands of organizations, it was crucial to adapt and change in a far more rapid way than they were able to.

Agility, flexibility, and adaptability, especially in the framework of an agile portfolio, help businesses address the significant challenges of developing and delivering software and applications in the shortest time possible, with the best opportunity to maintain lead times. When we take the agile approach and scale it to a portfolio, or even the enterprise level, we are empowering and enabling executives to be responsive and adaptive, while limiting the kneejerk or reactionary decision making that can often paralyze an organization.

Agile portfolio management (APM) enables faster business outcomes, improved quality, increased end-user satisfaction, and increased productivity.

12.5. Strategic Alignment

A centralized function of an organization is to develop the business strategy and invest in solutions that enable it. This is the primary responsibility of the executives who are accountable for business performance. As has been previously discussed, it is vital for effective organizations to establish and then communicate the strategic objectives of the organization. Subsequently, everything that the organization does should be focused on achieving those goals.

In the traditional portfolio, executives go through a project selection and prioritization process to ensure that the right work is performed. Within an organization that leverages an agile portfolio, the work is still focused on achieving the strategic objectives of the organization, but it is looked at from a different perspective. From the agile perspective, there are strategic themes that arise. Strategic themes are business objectives that provide unique characteristics focusing on changes to the strategy that affect a unique part of the portfolio.

Strategic themes are a way to communicate throughout the organization; from the enterprise level to the portfolios that provide solutions. They are typically simple and understated as all of the key stakeholders of the portfolio are familiar with the purpose and context of them. Further, these stakeholders establish and manage their own mission and vision that aligns with that of the enterprise.

These strategic themes are the result of collaboration between the enterprise and portfolio stakeholders. They collaborate to analyze and review potential inputs to arrive at an informed conclusion.

Some examples of strategic themes are:

- Reduce redundant applications to simplify processes;
- Make more effective use of limited space;
- Develop a mobile application to provide customers a one-stop solution; and
- Increase market penetration into the baby boomer population.

These themes are a vital communication method to relay the strategy to everyone involved in the portfolio. As with any advertising jingle, these themes are simple and memorable.

Strategic themes are key inputs to other aspects of the portfolio. They influence the portfolio backlog, value streams and budgets, solution trains, vision, and roadmap, which will be covered later.

12.5.1. Epics

This backlog, or list of next things to work on, is prioritized to provide business value, marketing differentiators, or business success. These are referred to as epics. Epics that constitute the portfolio backlog have advanced through analysis by stakeholders responsible for the backlog. Thus, they have been reviewed, analyzed, and approved for implementation. The effort and cost of epics is estimated in the analysis. Estimating then supports portfolio-level forecasting and roadmapping. This provides the enterprise a vision of the future adequate to support effective planning and execution.

12.5.2. Portfolio backlog

From an enterprise perspective, the portfolio backlog is the highest-level backlog. It is a list of prioritized items and future epics. They are intended to create a thorough portfolio solution set and must provide a stepping stone that works toward the strategic themes.

12.5.3. Budgets

Themes influence value stream budgets. In turn, they provide the spending and staffing-level allocations needed to achieve the strategic intent. In allocating resources, one must consider whether the investments in these value streams are in line with the changes to the current business goals. It is also important to ensure that the budget is the appropriate amount in regard to the intended solution.

Agile budgets consist of practices that limit overhead by funding value streams rather than projects, while keeping fiduciary responsibility governed. This happens in much the same way as operational budgets are developed. Executives responsible for funding evaluate the epics and value streams to determine if and how well they help to realize some set of technical solutions that enable the business strategy. To aid in this, each portfolio must work within the constraints of an approved budget, as the operating costs for solution development are a primary factor in economic success.

This is in contradiction to the traditional method of budget allocations. The budget being tied directly to results and key performance indicators (KPIs) and the marked ease of budget development typically proves to be a far better way of budget allocations and approvals. Agile budgeting addresses this without the typical overhead of traditional project-based funding and cost accounting. In this way, financially responsible executives have control over spending, yet programs are empowered for rapid decision making and flexible value delivery. Thus, businesses can be more responsive to changing needs and environments as well as professional and accountable management of development expenses.

12.6. Key Stakeholders

Epic owners are responsible for coordinating portfolio epics. They define the epic, the minimum viable product, and the business case. Later, when the epic is approved, they facilitate implementation.

If an epic is approved, the owner works directly with solution train and agile release train (ART) stakeholders to define the capabilities and features that will ultimately help the business realize the value. They may also have some responsibility to support the initiative as it moves farther into the pipeline.

Epic owners are responsible for formulating and elaborating the epic and analyzing cost and impact. They define a minimum viable product (MVP) if that is appropriate, and secure financial approval for the epic. In traditional project and program management, these tasks typically fall to a business analyst, architect, program manager, manager, or executive who understands both the business and technical impact of a large program.

When the epic is determined ready for implementation, the epic owner works with the solution train and ART teams to start development. The epic owner may then have some ongoing responsibilities for stewardship and follow up.

12.7. Agile and Project, Program, and Portfolio Management

The primary challenge of implementing an agile product process at the portfolio level is one of scaling up. Agile philosophies and the lean practices upon which they are based may be applied, and arguably should be applied, at all levels of governance and management.

From a portfolio perspective, the two key questions concerning incorporating any management approach are: Is the value to the organization significantly increased, and does the return on investment support the strategic goals of the portfolio and its parent enterprise? Within the small team environment, value is relatively easy to measure using agile-related metrics such as burn rate, team velocity, and features deployed. Work in progress can also provide a measure of organizational efficiency. However, rolling up these metrics to the portfolio, program, or even project level may be problematic if standard and consistent metrics are not used across the scores of teams involved in any moderate-sized project or program.

Finally, even though every team member should know their organization's strategic goals, the actual measure of benefits delivery is not usually made at the small team level or even the project level. Benefit delivery and the resulting calculation of return on investment is usually made at the portfolio or program level. Although it is acknowledged that where and how a company ties project and small team execution to benefits analysis and enterprise-wide return on investment considerations is a governance issue.

The governing management approach used by most organizations of any relative size incorporates some type of layered management structure beginning at the project level, extending to the program level, and reaching the top level of portfolio management. Superimposed above these management levels is some type of executive board or owner governance level where overall strategy, benefit delivery, and return on investment considerations are addressed. Lean practices recommend that these management layers be kept to a minimum. Generally, at least three layers are needed within an organization: a work execution level, some type of management level to pool and organize individual small team efforts, and finally, a governance level. As outlined above, this management level is usually divided into project, program, and portfolio levels of management.

Work is executed or performed within the project by small teams of individuals. Typical project management structures are made up of teams of about 10 or so individuals organized into work groups. These work groups are assigned work packages of approximately two to four weeks in duration taken from the project's work breakdown structure. In a similar fashion within an agile project using Scrum[136] processes, small teams of about six individuals select work from a sprint backlog and complete a minimally viable product or feature over the course of one to several sprints. Each sprint typically lasts two to four weeks. The two processes may be similar. However, within the agile framework, small teams are self-managing with only a facilitator present. Experienced, well-trained, and "performing"[137] teams are assumed. Outside of the agile environment, teams may be of any composition and governed using various management styles from dictatorial, to stewardship, to fully collaborative or self-leading.

Within a standard project, program, and portfolio structure, operations work is conducted as an ongoing effort separate from project work and is contained with programs or portfolio structures. The agile environment does not make a significant distinction between project and ongoing operations work since, at least for the Scrum methodology, development efforts are seen as ongoing. From the perspective of portfolio management, the incorporation of a DevOps approach has no effect on the overall portfolio approach since operations may be included in the portfolio's programs or directly included as its own element within the portfolio. However, using solely a DevOps agile approach may render the project layer of management redundant. This has significant implications for the management of DevOps work since it would then be managed within operations and not under a project management governance structure. However, the program or portfolio level of management would still be required within an organization making up more than a few development teams. This is because a single entity to manage and control the achievement of benefits and assure alignment of individual small team development activities and operations with the overall enterprise's strategic aims is still needed. Otherwise, return on investment metrics and calculations would not be possible across the enterprise. It is in this area where problems exist for specific agile processes as one goes from a single or perhaps two or three small teams to projects and programs consisting of scores of teams.

Agile processes are focused on small team management of fewer than 10 individuals and planning horizons of about one to two months at maximum. Within the Scrum methodology, the story point is used as the metric of choice for estimating the complexity of work activities. Since the estimate is based on a team consensus, there is no expectation or requirement that the definition of a story point will be consistent from one team to another. Additionally, story points are explicitly not related to work or effort hours by strict Scrum rules that govern the Scrum process. Further, the work effort is time-boxed and hence, a specific deliverable is not expected at the end of a sprint. Although ideally a minimal viable feature should be delivered at the end of every couple of sprints, the agile team or teams should deliver groups of features according to a published release plan if project work is being accomplished. Release planning is done one level above the agile team and usually covers no more than about half a year. Within the small team environment of only a couple of teams working within a limited planning window of only a couple of months, the lack of consistency between agile team metrics does not matter. However, for any effort above one or two small teams that lasts longer than approximately six months, consistent progress metrics between teams that will allow for work planning and cost estimating must be developed.

At this level of management, be it defined as a project, program, or operations, consistent metrics that will allow schedule, cost, and delivery predictions will be needed to develop product release schedules, benefit delivery projections, and return on investment calculations. Within agile-managed efforts, major product versions may be defined as increments or epics. A number of increments may also make up an epic. Epics are also defined as themes; however, the use of these terms is not consistent across the community. At a minimum, Scrum processes are composed of at least two and perhaps three levels of management. The story and epic are the most commonly used terms. Sometimes a third layer, the increment, theme, or some other term is used to define another layer if needed. The naming conventions are not consistent across the community and sometimes the terms epic, theme, and increment are interchanged. Interestingly, the complete project, program, and portfolio management space may be mapped to agile management processes via Table 19, which shows one of many possible mappings.

Table 19. Correspondence between Agile and Portfolio Management Governance Levels

	Agile	Portfolio Management
Level 0	Story (Scrum)	Task or Activity (work package)
Level 1	Feature Delivery (multiple sprints/theme) Increment (multiple features) Epic	Project
Level 2	Epic (assuming epics as multiple themes)	Program
Level 3		Portfolio
Level 4		Senior Executive

12.8. Scaling Techniques

Scaled Agile Framework (SAFe®) is a commercial approach for extending agile beyond the Scrum, as shown in level 0 of the above table. SAFe® uses four levels going from team at level 0, to program at level 1, to large solution at level 2, and finally, portfolio at level 3. SAFe® places the epic at its portfolio level, and although not explicitly stated, multiple features consisting of increments or themes would likely be found at either the large solution or program levels of the SAFe® structure. The SAFe® portfolio level of management corresponds most closely to the program level within the project, program, and portfolio space and the SAFe® program level most closely aligns with the project level of the project/program/portfolio space. Cost schedule and performance metrics begin to be tracked at the program level, leaving the team level to track just standard Scrum or Kanban work metrics.

Disciplined agile (DA) also extends the standard agile Scrum process, creating a three-phased project life cycle consisting of inception, construction, and transition. Project work is completed during the construction phase of the project life cycle through any number of agile processes, such as Scrum, extreme programming, unified process, or other methodologies. Disciplined agile thus establishes two levels of management, level 0 at the work level and level 1 at the program level. At least one other level is implied through the establishment of secondary roles for stakeholders that might not be involved in every effort. Roadmap definition, initial visioning, and funding are shown as an input to the inception phase and could be completed by secondary stakeholders not directly involved in the project execution.

What these and other agile extensions have in common is the recognition of the need for at least one, perhaps two management layers above the agile work level (level 0) to provide what is, in essence, a project or program management function that reports to senior management. This reporting is generally assumed to be done via some type of portfolio management structure where strategic considerations are aligned, value measured, and return on investment calculated.

12.9. Decision Cycles

One of the benefits of agile development processes is that they provide quick delivery of capabilities to customers. Design changes may be implemented quickly and efficiently with the almost constant involvement of the customer through a product owner, thereby increasing the likelihood of products and new features that are useful to the customer and deemed of high quality. For those using Scrum or Scrum-like processes, agile provides the ability for product developers to respond quickly to changing customer needs and through a two- to four-week sprint (change) cycle. This is a key attribute of the agile approach to decision or change management, and it is another example where agile processes have added significantly to the project management field in the mandating of a time-limited decision cycle that forces change during the development process.

Although the use of a mandated and limited decision cycle is unique to agile, the use and application of decision cycles as a decision and management tool is not. Edwards Deming[138] and Walter Shewhart[139] are usually credited with the PDCA (Plan, Do, Check, Act) cycle, although each one approached this process in a slightly different manner. The PDCA cycle involves running through the four-step process in a continuous fashion as much as a wheel turns with the accomplishment of each of the four steps. Building on Deming's and Shewhart's approaches, John Boyd[140] developed the OODA (Observe, Orient, Decide, Act) loop in connection with military operations. The trust of the OODA loop process is to achieve decisions through feedback loops between the "decide" and "observe" steps as quickly as possible. The goal is to make your decision cycle or OODA loop tighter or shorter than your competition's, thereby making decisions faster and adapting more quickly.

In terms of change within the portfolio, program, and project management space, we need to distinguish between what our decisions (or change) are operating on. At and particularly below the project level, change is usually focused on the unique product, service, or capability to be delivered. However, above the project level, the focus of the change begins to change. Process and enterprise alignment become considerations beyond just the delivery of an end item. Alignment and process considerations become more important when dealing with programs and very large projects and serve as a mechanism to limit complexity as a project becomes more complex. Operational considerations must also be accounted for. For project and program management efforts, interest in operations usually occurs at or near the time when production will begin. Within the agile process, it occurs anytime a feature or upgrade is deployed and within a DevOps environment; operational considerations must continuously be addressed. Finally, at and above the program level, benefit delivery, alignment to enterprise strategy, and particularly at the portfolio level, return on investment, become driving considerations for change as opposed to product development.

We will focus on what is being changed as opposed to the decision itself since it is the "what" that varies from management level to management level. From the above short discussion, we see three focus areas of decisions that development teams and management staffs must focus on. As shown in Table 20, they are: product or service, operations, and alignment decisions.

The area of product or service decisions is where agile processes provide the most potential for increased decision speed. This is because technical or other product design decisions are usually process based. That is, data are gathered and a design change is made through an optimization process of some type within a study environment that has been modeled or simplified to facilitate the decision process. Within the agile process, complexity is addressed through the use of stories, which are small packets of work that may be accomplished by a few individuals within days. Within this small packet of work, decisions are simplified due to the small number of people involved, the discreetness of the work, and the limited time frame of the specific effort. When using a Scrum or Scrum-like methodology, linkages to other work are handled within the sprint, and if needed, the scrum master may help facilitate a solution. Agile processes thus use the "divide and conquer" approach to driving complexity out of the decision process when possible.

A weakness of this approach is derived from its strengths. Within a standard Scrum process, there is no formal mechanism to work and coordinate change beyond the horizon of a rolling two or three sprint windows or between teams when working on a larger or more complex project. As described above, when working with multiple development

Table 20. Correspondence between Change and Decision Making at Various Management Levels

#	Agile	Portfolio Management Space	Decision Focus
Level 0	Story	Work Package	Product or Service
Level 1	Feature(s), Increment, Theme	Project	Product or Service
Level 2	Epic	Program	Operations or Alignment
Level 3		Portfolio	Alignment
Level 4		Senior Executive	Alignment

teams or on design issues that span or exceed the entire breadth of the release plan, a management level above the design team is usually established. This additional level is sometimes referred to as a "Scrum of Scrums" when dealing with a Scrum management effort. The problem is that the decision cycle of the "Scrum of Scrums" management level or the project team may extend as technical decisions within the Scrum transition to staffing decisions at a higher management level. The further away these design decisions are from the actual work, the more potential there is for delay within the decision cycle.

Typically, technical design issues beyond the planning and work window of agile processes would be managed by a systems engineering process within a project management structure. A systems engineering process is a highly iterative design or engineering set of activities that provides a structured framework in which to evolve, test, and prototype designs with the active involvement of all stakeholders, including product owners, through the use of integrated product teams. In fact, the Scrum process may be thought of as a highly tailored systems engineering process designed to work with small, highly skilled teams delivering limited or incremental improvements to existing products or services. The strength of a robust systems engineering process coupled with a rigorous change control system is its ability to handle complexity and projects of almost any level. However, its drawback is the overhead that a complete systems engineering and change control process bring to the project. Just as added agile structures above the Scrum working level may bring on decision delays through added overhead, so too may a robust systems engineering and change control process bring decision delays above the work package level.

Product or service design decisions should be process driven. Whether working within an agile development process or not, the fundamental driver to keeping product or service-related decision time to a minimum is to reduce management overhead and keep the decision maker as close as possible to the work. These processes are simply structured problem-solving methodologies designed to facilitate analysis and decision making. In other words, let the systems engineering or Scrum of Scrums process drive the decision.

However, the decision maker must also be able to coordinate actions across the project and account for time frames that encompass the entire project or epic. The above management problem may only be solved above the project or epic level by the establishment of clear management guidance through a governance definition process. This function is best performed at the portfolio level with coordination of senior executive management. The organization's general approach to product development should contain consistent guidance across portfolios and projects through a governance statement that provides program- and project-level managers flexibility in implementing specific management practices consistent with the supplied governance direction; in the case of product change decisions, a tailored structure decision process of some type (i.e., a Scrum-based or systems engineering process).

The second type of decision involves alignment of activities, goals, and objectives. At the program and portfolio levels, this alignment addresses strategic considerations and the delivery of benefits to the organization. At the portfolio level, return on investment is also addressed. These decisions may only be tangentially related to specific product or service design considerations. Business case and related financial analysis is usually the driving factor behind enterprise alignment decisions at the portfolio level. It is at this juncture where complexity is almost a given for any effort of even moderate size or duration. Like product design decisions, business case and financial analysis decisions are also highly technical and specialized. However, unlike the product design decisions, the decision process used by senior executives may be highly subjective. An individual's risk appetite, leadership style, and worldview based on a number of peripheral perceptions color the executive's decision process.

The nature of the decision environment at and above the portfolio level is thus not process driven as is typical at and below the program and project level of work. At the portfolio level and above may become perception driven by issues surrounding the interpretation of data provided by the business analyst or technical staffs. As such, specific process-oriented agile tools and techniques may not reduce the decision cycle because even if a clear analysis is present and options given, the senior executive staff may simply be unwilling to decide. That is not to say that an agile or lean process would have no effect on the actions of the senior support staff. On the contrary, lean and agile management processes should be incorporated at all management levels within the project, program, and portfolio management staff. However, the mere use of these tools and techniques will not guarantee a quick, streamlined decision process if the senior staff is unwilling to make a decision.

The following quote, paraphrased, comes to mind from a former senior-level student in a management class, "My senior executive service director is so risk averse, he would not sign his own stay of execution." So, what is one to do? The best that can be done is to implement overarching governance that mandates lean and agile practices, particularly at the level of senior management staff. The goal of such guidance would be to make quick decisions or have a tight OODA loop as part of the corporate culture of the organization. There will be tension between those who are risk averse and tend to experience "analysis paralysis" and those who never look before leaping. The role of the governance body chair (usually the company president, chief operating officer, or board chair) is to adjudicate actions between those two extremes. The role of the portfolio manager becomes one of providing the clear and unambiguous data that supports the senior-level decision process while helping the governance board chair in the aforementioned adjudication actions.

12.10. Product Requirements

An almost universal criticism of nonagile project management methods promoted by the agile community is the idea that product requirements may be completely defined up front as part of a comprehensive project initiation and planning process. As explained above, this criticism is based on generally nonexistent or faulty implementations of standard project management practices as outlined in the *PMBOK® Guide*. That is not to say that there are no projects that may be completely defined up front and that a linear design-build project life cycle is never appropriate. There are instances where a linear approach within a simple and straightforward development process will work and is the most cost-effective and efficient approach. However, we know that this is generally not the case in software development and is usually not recommended for any project of even limited complexity lasting for more than a few months. The problem here is the use of the term "requirements." This term is overused and usually ill-defined in most cases, which causes confusion when discussing the requirements elicitation as part of a project management process.

Requirements may be categorized into at least three major categories.[141] They are business, overall product requirements or system and subsystem requirements for the engineering-oriented, and design requirements. Product requirements must be directly traceable in a one-too-many relationship, extending from overall product requirements, to system and subsystem requirements, down to design requirements and specifications. As part of a systems engineering design process, these requirements may be documented within a requirements breakdown structure (RBS)[142] and linked to the project's work breakdown structure (WBS). Whatever process is used, it is not recommended to provide exhaustive specifications. Requirements should evolve from high-level to lower-level design specifications as the system design progresses. This design process may be done through any number of lean or agile processes, depending on the product being designed and the customer and design team's business processes.

Agile processes are primarily concerned with the requirements of the lowest two levels (work packages level and project level) including their design requirements and specifications. Generally, an RBS and WBS are not used in an agile process below the project level since design requirements are directly tied to user feature requirements through the user story or via a structured set of use cases. Whether use cases or stories are used is dependent on the specific programming method, and each type of communication has its own particular purpose.

Other artifacts are also sometimes used. Continuous and active changing of design requirements to support various user features are expected, encouraged, and embraced as part of any systems engineering development process and obviously this concept is fundamental to all agile approaches. Change as part of a development process is the vehicle by which an engineering or initial program concept evolves. Even under a strict waterfall project methodology, there would never be an expectation, perhaps with the exception of the software industry, that the engineering design process would start and proceed to completion with no changes, modifications, or enhancements. If that were the case, then why would a development process even begin?

Table 21 summarizes the various product requirements. There are no hard-and-fast rules as to what level of management is concerned with what type of requirement. In general, senior-level executive staff would be interested in business-related requirements. Portfolio-level managers would be interested in product and business-level requirements, whereas program-level managers, since they bridge a gap between the portfolio and project or operations execution, would likely be interested in all three types of requirements. However, program managers would likely focus on the product-level requirements and the management of major deliverables that bring value to the organization. At the project level and below, the focus is on design requirements. However, project managers are usually tasked with the delivery of some major product so

Table 21. Requirement Description

Requirement Type	Definition
Business Requirements Expectation is general stability over an annual planning window.	Highest level of requirements. Usually concerns overall product or system-level requirements along with external economic drivers and other business-related requirements. Focus is on the business case and overall product definition, and strategy-related and internal management requirements.
Product Requirements Expectation is some change as the product becomes better defined over time.	Defines the product to be developed. May be divided into multiple levels such as system and subsystem requirements. The focus is on defining the product and its overall functions. Product requirements define epic or major increment deliverables.
Design Requirements Expectation is frequent change and modification as the product is developed.	Detail requirements and specifications. Directly support the product development process and are usually contained within stories or use cases depending on the software development technique.

there would be interest in overall product requirements that fall within the scope of a particular project. Operational requirements are separate from development requirements and are not included in the chart.

There is also another set of requirements dealing with subproject, project, program, and portfolio management processes. These management requirements are usually standardized across an organization and are part of a governance management process not discussed here. Within the agile environment arena, process improvement is handled via sprint retrospective meetings that occur after each sprint or at the end of a time-boxed delivery of a feature. The retrospective deals primarily with internal small team interrelationships, but can include issues for elevation to the next management level up. Within nonagile methodologies, some type of continuous process improvement program should be in place either at the project or program level.

Taking the last in the above list first, it is the design requirements that must be developed and evolved through an iterative elicitation process throughout the design process. It is these design requirements that are of most interest to the agile practitioner as they are used to develop specific features described in various user stories. The change cycle or decision cycle associated with an agile development effort is about two to four weeks, depending on the iteration or sprint cycle. Even if a non-Scrum methodology-like process were used, agile management guidance still mandates frequent and short-term delivery and deployment of features. These design requirements would be tied to product requirements, and lower-level product requirements should be part of the story description.

Within a standard systems engineering process, the same type of customer-centered design process should be found. The major difference would be in the formal change cycle length, as even lean systems engineering processes do not envision formal change cycles of two to four weeks. Although the actual engineering development effort within the work package would be very similar to that done within an agile environment, and agile process may be incorporated into any systems engineering process to shorten the project's OODA loop. At the working level, design engineers or programmers should work essentially the same as those working within an agile environment.

Verification testing will likely be similar, whether working within an agile or nonagile environment. However, under agile processes, validation or operational testing has changed significantly. Verification and validation testing are merged and implemented within the sprint or as part of the development process. This change allows quicker releases and enables a DevOps environment.

For example, within the United States federal government, the U.S. Citizenship and Immigration Services (USCIS) is using a DevOps approach to move a formerly in-house verification program to Amazon Web Services. This large secure application program has been broken into small chunks of deployable code and then rebuilt, deployed, and tested in sprints. Each iterative sprint development is linked, resulting in USCIS achieving a continuous deployment of new capabilities within the cloud that incrementally moves the capability from in-house servers to the cloud while maintaining legacy interoperability. The combination of iterative development, testing, and deployment has allowed new capabilities to be delivered within weeks. USCIS now has the capability to deploy code repeatedly during the day.

The above example is typical of the positive aspects of implementing agile approaches. In any development effort, whether agile or not, if changing design requirements and iterative design cycles are embraced and encouraged at the working level, product delivery can be improved. Let's now move up one level to product or system/subsystem requirements.

This level describes the overall product that our project is to produce. Product requirements should remain fairly stable throughout the three to six months' time frame covered by the release-planning window. That is not to say change cannot happen should a competitor beat our company to market and our organization cannot be agile and able to change direction either strategically or tactically in a quick fashion.

However, if the basic definition of the effort is completely changing, that is, changes from one product type to another or significant redefinition of existing product work, then something is wrong. In agile terms, the product backlog at either the increment or epic level should be renegotiated with the product owner. In other words, changes a level above the sprint backlog, if working in Scrum, are affecting the orderly execution of the current and next planned sprints. In standard project management terms, it's time to renegotiate the project charter. A good project or program management, or a "Scrum of Scrums," structure facilitates the ordered change of requirements and redirection of the project given product-level requirements change above the single sprint team. It is at this level where most delays can occur in a systems engineering process where management must take care to ensure lean or agile processes are in place. The SAFe® methodology envisions this function taking place within the epic at the portfolio level of management, and this function maps, as expected, to the program level of the project, program, and portfolio space.

Finally, at the business level, business requirements and the overall product-level requirements that form the basis of the business case should be stable, at least within the six to 12 months' period that bounds delivery of major releases or epics. Ideally, at the portfolio level, strategic decisions and overall enterprise-level goals and objects should cover at least a one- to two-year period and many strategic planners recommend strategic planning horizons of three to five years. Financial considerations can change quickly, but generally overall economic indicators or trends that drive business case development at the strategic level do not change significantly in a 12-month period. The same considerations concerning the ability of management staff to adapt, change, and overcome, as outlined in the above paragraph, still hold. At the portfolio level of the project, program, and portfolio space requirements, whether they are business or product associated with specific epics or major increments, should not change significantly over the course of a year. As part of a corporate reaction to a changing business environment, particular epics or major program increments may change; again, all management levels should be lean and agile. However, there should be consistency within the enterprise's strategic requirements as it works diligently and over time toward meeting long-range strategic goals and objectives.

Requirements changes at the design level and below are expected and encouraged. It is here where agile processes have the most value. As one moves up the requirements chain, increasing stability is expected. Product requirements should be fairly stable, and at the business and overall product requirements levels, the general business environment should be stable, at least within the 12-month strategic planning window. In general, strategic planning and requirements should cover a three- to five-year period with only minor adjustments implemented, usually on an annual basis. Of course, there is always the possibility of a "Black Swan"[143] event. The above requirements structure is only loosely dependent on agile techniques, and from a portfolio management perspective, the use of agile processes will not impact the business and overall product-level requirements definition. However, when dealing with actual product development efforts involving the elicitation and evolution of product and design requirements, the adoption of lean and agile techniques have a great potential to streamline work and increase efficiencies at the project level of management and below.

12.11. Funds Management

Since the *Agile Manifesto* deals primarily with the execution of small teamwork, funding issues are not addressed within it. When initially created, the writers of the manifesto decided to focus on what small programming teams do in terms of their technical work. Typical management considerations such as budgeting, controlling expenditures, and aligning actions from the bottom up with enterprise-level strategic goals and objectives were left to others. From a portfolio management perspective, there is and will continue to be a requirement for senior executive management to report various fundamental business and accounting data to public or government entities on at least an annual basis.

As agile processes have matured, extensions to these processes have usually adopted lean management processes as a means to extend agile into the project, program, and portfolio management space. As described above, two such extensions are the SAFe® and DA processes. A comprehensive comparison of these and other agile extensions is beyond the scope of this section. However, these extensions have one thing in common, the recognition of the need to provide cross-team standardized reporting concerning the establishment, monitoring, and controlling of budgets and spending plans.

The requirement to provide standardized reporting has caused tension within the agile community concerning agile extensions into the project, program, and portfolio management space. In part, this is because of a strict adherence to philosophical considerations over practical management approaches. For example, one of the fundamental tenets of agile is story point estimation, which dictates that each team develops its own definition of a story point, and story points are explicitly not linked to time or duration. Further, the comparison of story points between teams should not be done. From the perspective of the small team operating below the project level, this does not represent a problem. However, the roll-up of cost data to the project, program, or portfolio levels becomes problematic unless the amount of work can be tied to specific deliverables over time and estimated into the future. From just a project level, this future usually involves time frames that are beyond the planning horizon of single, small agile teams. This process is still in relative renaissance so few examples of this in practice exist.

Reporting techniques include averaging data across teams, correlating story points with deliverables, time reporting after the fact, and the use of "rule of thumb" or subject matter expert estimates. These techniques, at least with respect to time, effort, and duration estimation, have been widely used within the project management community over decades. Extensive materials and robust tools and techniques are available. However, the agile community has generally not availed itself of the depth of existing estimating experience within the project management community. This has also resulted in tensions between agile practitioners working at the project level and below and project, program, and portfolio managers who have been tasked by senior management to provide standardized cost, schedule, and deliverable estimates, budgets, and spend plans.

These issues, whether internal to the agile community or between various levels of management above the agile development processes, are unnecessary. Cost and work data reporting is already addressed either by lean project management or any number of agile extension techniques. From an agile perspective, project- or program-level management should support the agile processes below them while collecting required data for reporting purposes to upper management levels. The portfolio, program, and project management space is not a monolithic management chain. Each level provides a function in terms of cost estimating, reporting, monitoring, and controlling. Funding issues involving estimating, monitoring, and controlling may be handled at the project and program levels of management. Reporting to senior-level management and addressing alignment and strategic concerning of return on investment may be handled by portfolio management staff. Whatever the tiered management structure used by an organization, the proper allocation management activities across the enterprise organization will free the agile working level at and below the project level to perform their work as originally envisioned by the creators of the *Agile Manifesto*.

12.12 Conclusion

To best understand how to apply agile at the portfolio level, it must be understood that much of what is agile at and above the project level of management is essentially lean management practices coupled with a mandated progressive management philosophy that directly involves the customer in product development. It also assumes highly trained and productive teams can work in a self-organizing and highly "performing" fashion. The critical attributes that distinguish agile from other project management practices are the involvement of the customer at the work team level and the mandating of self-forming and self-governing work teams. These two attributes are significant in creating the unique agile work environment.

Managing work within the project and program space concerns the delivery of products at the project level that create benefits for the organization through program execution or operational work, which is then aligned and supporting of enterprise strategic objectives and value delivery. Many agile approaches may be implemented within a work team whether that team is operating at level 0 within a development effort or at higher management levels within a project or operational endeavor. The end result should be a significant return on investment for the organization and unparalleled customer satisfaction through product delivery. From a product delivery perspective, agile processes are implemented at the working level of the project, program, and portfolio management space. Management processes at the project and program levels are thus focused on harmonizing work across the projects and programs, respectively, to deliver these products.

At the portfolio level, where work concerns staff or coordination actions to support portfolio-level and senior executive-level management decisions, the use of agile techniques is focused on streamlining staff actions. Individuals at any management level, be it project, program, portfolio, or operations, may use agile techniques such as Scrum or Kanban to manage and track their work. In short, project, program, and portfolio managers should be well-versed in progressive management approaches, lean practices, and agile tools and techniques so they may manage their staffs or contribute to staff activities effectively and efficiently. Work, whether product related as in the above paragraph or staff related as noted here, should be delivered in the most efficient and timely fashion possible.

As such, staffs may function using agile techniques, but their management product, specifically at the portfolio level, will at its base consist of metrics that allow senior executives to compare projects and programs across enterprise organizations that are much larger than the typical small team of individuals seen at the agile working level. These larger organizations require balancing effort and resources across portfolios and alignment of activities across portfolios and programs. All this is done within the context of meeting strategic goals based on a minimum of a two- to three-year planning horizon, which is beyond that considered under any agile approach. These actions support the senior executive management function and allow for a smooth and integrated functioning of the enterprise.

## CHAPTER 13

Dealing with Environmental Factors and Cross-Cultural Challenges in Portfolio Management

by Panos Chatzipanos

> Knowledge is of two kinds. We know the subject ourselves or we know where we can find information upon it.
>
> — **Samuel Johnson**

Human behavior and interaction, a primary cause of complexity, is of utmost significance for successful portfolio management. Research[144] has confirmed that the most significant change barriers to implementing organizational strategy exist when change initiatives conflict with the prevailing culture in the organization and its environment. Thus, portfolio management must regularly and consistently deal with the cultural aspects of risks, issues, situations, and problems. This aspect becomes paramount for innovative portfolio components. Today, innovation is a significant creator of added value for most organizations. A review of the extensive literature on the subject reveals that the term "innovative culture" is a major research topic, specifically, the cultural factors that create an organizational environment within which innovation and creativity can thrive. It is also a fact that organizational culture can be a sustainable, significant competitive advantage, which is usually hard to imitate.

In this chapter, cross-cultural challenges and their effects on portfolio management will be initially addressed. Then, aspects of organizational culture will be discussed. The discussion on ethnic cultural differences and the effects that these have on management is based primarily on the pioneering work done independently by Greg Hofstede and Erin Meyer. Readers interested in ethnic cultural aspects are referred to their work. References to their work are given in various subsections of this chapter. As already discussed, human behavior is of paramount importance for the portfolio manager. Human behavior highly depends on what people feel, have experienced, have learned, and thus have cultivated throughout their lifetimes. Culture, more than anything, ultimately determines human behavior and motivation. But what is culture? Let's discuss this briefly before discussing culture's relevance within portfolio management.

"Culture is the social programming of the mind that distinguishes one category of people from another," states the famous Dutch cultural expert Hofstede.[145] We all know that human groups being together for long periods of time develop a common existence. Humans have a culture in their genes, and although capable of generating great individuality within an organization, they can simultaneously contribute to the benefit of the whole group. In organizations, culture emerges over time, as repeated behaviors, common visions, principles, values, and goals. Success reinforces, promotes, and fixes these deep in the human brain. Thus, behavior determines culture and culture defines behavior. Often, an individual or a small group of people, usually during the first stages of the organizational life cycle, may determine fundamental cultural values based on their values, principles, beliefs, and experiences. Often, different cultures result in different behaviors.

People belong to many different cultures concurrently, and this fact usually enhances complexity. Therefore, people carry several layers of mental programming. These layers correspond to varying levels of culture. According to Hofstede, such cultural layers include:

- A national level according to one's country (or countries, for people who migrated during their lifetimes);
- Regional, ethnic, religious, linguistic, and other affiliation levels;

- A gender level;
- A generation level;
- A social class level, associated with educational opportunities and with a person's occupation or profession; and
- An organizational level incorporating departmental and corporate levels.

The mental programs from these various levels are not necessarily in harmony. In modern society, they are often conflicting in some ways: For example, religious values may conflict with social class values or with generation values; gender values may conflict with organizational values and derived practices. Conflicting mental programs within people make it more difficult to anticipate their behavior in a new situation.

13.1. Ethical Cultural Considerations for the Portfolio Manager

International organizations often boast of their experience and ability to cope with different national administrative cultures; for example, managing team members from Greece and Scandinavia and fostering a smooth operation of the team. Different cultural backgrounds may enhance creativity in pooling intellectual resources, but only if the members of the project or program team understand and take into account the underlying cultural differences. Greeks, for example, are known to be relaxed, friendly, exuberant, and emotional. In contrast, Scandinavians are known to enjoy being organized, communal, disciplined, logical, and task oriented. National cultures are determining values, beliefs, and mostly subconscious behaviors, having evolved for centuries; these are the result of living in a particular environment. Management involves awareness and consideration of these different cultural attributes in order to achieve efficient cooperation. In life, multiple forces and influences simultaneously act upon individuals and groups. These activities and the resulting complexity makes it difficult to determine how each of these forces shapes individual and group behaviors.

Cultural differences in leadership styles often create misunderstandings.[146] As an example, consider the average American thinking of a Japanese colleague as hierarchical while he himself is egalitarian. Yet the Japanese find Americans difficult to deal with. Although American bosses are outwardly egalitarian, they seem to the Japanese to be extremely autocratic in the way they make decisions—since usually for Americans, all provided input toward the decision may be thought as consultative since "the top man" alone finally decides. Japanese are more consensus oriented. It's common for people of different nationalities to engage with mutual incomprehension. Often, that is because managers fail to distinguish between the two most important dimensions of the cultural aspect of leadership: authority and decision making.

Authority has to do with how much attention and respect people pay to hierarchy. Following the example above, in this dimension, the Japanese are considerably more hierarchical than the Americans. The positions are reversed, however, when we look at the second dimension: decision making—who makes the decision. Does the "top man" decide, or does the relevant team decide collectively? In this dimension, the Japanese are more consensual than the Americans. Approaches to authority and decision making are most important within the cultural aspect of leadership. Moreover, if international managers confound the two, they often make mistakes in adapting their leadership styles to the cultures and situations at hand. Attitudes toward decision making impact multicountry teamwork. In a multicultural environment, how the role and functions of the leader are perceived by different national cultures is paramount. The reader is referred to E. Meyer's book, *The Culture Map*, for an analytical discussion of the above as well as recommendations toward dealing with major cultural and ethical issues.

Over the past century, the trend in most western countries has been the abandonment of hierarchical processes in the day-to-day management for a more collaborative and egalitarian approach. "Command and control" has been replaced with an authorized delegation. Managers have been trained to refrain from telling their employees what to do and instead move to "management by objectives," encouragement of openness and transparency, 360-degree assessments, performance metrics, and continuous employee feedback. Company hierarchy further dissolved when, in certain organizations, top managers started having impromptu discussions with people at all levels without even letting their superiors know. Attitude toward authority is one of the most striking points of difference across cultures. As Meyer notes in her book, in Nigeria a child learns to kneel or even lie down as a sign of respect when an elder enters the room. In Sweden, a student calls his teachers by their first names and, without implying any disrespect, feels free to contradict them in front of all others. Thus, the management approach that works in Lagos may not get the best results in Stockholm or New York.

Understanding this disconnect is important. In many countries, including those with large emerging economies, the prevailing cultures are ones that hierarchy and respect to authority are amalgamated within the national identity. The management orthodoxy of pushing authority down in the organization does not fit easily into the business and organizational context of some nations. Thus, portfolio components executed in these countries may trip up Western organizations, particularly on their first projects abroad particularly if such projects are executed in a consortium with a local organization.

On the other hand, in Western cultures, for decades now, organizations have been training their employees in egalitarian leadership methods.[147] As an example, contemplate the culture of encouraging the workforce to show initiative, or teaching the executives to leave their doors open, accept, consider, and discuss multiple feedback, set objectives rather than issue decisions, and so forth. People from different cultures may perceive the above encouragements as ineffective and simultaneously arrogant because under such initiatives the senior executive does not take the time to explain to his employees in detail what they direct them to do and how they want things done. Such completely different attitudes toward hierarchy lead to different behaviors. Many managers, being aware of the above, assume that in more hierarchical societies, decisions will be made at the top by the person in charge, and in more egalitarian cultures, decisions will be reached by group consensus. Yet, on a worldwide scale, research indicates that hierarchies and decision-making methods are not always correlated. Unless cultural synergy is built, there usually is cultural conflict. Confrontations between people, groups, societies, and nations have been ubiquitous throughout history worldwide.

Simultaneously, the ever-expanding common problems demand cooperation, collaboration, and teamwork for their solution. The project management discipline creates such a common language for project-based work. But sometimes the existence of this common language is not enough. Awareness and understanding of values and communication styles of diverse people, groups, and societies is paramount to cooperation. Moreover, today more than ever, cooperation is key for change initiatives that the portfolio encompasses in order to obtain organizational growth, sustainability, and ultimately, successful delivery or strategic objectives. Culture entails the patterns of thinking, feeling, and acting shared by people who live under the same contextual conditions. The shared environment is where this collective phenomenon takes place. According to Hofstede[148] "culture is learned, not innate. It is derived from an individual's environment much more than from one's genes." For a portfolio having a multitude of international components, awareness of cultural differences and successful navigation through these may prove quite important for the portfolio manager.

13.2. Navigating Multicultural Issues within a Portfolio, Persuading in a Multicultural Portfolio Environment, and Managing Human Capital

The discussion so far illustrates that portfolio components that involve team parties from two or more countries may encounter the problem of cultural fit. International projects may involve many different projects, executed in various countries often with a multinational team having a large range of features, emergent issues, and risks. Technology such as video conferencing, web communication applications, mobile devices, and so forth, have considerably reduced direct face-to-face communication in many international projects. Cultural differences may become quite important in such multinational work environments, enhancing complexity and giving rise to additional risks and issues.

Many people assume that portfolio management is a discipline with global rules applied uniformly worldwide. This approach views portfolio management only as an applied science, as a mechanical system applied universally. As discussed in previous chapters, although most principles, processes, and good practices apply globally to most portfolios, most portfolios are complex adaptive systems. Thus, they also should be understood and managed as such. Further to the inherent complexity of the portfolio itself, portfolio management has certain aspects that are applied in practice differently by different cultures. This fact may enhance the complexity that the practitioner must navigate.

Portfolio components having an international nature may come in many forms, for example, projects in one country for a foreign client, portfolio components having multinational teams, projects in one country involving foreign contractors and/or suppliers or consultants, working as a contractor in a foreign country for an international client, multinational consortiums, and joint ventures, to name a few. Executing portfolio components under conditions like the ones described above may lead to situations, that require awareness and a proactive mindset, such as:

- Working with a client or a subcontractor of a different culture, with an alien way of doing business; for example, when working as a contractor overseas.
- The necessity to understand, appreciate, and accommodate local traditions. Be cautious of the possibility of unintentionally offending people.
- Under fewer shared cultural and commercial assumptions, the chances of a damaging misunderstanding are much greater.
- The applicable contract law is usually of the country where most of the work is to be executed. The observance and maintenance of national legislation, rules, and prevailing business conduct practices is usually a contractual requirement.
- Complex multinational contractual and funding arrangements; multinational project teams.

Research indicates that for some cultures—for example, northern European ones—the preference is for the information to be spelled out, assuming that unless things are stated, these may become vague, imprecise, or inexact, and thus a source for disputes. If such clarity cannot be communicated, practitioners need to concentrate on the common areas that may cause disagreement. A different perspective favored by the many Asian cultures is to focus on the common interest at the center of most objectives and base communications on this. Building sufficiently documented infrastructure to provide reference and a way of working as an efficient team is essential. Conflicts of interest are expected to be worked out gradually, preferably one at a time, as common objectives are more and more appreciated by the whole multinational team. The aim is to build and preserve a relationship that will realize the portfolio component's purpose.

Thus, for portfolio components in which the influence of multicultural issues is considered prominent, it is essential that the portfolio management organizational structure be set up to account and navigate cultural aspects and differences primarily through efficient, transparent communications.

Cultural characteristics are usually classified in three levels:

- Societal/ethnic characteristics,
- Market/professional characteristics, and
- Organizational characteristics.

Organizational culture is sometimes the dominant culture and may eventually—after individuals spend long periods in the same organization—surpass societal or ethnic culture characteristics. Although organizational culture is shaped by multiple forces, both internal and external to the organization, it is primarily the culture that can gradually change in a relatively short duration. Change in ethnic cultures may take generations while change in market culture may be often uncontrollable and abrupt.

G. Hofstede[149] identified that our assumptions are based on our education, competencies, and experiences based on our family, school, gender, professional, social, regional, religious, and ethnic background. These attributes influence our behavior as teams and as individuals both within the organization we work and socially. When working with multicultural teams and groups, the portfolio manager needs to know about the approaches of different cultures to be able to predict behaviors and the complexity that human behavior introduces, to have the flexibility to productively work with the various individuals, and to give or take no offense from misunderstandings due to the inevitable existing cultural differences. Hofstede identified and evaluated four principal characteristics or dimensions of cultural difference.[150] Briefly, these dimensions are:

- **Power distance:** The extent to which the less powerful people in a group accept inequality in power and accept it as the way things are. Power distance is associated with paternalism. In Eastern cultures, paternalism is one of the most desired characteristics of senior management. In Western societies, paternalism is viewed negatively since in the Western cultures, paternalism is usually associated with authoritarianism. Often a paternalistic manager is viewed as a "benevolent dictator" in Western societies. Thus, in certain societies, the perception of a paternalistic figure is of an authoritative and manipulative nature whereas in other societies is of a caring and considerate nature. The largest cultural differences among countries have been measured to occur in the power distance/paternalism dimension.[151] Low power distance signifies egalitarian values and the society's quest toward reduced status difference and a more equal, more "normal" distribution of power. Fatalism can be quite often explained by historical experiences.

- **Individualism:** The extent to which individuals primarily look after their interest and the interest of their immediate family. Individualism is directly related to the cultural dimension of team loyalty and loyalty toward the community.
- **Uncertainty avoidance:** The range to which people are anxious about situations they consider to be unstructured, unpredictable, or unclear, and the extent to which they try to avoid such situations by adopting strict codes of behavior and by believing in "absolute truths." This parameter is also associated with fatalism. Fatalism is the belief that whatever happens was ordained to happen. Under this mentality, since it is not possible to control the outcomes of one's actions, making repetitive efforts to achieve something, making long-term plans, and being proactive may prove to be futile exercises.
- **Masculinity:** The extent to which the biological existence of two sexes is used to define different roles for men and women.

Jessen[152] notes that power difference, individualism, and uncertainty avoidance may change during long time frames such as the portfolio life cycle. Once the portfolio manager is aware of the above dimensions, navigating and mitigating plans can be made to reduce their effect on the progress of the particular portfolio component(s). During initiation, power distance should be high, since this is when the portfolio manager must focus on prioritization requirements, alignment to organizational strategic objectives, resource distribution, and so forth. Individualism should also be high, as there is a need for creativity and innovative thinking during this stage. Uncertainty avoidance should be low, as feasibility demands the ability to think in new directions and uncover new solutions, which often means risk, change, and unpredictability. For cultures that do not exhibit these characteristics, extra care should be taken to dampen such cultural influences.

During the planning, and particularly during the execution phases of each of the portfolio components, changes will occur. Power distance will be reduced as hierarchy levels decrease and as teamwork becomes, to an extent, egalitarian. As noted above, hierarchies and decision making are two different characteristics in most cultures. The main purpose of planning and execution for each portfolio component is to ensure the delivery of the prescribed component outcomes and that the derived benefits from the execution of the component are achieved. The project manager and team members of each portfolio component are the best people to decide the method of achieving success for their program or project. The portfolio manager, in many cases, should provide awareness on cultural issues and risks as well as guidance.

Meyer also describes cultural differences between nations. These differences primarily affect the ways we communicate, evaluate, decide, trust, disagree, persuade, and so on. Meyer identifies and explains eight scales of cultural differences based on these human behaviors. Awareness of the causes of individual behavior due to national culture may prove to be very important to the portfolio manager who must successfully deliver a portfolio with multinational, multicultural components. Moreover, the competency of persuasion is paramount for a portfolio manager. Without the ability to persuade clients, executives, colleagues, program and project managers, functional managers, and team members, management functions become ineffective and inefficient. As Meyer underlines, "the ways you seek to persuade others and the kinds of arguments you find persuasive, are deeply rooted in your culture's philosophical, religious, and educational assumptions and attitudes. Far from being universal, then, the art of persuasion is one that is profoundly culture-based."

One needs a different approach when dealing with people who focus first on practicalities (e.g., Americans) than people who focus first on theory (e.g., French or Germans). This is mainly due to the different educational systems. The reasoning behind people who focus first on practical considerations is usually referred to as applications-first reasoning (also known as deductive reasoning). The reasoning behind people who focus first on theoretical considerations is usually referred to as principles-first reasoning (also known as inductive reasoning). The first type of reasoning derives conclusions based on a pattern of factual observations from the real world, whereas the second type of reasoning derives conclusions or facts from general principles or concepts. The large majority of professional people are capable of using both types of reasoning for reaching conclusions. But for each individual, the dominant type of reasoning is one of the two. And this primarily depends on the way each individual has been taught, based on their culture's educational structure. Thus, both communication and persuasion problems may arise simply by different models of reasoning based on cultural differences. Applications-first countries include the United States, Canada, Australia, and, slightly less, the United Kingdom and the Netherlands, while principles-first countries include France, Italy, Spain, Russia, and, slightly less, Germany. In the middle of the scale are countries such as Brazil, Argentina, Mexico, Sweden, and Denmark. Very important toward understanding such comparisons is cultural relativity. Where a particular country is situated on the scale matters less than where two cultures fall relative to one another.

The Asian cultures have an entirely different frame of reference unrelated to levels of persuasion. A persuading scale is based on a specific—usually linear and proportional—approach to thinking. Asian cultures are based on holistic thinking, emphasizing interdependencies and interconnectedness of all things. Thus, in a Western culture, when communicating with someone, one must concentrate on providing very detailed and segmented information while in an Asian culture. When the portfolio manager needs to persuade, motivate, or manage individuals or teams, they will be much more successful if they take the time to explain the big picture, show how all the parts fit together, and illustrate dependencies between the parts as well as the effects of these. Another example of considerable differences in perception resulting from ethnic cultures has been presented by Meyer.[153] Referenced briefly, for an American a decision is perceived as simply an agreement to continue discussions. But for a German, that same decision is a final commitment to march forward on a plan. This can cause a lot of confusion.

Therefore, when both conditions exist (egalitarian culture and consensual decision making) the boss won't jump in and decide unless there is a major emergency. To get the collaboration on track, the portfolio manager may organize a meeting on cultural differences. All team members may discuss their assumptions about how decisions should be made and what the word "decision" means in each of their cultures. When there is awareness of cultural differences, and cultural differences are brought to the surface and understood, collaboration/teamwork may benefit considerably. Consequently, making a clear distinction between attitudes toward authority (from hierarchical to egalitarian) and attitudes toward decision making (from top-down to consensual) enhances the portfolio manager's capability to successfully oversee the management of portfolio components having a multinational, multicultural dimension. For example, if the key portfolio component stakeholders come from egalitarian and consensual cultures, the portfolio manager must be aware that consensual decision making may be a great incentive enhancer in principle, but people from fundamentally nonconsensual cultures can find the whole process deterring, time consuming, frustrating, and so one.

Thus, in such cases, the portfolio manager should expect decision making to take longer and to involve more meetings and correspondence. The portfolio manager should be aware that they are considered more as a facilitator and not as a decider and must not push, if the circumstances allow, for quick resolutions. It may be better to steer for the best possible solution since in this cultural context, it is difficult to change decisions once these are taken. It is advisable for the practitioners to investigate and then decide whether for each portfolio component it will be better to adjust to the cultural norms of most team members rather than expect the team to adjust to their cultural norms.

Consequently, the portfolio manager must be aware of the existing cultural differences and how these affect the particular portfolio component. They must also be informed enough and adaptable enough to choose which style will work best in which cultural context and then deliberately decide how to adapt (or not) to get the best possible results. Further, they must possess the necessary emotional intelligence to appreciate the fact that all human interactions are influenced and usually determined by the patterns of the multiple experiences of the individual. Furthermore, they should have the necessary skills to understand, navigate, and harness human behaviors both personal and collective.

13.3. Component Scheduling of a Multinational Portfolio – Cross-Cultural Perceptions of Time

Time, more than anything else, defines almost all portfolio components once they are prioritized and planned, becoming time-bound endeavors. It is clear that there are other important constraints for each portfolio component, which need continuous monitoring and balancing, but time is usually the most important constraint. Time, of course, is regular, linear, and proportional; time is a constant. It is a quantitative entity that can be measured with very high precision. In dealing with portfolio components, we understand time as it is accurately measured in durations, schedules, milestones, timelines, and so on. All these are linear dimensions, and naturally, our perception of time is linear, regular, reliable, and distinguishable. But should we only consider time's true dimension when dealing with portfolio management?

The ancient Greeks had two perceptions of time, named "Chronos" and "Kairos." Chronos time is regular and linear—as science defines time. Kairos time is not—since human perception of time may vary considerably from the exact period that a mechanical device is designed to measure accurately. Kairos describes what we perceive as time passed when we are completely absorbed by an endeavor. To the ancient Greeks, Kairos described both qualitative time and opportune time, a time window during which decisions, actions, and deeds are most advantageous. Kairos has to do with deciding or acting at the most opportune moment according to the situation in hand, one's resources, and one's capabilities. For a detailed treatise of the concept of Kairos and complexity in project-based work, the reader is referred to *Kairos* by Kaye Remington.[154]

We all know stories about southern Europeans being free with time and northern Europeans being punctual. Many people say that this is implanted in the respective DNAs due to the length of the day during the long winter months of Northern Europe—for thousands of years, farmers could not afford to waste the short winter days. Thus, attitudes to time reveal different cultural programming. Germans, for example, believe events are controlled by planning and respecting deadlines. Things must be in order. Time is limited and cannot be wasted. Keeping people waiting is also insulting; it implies that the people who are waiting are not busy or do not have important things to do and therefore they are unimportant.

Other national cultures have considerably more relaxed beliefs toward the above concept. The example, though, illustrates that a project leader in Germany usually meets fewer problems than a project leader in a southern European country, for example, when stressing to his colleagues or his stakeholders the importance of following schedules or the importance of missed deadlines. Under the German culture, plans must be carefully thought out and followed. Scheduling of social events is another example. Most northern Europeans like to plan well in advance; most southern Europeans find this too restrictive and like to arrange their social lives at the last minute—and do what they feel like doing at that particular time. In other parts of the world, in most Asian countries, for example, time is seen through much longer lenses. As time flows, things come together at appropriate intervals. Emphasis is placed on doing things once and properly, particularly establishing sustainable relationships. Doing things as they arise means interruptions, which derail plans. Deadlines are perceived as movable because it is more important to ensure relevant issues are taken care of when they occur so that continuity is maintained.

Both "Chronos" and "Kairos" are important concepts relating to how we use time in project-based work. We need to balance the pressure associated with achieving goals against the clock with the need for social time (Kairos) that promotes learning and knowledge transfer. States of flow that enhance creative problem solving should also be valued. Practitioners should recognize that different stakeholders may experience and perceive time differently so that they can address differences early rather than later. They also need to take into account Kairos as well as Chronos in the way time is conceptualized—and scheduled—in managing the various portfolio subsystems. To be fully utilized, Kairos requires more flexible approaches than the time management processes that are traditionally associated with project time management.

Certainly, milestones must be achieved, but the portfolio manager also needs to work with emergence to navigate complex risks, solve multidimensional problems in dynamic situations, motivate teams, and so on. To successfully perform this work, one must also appreciate the concept of Kairos. Technical project management methodologies break each portfolio component into discrete, measurable chunks that can be delivered to a linear timeline or schedule. This idea has proven to be extremely useful but, like all good ideas, there is also a downside. This downside may be accounted for once the practitioner utilizes the above in parallel and acknowledges that some stakeholders may perceive time differently. At very critical moments, Kairos may prove to be more important than Chronos—and sticking to the schedule. Exposure to emotionally charged information and situations will create new arguments and instigate new initiatives and projects to provide solutions. Different cultures are stricter or more flexible with running time or with the set time for a particular event or task from other cultures. Knowing that people associated with the whole portfolio or any one of its components have different perceptions of time helps the portfolio manager develop more realistic milestones, provide targeted feedback advice, and account for iteration and realignment of people and ideas as the project progresses.

In summary, when working in a complex environment, time is perceived as relative to the person receiving it. Therefore, different people associated with the portfolio or with a certain component of that portfolio will experience the schedule, pace of activities, and overall progress differently. These events on the schedule can actually appear to speed up or slow down as emergence become stronger or weaker. Understanding these differences might be one important key to navigating complexity. This means actively working with linear time as well as social time—understanding how to swim with the tide rather than against it. Arguments associated with a particular issue will modify and develop, and more effective solutions may emerge as people change their minds, beliefs, interests, locations, communities, and alliances. Moreover, this has to do with navigating cultural differences under a collaborative, transparent approach. Sometimes under high complexity and for relatively short periods, the perception of time is better to be in Kairos terms and not Chronos. As risk patterns emerge, the portfolio manager must be aware of the potential for rapid escalation. Such awareness requires the use of visualization tools, which assist the portfolio manager in recognizing patterns as they build and escalate. The linear risk analysis would not suffice. The portfolio manager often has to sense the moment and thus communicate the right thing, at the right moment, to the right stakeholder.

13.4. Organizational Culture – Performance of Organizational Change through a Cultural Lens

In organizations that encourage individualistic behavior or have a solidly functional organizational structure, most people work as individuals and not as teams. Organizational assessment techniques, which reward individual performance more than team performance reinforce individualistic, functional work. The consequence of this is usually a decrease in efficiency. New people joining must learn the organizational jargon plus means and ways of "doing things" in the particular organization before they can work efficiently. These organizational traits need to be accepted and learned by newcomers in order to collaborate efficiently. Cultural differences in the last decades are being considered as critical contingency variables toward understanding organizational behavior. Such variables predominantly exist in portfolios having multinational components. Moreover, it is now widely accepted that many human resource management practices and techniques that have evolved in the context of Western principles and values may not be adequate in other sociocultural environments.

Portfolio managers must appreciate that managing human capital working in other countries requires an understanding of both the internal and external environments of their organization in that particular country. The internal environment is represented by the organizational culture, whereas the cultural influences from the external environment are dependent on market characteristics, nature of the industry, resource availability, and so on. Both of these environmental forces are, in turn, influenced by the societal-cultural and political context (e.g., power distance, paternalism, historical, social, political forces, etc.). In this chapter, culture is defined as collective or communal patterns, assumptions, values, and beliefs, plus the norms of behavior that arise from these, which may affect the portfolio or one of its components. Internal organizational culture also includes some managerial assumptions flowing throughout the organization.

One challenge that portfolio managers often face when they are involved in selecting managers is being able to select individuals who have the competence to balance and evolve the demands of the cultural interfaces. These interfaces include those between their "home" organization, the client group, the various stakeholders of the portfolio components, and the various team members. Many organizations that work internationally report that to be successful they had to modify their thinking and working practices. Cross-cultural working is a two-way street; it is not colonization. Portfolio managers and project leaders may have to respect values leading to behaviors alien to them, but important to the individuals and society to which they belong. Assuming things will be done "our way" only pushes differences underground, so that they become embedded blockages. Such conduct quickly creates an atmosphere of winners and losers, which can prejudice efficient delivery.

For teams to work efficiently, particularly cross-cultural teams, the roles and responsibilities of the manager and the team members, both at the individual and the collective level, must always be clear and agreed upon. If the team is composed of people from different cultures, then expectations of leadership, hierarchies, collaborations, and membership usually differ. For this reason, clarifying degrees of equality, responsibility, and accountability of the sponsor, the manager, and the members of the team up front is paramount. So, team start-up and team building are vital to success. The activities well-known for team-building events are just as important, but extra dimensions need to be added for global teams. There are at least three dimensions that should be considered and transparent procedures to be established to achieve high performance.

- Ability to respect established ways of working styles;
- Awareness of one's own cultural programming; and
- Awareness of others' cultural programming.

The ability to respect established ways of working means building a team culture where cross-cultural issues are openly discussed. The result of such discussions is the development of appropriate ways of conducting the required work, so that all needs are integrated into the agreed-upon procedures. In addition to formal team-building sessions, informal contacts between team members, suppliers, clients, and other stakeholders establish and develop networks by creating links that enhance mutual understanding and respect. In egalitarian cultures, informal relationships mean getting to know individuals outside formal work protocol, and are considered more important than formal relationships. New communications technologies are powerful tools for project managers, but they frequently fail to live up to their promise. The key lesson is to not fall into the trap of believing that email, electronic and video conferencing, and groupware get people "really" communicating. Exchanging information is fine, but for building trust, much deeper communications are necessary. The personal relationships and networks are ideally built in parallel to formal relationships and information exchange. Available technologies can help significantly to develop such social networks.

The character of any team is predominantly determined by the quality of its senior personnel. This is particularly the case in international projects, where there is less toleration of personalities who do not fit in. A good team usually does not just happen. It is achieved by hard work, particularly by the leader, and this job is best done before mobilization for the global project. The selection of the project team itself also requires careful consideration in global projects, particularly the ability to work well with others. This is probably the most important characteristic. Downturns on global projects are caused much more often by poor interpersonal relationships than noncapability of technical skills. Character deficiencies are more detrimental in the context of a global project—portfolio component—than they are in the home office.

Ethnic cultures have different concepts of the role of personal relationships in business. Take, for example,[155] the Swedes and the Saudis. For the Swedes, business is done with an organization. For the Saudis, business is done with a person you know and trust. Thus, for example, if business must be conducted by people from these two cultures, it is advisable that initial contacts be made in the presence of an intermediary, someone who is known and trusted by both parties. At the root of the difference between these cultures is a fundamental issue in human societies: the part of the individual versus the part of the group. In an individualist culture, when people meet, they feel a need to communicate orally. Silence is considered abnormal. Social conversations can be depressingly banal, but they are compulsory. In a collectivist culture, the fact of being together is emotionally sufficient; there is no compulsion to talk unless there is information to be transferred.

In conclusion, issues and problems for portfolio components that have a global nature may be created by:

- Culture (ethnic, market, organizational);
- Organization, leadership, management, and communication;
- Productivity, distance, and logistics; and
- Differences in local legislation and regulation.

As discussed in Section 13.2 above, the dimensions of cultural difference include:

- Uncertainty avoidance,
- Power distance,
- Individualism,
- Masculinity,
- Role of time, and
- Consideration of detail.

These must be accounted for to manage cultural differences. To manage these differences, portfolio managers also need to:

- Become actively involved in the selection of appropriate project managers and key personnel;
- Be aware of the "cultural" programming of themselves and others;
- Use appropriate leadership styles, accommodating the various national cultures involved;
- Discuss and respect established ways of working;

- Accelerate personal cross-border network development;
- Use appropriate language, use the common language of the project management discipline;
- Use cross-border coaches;
- Choose a capable local partner, preferably having multicultural experiences; and
- Develop a transparent communications infrastructure.

## CHAPTER 14

Current Trends in Portfolio Management

by Te Wu

> The important thing is not to stop questioning. Curiosity has its own reason for existing.
> — **Albert Einstein**

Portfolio management is both old and new. Since the dawn of business strategy in the 1960s and 1970s, management thinkers have prominently noted the importance of portfolio management. Igor Ansoff is often noted as the "father of modern strategic thinking," and co-authored an article with Dr. James Leontiades titled "Strategic Portfolio Management" in 1976 in the *Journal of General Management*. In this article, Ansoff and Leontiades discussed the drastic changes of the past twenty years and the need for organizations to adopt a more organized approach to managing growth, resources, and trade-offs to advance their enterprises further. These views of managing rapid change, driving toward greater growth, and improving alignment between firms and their environment are as true today as they were yesterday.

Even though portfolio management has been widely adopted and popular in "financial" portfolio management, organizationally and in project management, portfolio management is new in most organizations, but the rate of adoption has quickened. The recognition of the value of portfolio management, as discussed in the previous chapters, has been widely recognized, and portfolio management today is viewed as one of the most critical disciplines for connecting organizational strategies with business execution. The acceptance of its value has led to the active adoption of portfolio management by enterprises across the globe, and the effects have been positive. Today, organizations are reporting a 20 percent reduction in wasted financial investments on projects.[156] Furthermore, 61 percent of organizations feel that their project success rate has improved over the past two years, and there has been an increase in the number of organizations that manage their projects within a portfolio structure.[157]

While portfolio management is more clearly defined today than at the time of its inception, the discipline is still in a malleable state. There are some important trends shaping the future of portfolio management. This chapter highlights six of these trends that are shaping portfolio management.

1. Taking agile from project to portfolio to enterprise
2. Using technology to manage emergent risks
3. Portfolio management drives innovation and ideation
4. PMO and strategic execution
5. Achieving benefits realization at the organizational level
6. Importance of people in portfolio management

14.1. Taking Agile from Project to Portfolio to Enterprise

In 2011, the term "agile project management" surpassed the term "agile software development" for the very first time on Google Trends.[158] However, agile practices are no longer sufficient without agility across the entire portfolio. As Chapter 12 on agile portfolio management discussed, the agile principles are now being extended to portfolio management. There is a growing need to stretch the principles of agility beyond projects and teams and toward the broader portfolio and enterprise management.[159] However, this extension requires complementary changes to strategy, processes, and culture.

From a strategy perspective, being agile requires a considerable change to how the organization conducts strategy. For organizations that practice deliberate strategy, it needs to shift toward a more emergent model in which organizations constantly sense the environment and changes, learn from the successes and failures, and adapt its strategy. With the new emergent strategy, organizations inevitably would have to redesign some core business processes, such as strategic planning, annual budgeting, product development, production and operational planning, and resource management. For example, the budgeting processes would likely shift from annual to a shorter duration and possibly to continuous budgeting. To enhance the adoption of this new reality, organizations need to consider more fundamental changes to their culture and move from the traditional planning and execution style to a more learning and adoption style in which organizations learn to fail early, fail fast, recover, and progress.

Organizations that embrace organization-wide agility are consistently more likely to complete projects on time, within budget, and having met the original project goals. Furthermore, the trend reflects an increasingly blurred line between the disciplines of change management and portfolio management to achieve this agility.

See Chapter 12 on agile portfolio management for more information.

14.2. Using Technology to Manage Emergent Risks

Commonly, technology is a disrupter with vast implications. Consider the prediction that global robotics spending will grow by US$52 billion between 2010 and 2025, and that by 2025 the share of tasks performed by robots will increase to 25 percent from a global manufacturing industry average of around 10 percent.[160] This kind of disruption is why over 80 percent of CEOs identify technological advancement as the primary global trend that will transform their businesses.[161] For firms, technology is becoming one of the prime reasons for the necessity of portfolio management to make sound investment decisions.

Organizationally, with this rapid pace of change, organizations are using technology to create insights, leveraging the fuzzy data in the marketplace and embracing technologies as opportunities rather than threats.[162] Since portfolios often represent a significant investment of organizational resources with a greater breadth of impact across organizations, portfolios are more susceptible to unknown-unknowns. This is where technology can play a much more significant role to help organizations "discover" the previous unknown-unknowns, also known as emergent risks, and analyze them for potential implications on the portfolio.

Portfolio information technology and applications are providing predictive analytics, and cloud computing and big data are gaining popularity as a means to competitive technological parity in portfolio management.[163] Furthermore, portfolio management systems are becoming more powerful to enable organizations to manage more complex portfolios. Through leveraging technology, the breadth of coverage and the speed of analysis will greatly enhance the portfolio manager's responsibility of anticipating risks rather than be surprised by them.

14.3. Portfolio Management Drives Innovation and Ideation

There has been a growth in the number of organizations implementing portfolio management over the past few years, and the primary reason is so the sponsoring organizations can undertake more of the "right" projects and programs. A similar approach is gaining recognition in the innovation value chain. Business is taking a decided focus on innovation strategies. This means that organizations are implementing portfolio management, not only to manage projects once products are in development, but also to manage the selection of products and ideas *before* they reach development.[164] Portfolio management is being applied to the process of selecting the right strategically beneficial innovations before they get to the front-end stages of implementation.

Building on the earlier trend of leveraging technology to discover emergent risks, portfolio managers can work with innovation or product managers to determine sound decision criteria, conduct deeper analysis, analyze data quicker, prioritize options and features, and improve portfolio prioritization. For example, an innovative midsize manufacturing company with about 6,000 employees and a revenue of US$6 billion examined its project environment and found nearly 2,900 active projects across the company. A significant portion of those projects is product related. Upon closer examination, the firm quickly realized that there were significant overlaps and redundancies, in addition to no clear prioritization, especially at the organizational level. This represented a significant waste or, at the minimum, ineffective resource utilization. The company leveraged the portfolio management process to be more focused on high-priority and high-value projects and greatly reduce the number of active ones.

By extending coverage of the portfolio to encompass ideation through operations, organizations with fresh, bold, and creative ideas will likely achieve more and compete well against organizations that are largely stuck in traditional processes.

14.4. PMO and Strategic Execution

With the help of portfolio management, project success rates appear to be on the rise. However, many projects still fail to reach their objectives, and organizational leadership is largely attributing this to strategic alignment (or lack thereof). In fact, a recent study has shown that portfolio management performance is directly influenced and positively related to strengthening the strategic alignment between projects and business strategy.[165] For this reason, organizational leadership is bridging the gap between strategy and execution by cascading clear strategic objectives down to the project level with portfolio management serving as a bridge between concepts and reality.

For many if not most organizations, the key to closing this gap is the creation and maturity of the project management office (PMO). In a Gartner project portfolio management and IT governance summit, nearly half of CEOs identified PMOs as an integral part of "getting things done."[166] As such, the percentage of organizations with a PMO has followed an upward trend since 2007 (61 percent), with over 70 percent of organizations using a PMO today.[167] These organizations benefit from (on average) a 38 percent higher project success rate than those organizations without a PMO.

Consequently, the PMO has been undergoing a major shift in its value proposition. Before 2000, most of the PMOs contributed tactical value to their organizations by concentrating on monitoring and controlling or becoming a clearinghouse for project management-related training and competency development. Gradually, the emphasis of PMOs has moved toward more directing of projects, creating consistency of execution through methodology development and risk management. In recent years, the value of PMOs has progressed toward making strategic contributions by supporting project portfolio management, providing enterprise governance of projects, and working closely with C-suites.

14.5. Achieving Benefits Realization at the Organizational Level

The shocking reality is that only 21 percent of projects are consistently delivering on their benefits.[168] This is why benefits realization is gaining increased attention as a powerful way to align an organization's strategy with its portfolios of projects, in turn resulting in greater benefits realized.

There has been a marked increase over the past four years in the number of organizations who report having formal benefits measurement and realization processes.[169] There are many challenges with implementing benefits management. For example, in most organizations, projects require some level of business justifications or business cases. Yet, to make projects more attractive, inflating or exaggerating the project benefits are rather common in many organizations. Since the benefits from these justifications and business cases are rarely tracked systematically, project benefits are often difficult to compare with the original intention.

When this phenomenon of exaggerating benefits in the business becomes prevalent, the negative implication across the organization can be vast. However, with the advancement of portfolio management, there are significant improvements. Today, more than half of organizations report that they review project portfolio outcomes against the organizational strategy.[170] Similarly, more organizations are reporting that projects consistently achieve the realization of their planned benefits. There is still significant room for improvement as organizations instill the greater discipline of managing benefits and values across their enterprise.

14.6. Importance of People in Portfolio Management

The investment in and development of people has gained significant interest of late. Organizations are recognizing the importance of project and portfolio management practitioners, and active leadership in ensuring the successful execution of strategy through project portfolios. This trend spans from the active role of project sponsors and the inclusion of executive-level leadership in project and portfolio execution, all the way to increased training and talent creation within project teams. Nearly 50 percent of organizations today implement ongoing project management training,[171] and organizations are making use of tools for team collaboration. However, career planning for portfolio managers continues to lag and is generally undertaken by fewer than 20 percent of organizations.[172]

Still, organizations are starting to realize this gap. For example, in the recent passing of the Program Management Improvement Accountability Act (PMIAA) enacted by the United States in December 2016, this law explicitly requires the U.S. federal government to formalize a clear career path in portfolio, program, and project management training. While this act is still in its infancy, and how it will be executed is still being discussed at the time of writing, the author expects that the United States government will move toward a more formal and structured process of creating official job series for federal employees, formalizing job criteria for the various project management-related positions, and developing a clear career path for its people. However, since state and municipal governments, as well as other nationals, often emulate or even piggyback off of U.S. laws, the true implication of PMIAA can only be guessed at this point. However, one thing is clear, the emphasis on people will only become stronger over time.

Conclusion

Project portfolio management has undergone a significant evolution over the past few years, and improvements in project success rates may be evidence of its effectiveness. However, the current global trends facing portfolio management indicate that this discipline is still growing and developing. Trends toward a more agile, more technologically savvy, more innovative approach to portfolio management are shifting the boundaries yet again. Today, portfolio management has become a critical and practical tool for executing strategy and realizing benefits. Portfolio management will likely continue to transform with the changing needs of organizations, and the advancing means of technology.

To further advance portfolio management, we are creating an "Project Portfolio Management Forum" (PPMF) to focus on the challenges and opportunities in portfolio and program management. This forum is being created in multiple phases. At the time of writing, a core team of 30 professionals and academics have agreed to work together to establish an agenda. The team is also planning to create a comprehensive report on the state of project portfolio management. If you are interested in joining this group, please complete the short form at www.implementppm.com/join-ppmf.

References and Endnotes

[1] Wu, T. *The Sensible Guide to Passing the PfMP Exam – 1st Edition.* (New York: iExperi Press, 2014), Table 11, page 45.

[2] Project Management Institute. *The Standard for Portfolio Management – Fourth Edition.* (Newtown Square, PA: Project Management Institute, 2017), page 7.

[3] Ibid.

[4] Ibid., Figure 2-1, page 22.

[5] Ibid., Figure 2-2, page 23.

[6] Project Management Institute. *Governance of Portfolios, Programs, and Projects: A Practice Guide.* (Newtown Square, PA: Project Management Institute, 2017), Figure 3-1, page 43.

[7] Craddock, W. T. PMI White Paper, "Change Management in the Strategic Alignment of Project Portfolios." Project Management Institute. May 2015 Figure 5, page 6. https://www.pmi.org/learning/library/change-management-strategic-alignment-project-portfolios-11137.

[8] Project Management Institute. *Pulse of the Profession®: Portfolio Management.* Newtown Square, PA: Project Management Institute, 2012.

[9] Project Management Institute. *The Standard for Portfolio Management – Fourth Edition.* (Newtown Square, PA: Project Management Institute, 2017), page 7.

[10] Project Management Institute. *Delivering on Strategy: The Power of Project Portfolio Management [report].* (Newtown Square, PA: Project Management Institute, 2015). Retrieved from https://www.pmi.org/-/media/pmi/documents/public/pdf/learning/thought-leadership/deliver-strategy-portfolio-management.pdf.

[11] Garfein, S. J. "Strategic Portfolio Management: The Key to the Executive Suite." Paper presented at PMI® Global Congress 2008—EMEA, St. Julian's, Malta. (Project Management Institute, 2008).

[12] Rumelt, R. *Good Strategy, Bad Strategy – The Difference and Why it Matters.* London, UK: Profile Books, 2011.

[13] Kornberger, M. "Clausewitz: On Strategy." *Business History*, 55:7 (2013).

[14] Hrebiniak, L. G. *Making Strategy Work*. Upper Saddle River, NJ: Wharton School Publishing, 2005.

[15] Lafley, A. G., and R. L. Martin. *Playing to Win: How Strategy Really Works*. Cambridge, MA: HBR Press 2013.

[16] Project Management Institute. *PMI's Pulse of the Profession® In-Depth Report: The Impact of PMOs on Strategy Implementation*. Newtown Square, PA: Project Management Institute, November 2013.

[17] Mankins, M. C., and R. Steele. "Turning Great Strategy into Great Performance." *Harvard Business Review*, July-August 2005.

[18] Garfein, S. J. "Expanding Strategic Throughput: A New Perspective on Closing the Gap Between Strategy and Results." Paper presented at PMI® Global Congress 2009—EMEA, Amsterdam, North Holland, The Netherlands. (Project Management Institute, 2009).

[19] Garfein, S. J. and D. Toit. "Strategic Portfolio Management at Hydromax: Closing the Gap Between Strategy and Results—A Case Study." Paper presented at PMI® Global Congress 2006—North America, Seattle, WA. (Project Management Institute, 2006).

[20] Porter, M. E. *Competitive Advantage: Creating and Sustaining Superior Performance*. New York: The Free Press, 1985.

[21] Porter, M. E. "The Five Competitive Forces that Shape Strategy." *Harvard Business Review*, January 2008.

[22] Moore, K. "The Emergent Way: How to Achieve Meaningful Growth in an Era of Flat Growth." *Ivey Business Journal*, November/December, 2011.

[23] Mintzberg, H., B. Ahlstrand, and J. Lampel. *Strategy Safari: A Guided Tour of the Wilds of Strategic Management*. New York: The Free Press, 1998.

[24] Argyris, C. *On Organizational Learning*. Hoboken, NJ: Wiley-Blackwell, 1999.

[25] An Interview with Chris Argyris. https://www.strategy-business.com/article/9887?gko=c19c5.

[26] Risk tolerance may be simply thought as the defined and accepted minimum and maximum levels or each particular risk beyond which the organization is not willing to lose.

[27] Project Management Institute. *The Standard for Portfolio Management* – Third Edition. Newtown Square, PA: Project Management Institute, 2013.

[28] Adopted from PMO Advisory, a PMI Global R.E.P. (#4172), Portfolio Management Professional Training content.

bibliography / endnotes section

[29] Project Management Institute. *The Standard for Portfolio Management* – Fourth Edition. (Newtown Square, PA: Project Management Institute, 2017), Section 4.2, page 43.

[30] The PMI foundational standards include: *The Standard for Portfolio Management, The Standard for Program Management*, and *A Guide to the Project Management Body of Knowledge (PMBOK® Guide)*.

[31] Small teams are taken to be about six to 10 people or less. Generally, work packages within a project are assigned to teams of about 10 or so individuals. These teams are led by a group or section leader who is part of the project personnel structure. The project manager manages "above" the work packages by coordinating actions of multiple team leads. Workflow may be managed using lean or agile techniques such as Kanban. Using a specific agile technique, Scrum teams consist of about six or so individuals. These teams are self-managing and facilitated by a scrum master. See footnote 6.

[32] IPMA Organizational Competence Baseline, International Project Management Association (IPMA®). C/O Advokatuburo Maurer & Stage, fraumunsterstrasse 17, Postfach 2018, Ch-8022 Zurich, Switzerland

[33] See the *Agile Manifesto* website at http://agilemanifesto.org/.

[34] There are many agile management systems. Scrum is an iterative development process that depends on experienced self-governing teams to deliver products over short increments of a few weeks to a couple of months. Kanban is a workflow management technique that focuses on work in progress as a means of focusing teams to deliver items quickly.

[35] Project Management Institute. *The Standard for Portfolio Management* – Fourth Edition. (Newtown Square, PA: Project Management Institute, 2017), Section 1.3, page 3. Also, see Table 1-1 on page 6.

[36] For a complete discussion on emergence and complexity, see the following:

- Gharajedaghi, J. *Systems Thinking: Managing Chaos and Complexity: A Platform for Designing Business Architecture.* Burlington, MA: Elsevier, 2011.
- Kerr, D. *An Introductory Guide to Systems Thinking* [Kindle Edition version]. Cheshire, UK: Watts Works Consulting Ltd., 2012.
- Project Management Institute. *Navigating Complexity: A Practice Guide.* Newtown Square, PA: Project Management Institute, 2014.

[37] Project Management Institute. *The Standard for Portfolio Management* – Fourth Edition. (Newtown Square, PA: Project Management Institute, 2017), page 9.

[38] Government Accountability Project. *Why Whistleblowers Wait*. Accessed July 2017 via https://www.whistleblower.org/sites/default/files/GAP_Report_Why_Whistleblowers_Wait.pdf, Government Accountability Project, Washington D.C., page 9, citing Pacella, Jennifer. "Inside or Out? The Dodd-Frank Whistleblower Program's Anti-Retaliation Protections for Internal Reporting." *Temple Law Review*. 86, 4 (2014): 721–761, 755, citing Mayer, David et al. "Encouraging Employees to Report Unethical Conduct Internally: It Takes a Village." *Organizational Behavior and Human Decision Processes* 121 (2013): 91,10001.

[39] Gharajedaghi, J. *Systems Thinking: Managing Chaos and Complexity – The Third Edition*. Burlington, MA: Elsevier, 2011. The author outlines the following attributes of complex systems as openness, purposefulness, multidimensionality, emergent property, and counterintuitive behavior.

[40] Project Management Institute. *The Standard for Portfolio Management* – Fourth Edition. (Newtown Square, PA: Project Management Institute, 2017), Section 4.4.1, page 44.

[41] The work of portfolio management is primarily a staff function. Product development, delivery, and operational work is conducted within the portfolio through its programs, projects, and operating entities. As such, from an execution perspective, development; delivery; and operational work cannot be taken on by the portfolio management staff. In terms of program, project, and operational effort, the responsibility stops at the portfolio management level. The same can be said for work passed to senior executive management. Their primary function is strategic analysis and strategic and operational decision making. Execution is left to the component within various portfolios.

[42] See Block P. Stewardship. Berrett-Koehler Publishers, San Francisco, 1993. The author provides a stewardship model for management that was innovative at the time. This model has since been adopted within the agile and project management communities. The practice of self-forming and self-guided teams working under a mentor or facilitator is no longer unusual. However, such teams require experienced personnel trained to work in such an environment

[43] Not all projects are required to be nested within a program. Project managers report directly to portfolio managers or other mangers within the organization.

[44] For example, a sports company may choose to continue a low-profitable line of sneakers to maintain brand presence in a particular market.

[45] Many hierarchical structures exist to describe the flow of information within organizations. The list of data, information, and knowledge proposes a three-tiered structure to abstract data held by an organization. The lowest level of data refers to raw data such as the numbers 15054839582. With some simple formatting, this data may be transformed into information such as 1-505-483-9528. We now have the information that this is a U.S. phone number with a likely location in New Mexico. Finally, this information may be further transformed in knowledge by knowing this is the number to call, say, computer systems support at a local bank in Albuquerque.

[46] See Project Management Institute. *Navigating Complexity: A Practice Guide.* (Newtown Square, PA: Project Management Institute, 2014) for a complete discussion of complexity within the project management domain.

[47] These steps are paraphrased from *The Standard for Portfolio Management* – Third Edition. With the publication of the fourth edition of *The Standard for Portfolio Management*, a break was made from the previous prescriptive standards. Complexity was acknowledged as a significant driver of management considerations at the portfolio level.

[48] Project Management Institute. *The Standard for Portfolio Management* – Fourth Edition. (Newtown Square, PA: Project Management Institute, 2017), Section 1.6, page 5.

[49] Ibid.

[50] Project Management Institute. *Navigating Complexity: A Practice Guide.* Newtown Square, PA: Project Management Institute, 2014.

[51] Adopted from PMO Advisory, a PMI Global Registered Education Provider, Portfolio Management Training course.

[52] Ibid.

[53] Project Management Institute. *The Standard for Portfolio Management* – Fourth Edition. (Newtown Square, PA: Project Management Institute, 2017), Section 7.1, page 75.

[54] Ibid., page 76.

[55] Ibid., Figure 8-1, page 90.

[56] The term "fuzzy" refers to fuzzy logic, an approach to reasoning that is not based on Boolean logic, in which an item or proposition exists either in one set or another, say "yes" or "no." Fuzzy logic was refined in the early 1960s to try to develop computer programs that operated

like human thinking. *Decisions under risk* refers to a body of decision processes that acknowledges the limits of data in any application and seeks to establish processes and tools to facilitate decision processes that recognize this limitation. Studies in complexity try to describe the underlying environment that leads to the need for decisions under risk and the application of fuzzy logic. Complexity is more than being complicated, as a well-defined management environment may be complicated but not complex. For example, the mathematical equations that govern the orbit of the moon around the earth are complicated and non-linear for those familiar with orbital mechanics. However, they are also well-defined. Various relationships and data are bounded and the future outcomes are highly predictable. This represents a complicated system, but not complexity as discussed within the field of complexity.

[57] Below is a selective list of books dealing with risk management:

- Bible, Michael and Susan Bivins. *Mastering Project Portfolio Management, A Systems Approach to Achieving Strategic Objectives.* Plantation, FL: J Ross Publishing Inc., 2011. ISBN 978-1-60427-066-2
- Hulett, David. *Integrated Cost-Schedule Risk Analysis.* Farnham, UK: Gower Publishing, 2011, ISBN 978-0-566-09166-7 and *Practical Schedule Risk Analysis.* Farnham, UK: Gower Publishing, 2009, ISBN 978-0-566-08790-5
- Moore, Simon. *Strategic Project Portfolio Management, Enabling a Productive Organization.* Hoboken, NJ: John Wiley & Sons, 2010, ISBN 978-0-470-48195-0
- Project Management Institute. *Practice Standard for Project Risk Management.* Newtown Square, PA: Project Management Institute 2009, ISBN 978-1-933890-38-8
- Vose, David. *Risk Analysis, A Quantitative Guide*, Third Edition. Hoboken, NJ: John Wiley & Sons, Ltd., 2008, ISBN 978-0-470-51284-5

[58] Section 8.4.2 of *The Standard for Portfolio Management* – Fourth Edition has a long discussion, which is not repeated in this chapter, on risk perception and how individual risk appetite contributes to an overall risk culture within an organization.

[59] DevOps is a software delivery approach conducted as part of an agile delivery process where the code development, test, and deployment processes are combined into one delivery action resulting in new

capabilities being delivered without noticeable interruption to the on-going operation of the system. An example of a DevOps environment is the continuous updating of a sales website with new price information or enhanced ordering capabilities without noticeable downtime or interruption of commerce.

[60] See Chapter 12 of this book on agile portfolio practices for a discussion of extended agile principles above the small team level.

[61] Project Management Institute. *The Standard for Portfolio Management* – Fourth Edition. (Newtown Square, PA: Project Management Institute, 2017), page 95.

[62] Ibid., Section 5.3, page 52.

[63] Ibid., Section 7.7, page 80.

[64] Ibid., Section 7.8, page 82.

[65] See Chapter 12 of this book for a short explanation of SAFe® Agile.

[66] Project Management Institute. *The Standard for Portfolio Management* – Fourth Edition. (Newtown Square, PA: Project Management Institute, 2017), Figure 4-1, page 45.

[67] Project Management Institute. *A Guide to the Project Management Body of Knowledge (PMBOK® Guide)* – Sixth Edition. (Newtown Square, PA: Project Management Institute, 2017), Figure 11-1, Section 11, page 396.

[68] Project Management Institute. *The Standard for Portfolio Management* – Fourth Edition. (Newtown Square, PA: Project Management Institute, 2017), page 103.

[69] The Tulip collapse is a classic example of investor mania and is mentioned here to emphasize that extreme, usually negative, risk events are not a recent phenomenon.

[70] The results of the high-impact but very low probability of certain catastrophic events is discussed in *The Black Swan*, by Nassim Taleb, Random House, 2010. Portfolio and senior-level managers must be aware of the possible impact of these types of events and understand the potential impacts.

[71] The Standish Group, a consultancy, has published a project success report for the information technology industry since the 1990s. For more information, visit www.standishgroup.com.

[72] PMO Advisory, a PMI Global Registered Education Provider, has been examining strategic business execution since 2012. For more information about the company and its research, visit www.pmoadvisory.com.

[73] Lombardo, M. M. and R. W. Eichinger. *Career Architect® Development Planner* – 5th Edition. Lominger International: A Korn/Ferry Company, 2010.

[74] Ackoff, R. L. *Re-Creating the Corporation: A Design of Organizations for the 21st Century*. Oxford: Oxford University Press, 1999.

[75] Project Management Institute. *The Standard for Portfolio Management* – Fourth Edition. Newtown Square, PA: Project Management Institute, 2017.

[76] Sauser, B., J. Boardman, and A. Gorod. *System of Systems Management – Innovations for the 21st Century*. Edited by Mo Jamshidi. Hoboken, NJ: Wiley, 2008.

[77] Syed, G. and S. Sankaran. "Investigating an Interpretive Framework to Manage Complex Information Technology Projects," IRNOP IX Conference, Berlin, October 11–13, 2009.

[78] Sankaran, S., T. Haslett, and J. Sheffield. "Systems Thinking Approaches to Address Complex Issues in Project Management." Paper presented at PMI® Global Congress 2010—Asia Pacific, Melbourne, Victoria, Australia (Project Management Institute, 2010).

[79] Martinsuo, M., and P. Lehtonen. "Role of Single-Project Management in Achieving Portfolio Management Efficiency." *International Journal of Project Management*, 25, 1 (2007): 56–65.

[80] McConell, S. *Rapid Development: Taming Wild Software Schedules*. Redmond: Microsoft Press, 1996.

[81] Kim, D. H. *Introduction to Systems Thinking*. Innovations in Management Series. Waltham, MA: Pegasus Communications, 1999.

[82] Turner, J. R., and R. A. Cochrane. "Goals-and-Methods: Coping with Projects with Ill-Defined Goals and/or Methods of Achieving Them." *International Journal of Project Management*, 11, 2 (1993): 93–102.

[83] Crawford, L., B. Hobbs, and J. R. Turner. "Project Categorization Systems and Their Use in organizations. PMI Research on Categorization of Projects: An Empirical Study." In Slevin, D. P., C. David, and J. K. Pinto (eds.) *Innovations: Project Management Research*. Newtown Square, PA: Project Management Institute, 2004.

[84] Senge, P. *The Fifth Discipline: The Art and Practice of the Learning Organizations*. New York: Doubleday, 1990.

[85] Pollack, J. "The Changing Paradigms of Project Management." *International Journal of Project Management*, 25, 3 (2007): 266–274.

[86] Winter, M. and P. Checkland. "Soft Systems: A Fresh Perspective on Project Management." *Civil Engineering*, 15, 4 (2003): 187–192.

[87] Cicmil, S., T. Cooke-Davies, L. Crawford, L., and K. Richardson. *Exploring the Complexity of Projects: Implications of Complexity Theory for Project Management Practice*. Newtown Square, PA: Project Management Institute, 2009.

[88] Morris, P. W. *Reconstructing Project Management*. Oxford, UK: Wiley-Blackwell, 2013.

[89] Maani, K. E., and R. Y. Cavana. *Systems Thinking, System Dynamics: Managing Change and Complexity*. North Shore, New Zealand: Pearson Education, 2006.

[90] Remington, K. and J. Pollack. *Tools for Complex Projects*. Aldershot: Gower, 2008.

[91] Williams, T. *Modelling Complex Projects*. London, UK: Wiley, 2002.

[92] Project Management Institute. *Navigating Complexity: A Practice Guide*. Newtown Square, PA: Project Management Institute, 2014.

[93] Oehmen, J., C. Thuesen, P. P. Ruiz, and J. Geraldi. "Complexity Management for Projects, Programmes, and Portfolios: An Engineering Systems Perspective." Paper presented at PMI® Global Congress 2015—EMEA, London, England. (Project Management Institute, 2015).

[94] Sheffield, J., S. Sankaran, T. Haslett. "Systems Thinking Approaches to Address Complex Issues in Project Management," Paper presented at PMI® Global Congress 2010—Asia Pacific, Melbourne, Victoria, Australia. (Project Management Institute, 2010).

[95] **Law of Requisite Variety:** May be stated for portfolio management as follows: The way in which systems operating in changing environments succeed in maintaining variables critical for their sustainable existence within tightly defined limits. Ashby's "Law" of Requisite Variety states that for a system to be stable, the number of states that its control mechanism is capable of attaining (its variety) must be greater than or equal to the number of states in the system being controlled. If a system is to be able to deal successfully with the diversity of challenges that its environment produces, then it needs to have a repertoire of responses, which is at least as varied as the issues created by the environment. So, a viable system is one that can handle the variability of its environment. Or, as Ashby put it, only variety can absorb variety. Until recently, organizations coped with environmental challenges mainly by measures to reduce the variety with which they had to cope. Mass production, for example, reduced the variety of its environment by limiting the range of choice available to consumers: Product standardization was essentially an extrapolation of Henry Ford's slogan that customers could have the Model T in any color so long as it was black. But the rise of the internet has made variety reduction increasingly difficult. By any metric that one chooses, for example, the density of interactions between system components, the pace of change, the degree of connectivity, etc., the global contemporary

information ecosystem as its various subsystems are orders of magnitude more complex than they were only 30 years ago. And variety, in Ashby's terms, has increased in proportion to complexity. Given that variety reduction seems very difficult nowadays, the implication is that many of our organizations—ones that have evolved to cope with much lower levels of variety—are no longer capable of working effectively and efficiently. Thus, the path back to viability requires that new ways of increasing their variety must be found. And the current challenge is to find them. It has been proven that the persons or the control system with the most flexibility of behavior will control the referenced system. The portfolio manager must possess essential awareness for this common phenomenon and proactively have planned for a sufficiently large variety of well-planned actions in order to ensure a sufficiently small variety in the outcomes of his most essential variable—the strategic objectives of his portfolio.

[96] Glouberman, S. and B. Zimmerman. "Complicated and Complex Systems: What Would Successful Reform of Medicare Look Like?" *Romanov Papers: Changing Healthcare in Canada*, Vol. 2, Forest, P.-G., G. P. Marchildon, and T. McIntosh (eds.). Toronto: University of Toronto Press, 2014.

[97] Snowden, D. J. "Complex Acts of Knowing—Paradox and Descriptive Self-Awareness." IBM Global Services, July 2002.

[98] Snowden, D. J. and M. E. Boone. "A Leader's Framework for Decision Making." *Harvard Business Review*, November, 2007.

[99] Brooks, F. *The Mythical Man-Month*. Boston, MA: Addison-Wesley, 1995.

[100] Ackoff, R. L. *Creating the Corporate Future*. Hoboken, NJ: Wiley, 1981.

[101] Christakis, A. and K. Baush. *How People Harness Their Collective Wisdom and Power to Construct the Future in Co-Laboratories of Democracy*. Charlotte, NC: Information Age Publishing, Inc., 2006.

[102] Fernández-Aráoz, C. *It's Not the How or the What But the Who: Succeed by Surrounding Yourself with the Best*. Brighton, MA: Harvard Business Press, 2014.

[103] Project Management Institute. *The Standard for Portfolio Management* – Fourth Edition. Newtown Square, PA: Project Management Institute, 2017.

[104] Project Management Institute. *Navigating Complexity: A Practice Guide*. Newtown Square, PA: Project Management Institute, 2014.

[105] "Embracing Complexity" especially the Spotlight section entitled "Managing Complex Organizations," *Harvard Business Review*, September 2011.

[106] Cavanagh, M. *Second Order Project Management*. London: Routledge, 2012.

[107] Senge P. *The Fifth Discipline*. New York: Doubleday, 2006.

[108] Zero-sum is a situation in game theory in which one person's gain is equivalent to another's loss, so the net change in wealth or benefit is zero.

[109] This is mathematically expressed by Metcalfe's formula: $n*(n-1)/2$.

[110] Remington, K. and J. Pollack. *Tools for Complex Projects*. Farnham, UK: Ashgate, 2008.

[111] Kahneman, D. *Thinking Fast and Slow*. New York: Farrar, Straus and Giroux, 2011.

[112] Works of D. Kahneman, https://worldcat.org/identities/lccn-n81 -55169/

[113] Simon, H.A. "A Behavioral Model of Rational Choice." *Quarterly Journal of Economics*, 69 (1995): 99–118.

[114] Ware, C. *Information Visualization: Perception for Design, 3rd Edition*. Amsterdam: Morgan Kaufmann, 2012.

[115] Weick, K.E., K. M. Sutcliffe, and D. Obstfeld. "Organizing and the Process of Sensemaking." *Organization Science*, 16, 4 (2005): 409.

[116] For an extended discussion of the causes of complexity, the practitioner is referred to PMI's *Navigating Complexity: A Practice Guide* and other PMI publications on complexity included in the references of this book.

[117] Brief descriptions of all terms of human behavior mentioned below are included in the Glossary.

[118] There are known knowns. These are things we know that we know. There are known unknowns. That is to say, there are things that we know we don't know. But there are also unknown unknowns. These are things we don't know we don't know. https://www.brainyquote.com/quotes /donald_rumsfeld_148142.

[119] Kim, S D. "Characterizing Unknown Unknowns." Paper presented at PMI® Global Congress 2012—North America, Vancouver, British Columbia, Canada. (Project Management Institute, 2012).

[120] Project Management Institute. *Governance of Portfolios, Programs, and Projects: A Practice Guide*. Newtown Square, PA: Project Management Institute, 2016.

[121] Project Management Institute. *Governance of Portfolios, Programs, and Projects: A Practice Guide.* (Newtown Square, PA: Project Management Institute, 2016), Figure 1-3, page 9.

[122] Chatzipanos, P. A., E. Lykouropoulos, and N. Zygouris. "Complexity in Projects of Greek State Reforms: National Cadaster." Paper presented at PMI® Global Congress 2014—North America, Phoenix, AZ. (Project Management Institute, 2014).

[123] Chatzipanos, P. A., and T. Giotis. "Cognitive Biases as Project & Program Complexity Enhancers: The Astypalea Project." Paper presented at PMI® Global Congress 2014—EMEA, Dubai, United Arab Emirates. (Project Management Institute, 2014).

[124] Snowden, D.J. "What is Sense-Making?" http://cognitive-edge .com/blog/what-is-sense-making/, June 7, 2008.

[125] Klein, G., Phillips J. K., Raill E. L., and Peluso D. A. "a data-frame theory of sensemaking. In R. R. Hoffman (Ed.), Expertise out of context: Proceedings of the sixth international conference on naturalistic decision making (pp.113-158). New York, NY, Taylor & Francis, 2007.

[126] Goffman, E. "Frame Analysis: An Essay on the Organization of Experience," Cambridge, MA, Harvard University Press, 1974.

[127] Weick K. E., Sutcliffe, K. M., Obstfeld. "Organizing and the Process of Sensemaking," Organizational Science, Vol 16, No. 4. July-August 2005.

[128] Maitlis, S. and M. Christianson. "Sensemaking in Organizations: Taking Stock and Moving Forward." *Academy of Management Annals*, 8, 1 (2014): 57–125.

[129] Kurtz, C.F. and D. J. Snowden. "The New Dynamics of Strategy—Sense-Making in a Complex and Complicated World." *IBM Systems Journal*, 42, 3 (2003).

[130] Geraldi, J., and M. Arlt. "Confident and 'Wrong'? Towards a Mindful Use of Visuals in Project Portfolio Decisions." Paper presented at IRNOP 2015 Conference. (London: IRNOP 2015 Conference, 2015).

[131] Project Management Institute. *Complexity Management for Projects, Programs, and Portfolios: An Engineering Systems Perspective.* (Newtown Square, PA: Project Management Institute, 2015), Figure 1, page 10.

[132] Project Management Institute. *A Guide to the Project Management Body of Knowledge (PMBOK® Guide) – Sixth Edition.* Newtown Square, PA: Project Management Institute, 2017.

[133] http://www.agilemanifesto.org

[134] Project Management Institute. *Agile Practice Guide*. Newtown Square, PA: Project Management Institute, 2017.

[135] Ibid, page 18.

[136] For brevity, Scrum processes are discussed. Other agile processes exist; however, Scrum is the most common and most other agile work processes incorporate scrum techniques.

[137] See Bruce Tuckman's June 1965 article in *Psychological Bulletin* (63: 384–399), "Developmental Sequence in Small Groups."

[138] Deming, W. Edwards. *Out of the Crisis*. (Cambridge, MA: Massachusetts Institute of Technology, Center for Advanced Engineering Study, 1986), page. 88.

[139] Shewhart, W. A., and W. E. Deming. *Statistical Method from the Viewpoint of Quality Control*. New York: Dover, 2011.

[140] Boyd, J. R. *Destruction and Creation (PDF)*. (U.S. Army Command and General Staff College, September 3, 1976).

[141] Other categorizations exist. The intent is not to offer this list as comprehensive nor definitive.

[142] RBS may also refer to the risk breakdown structure. Three interrelated documents fully describe the characteristics of most projects. They are the WBS and the two RBSs. Within the WBS is the project's budget. This budget is tied to specific deliverables within the WBS and associated with the project's requirements and risks via the linkages between the WBS and RBSs.

[143] Taleb, N. *The Black Swan*. New York: Random House, 2007. Describes very highly unlikely events that have significant or extreme consequences.

[144] Reisyan, G.D. *Neuro-Organizational Culture*. New York: Springer, 2016.

[145] Hofstede, G., G. J. Hofstede, and M. Minkov. *Cultures and Organizations—Software of the Mind*. New York: McGraw-Hill, 2010.

[146] Meyer, E. *The Culture Map*. New York: Public Affairs, 2014.

[147] Ferguson, N. *Civilization: The West and the Rest*. New York: Penguin, 2011.

[148] Hofstede, G. *Culture's Consequences: Comparing Values, Behaviors, Institutions, and Organizations Across Nations*. London: Sage Publications, 2001.

[149] Ibid.

[150] Values for each dimension for most countries can be found on the internet at: https://geert-hofstede.com/countries.html.

[151] Aycan, Z., R. N. Kanungo, M. Mendonca, K. Yu, J. Deller, G. Stahl, and A. Kurshid. "Impact of Culture on Human Resource Management Practices—A 10-Country Comparison." *Journal of Applied Psychology*, 49, 1 (2000).

[152] Jessen, S-A. *The Nature of Project Leadership*. Oslo, Norway: Scandinavian University Press, 1993.

[153] Meyer, E. "Being the Boss in Brussels, Boston, and Beijing." *Harvard Business Review*, July–August, 2017.

[154] Remington, K. *Kairos: Harnessing Time and Emergence in Complex Projects*. Australia: International Centre for Complex Project Management, 2013.

[155] http://www.odat.nl/training_icw_en/demo/pagina.php?pa=10

[156] Project Management Institute. *Pulse of the Profession®: 9th Global Project Management Survey*. (Newtown Square, PA: Project Management Institute, 2017). https://www.pmi.org/-/media/pmi/documents/public/pdf/learning/thought-leadership/pulse/pulse-of-the-profession-2017.pdf.

[157] KPMG Project Management Survey. *Driving Business Performance*, (2017). https://assets.kpmg.com/content/dam/kpmg/nz/pdf/July/project managementsurvey-kpmg-nz.pdf.

[158] Stettina, C. J. and J. Horz. "Agile Portfolio Management: An Empirical Perspective on the Practice in Use." *International Journal of Project Management*, 33, 1 (2014).

[159] Deloitte Development LLC. *Agile and Project Portfolio Management (PPM)*, (2017). https://www2.deloitte.com/content/dam/Deloitte/us/Documents/technology/us-cons-agile-and-project-portfolio-management.pdf

[160] Project Management Institute. *Pulse of the Profession®: 9th Global Project Management Survey*. (Newtown Square, PA: Project Management Institute, 2017). https://www.pmi.org/-/media/pmi/documents/public/pdf/learning/thought-leadership/pulse/pulse-of-the-profession-2017.pdf.

[161] PwC Point of View, Enterprise Portfolio and Program Management, (2015).

[162] Kokshagina, O., P. Masson, and B. Weil. "Portfolio Management in Double Unknown Situations: Technological Platforms and the Role of Cross-Application Managers." *Creativity and Innovation Management*. Hoboken, NJ: Wiley Online, 2015. https://onlinelibrary.wiley.com/doi/full/10.1111/caim.12121.

[163] Chakraborty P., "State of Project Portfolio Management in 2016." *IT Governance, Project Portfolio Management*, (November 16, 2016). Retrieved from: http://aits.org/2016/11/state-project-portfolio-management -2016/.

[164] Kock, A., W. Heising, and H. G. Gemuending. "How Ideation Portfolio Management Influences Front-End Success." *Journal of Product Innovation Management*. (New York: Wiley Online, September 2014). https://doi.org/10.1111/jpim.12217

[165] Filippov, S., Mooi, R. Weg, and L. J. Westen. "Strategic Alignment of the Project Portfolio: An Empirical Investigation." Paper presented at PMI® Research and Education Conference, Limerick, Munster, Ireland (Project Management Institute, 2012). https://www.pmi.org/learning /library/strategic-alignment-project-portfolio-6387

[166] Gartner. Annual Gartner Program and Portfolio Management Summit (Orlando: Gartner, June 2017).

[167] Project Management Institute. *Pulse of the Profession®: 9th Global Project Management Survey*. (Newtown Square, PA: Project Management Institute, 2017). https://www.pmi.org/-/media/pmi/documents /public/pdf/learning/thought-leadership/pulse/pulse-of-the-profession -2017.pdf.

[168] KPMG Project Management Survey. *Driving Business Performance*. (2017). https://assets.kpmg.com/content/dam/kpmg/nz/pdf/July/project managementsurvey-kpmg-nz.pdf.

[169] Ibid.

[170] Ibid.

[171] Ibid.

[172] Ibid.

Index

risk *(continued)*
  response, 169
  stakeholder engagement, 124, 165
  threshold, 56
  tolerance, 58
risk management, 56, 143
  across project, program, and
    portfolio, 150
  balancing capacity and
    capability, 156
  capability assessment, 156
  capability development, 156
  capacity planning, 155
  context, 144
  organizational capabilities, 105,
    155
  overhead, 169
  performance reporting and
    analytics, 155
  risk focus, 149
  stakeholders, 165
  structural risk area, 154
  subordinate-level guidance, 161
  supply and demand
    management, 154
  tools and techniques, 147

S
S.M.A.R.T., 43, 49
SAFe®, 162, 240, 249, 250
scenario analysis, 102
skill
  facilitation, 34
  soft, 13
  technical, 13
sponsorship, 11
stakeholder management, 117, 128
  activities, 117
  communication plan, 117, 125
  engagement plan, 125
  identify, 117, 118

importance, 117
prioritize, 117, 119
strategic alignment, 64
strategic business execution
  core disciplines, 175
  framework, 178
  individual competencies, 182
  integrating processes, 184
strategic execution, 43, 279
strategic goals and objectives, 57
strategic operating plan, 57
strategy
  deliberate, 64
  emergent, 64
  organizational learning, 64
  well-defined, 51
strategy alignment, 47, 64
strategy map, 54
supply and demand
  monitor, control, and optimize,
    104
supply and demand analysis, 101
supply and demand management, 101
system stability, 19
systems thinking, 187, 194
  frame of reference, 188
  portfolio management, 192
  portfolio management and
    environment, 196
  simple, complicated, and
    complex, 198

T
technology, 214, 277
transparency, 10

V
value management, 131, 134
  balance, 134
  monitoring and measure, 140
  principles, 132

Biographies

Our Team

This book is a collaborative "labor of affection" by a team of portfolio management practitioners. These individuals have contributed selflessly to the writing, reviewing, and editing of this book.

Steve Butler, MoP, Prince2, Chartered IT Professional, PMP, PfMP

Steve Butler is a dynamic PMO manager and globally recognized expert in the field of portfolio management. He offers deep cross-industry knowledge of PMO design, implementation, and management, and significant experience successfully linking broad strategic objectives into specific initiatives that drive tangible change. Selective highlights of Mr. Butler's work include the following:

- Worked with organizations such as the UK Financial Conduct Authority, Allen & Overy, Credit Suisse, Barclays Wealth, HSBC, the FT, the NHS, Vodafone, Orange, Gazprom, Zurich Insurance, and Old Mutual Wealth—and with PMI
- Current chair of the UK Portfolio Management Forum
- Member of the core committee that wrote PMI's *The Standard for Portfolio Management* – Fourth Edition
- Core member of the governance board that created the Portfolio Management Professional (PfMP)® certification, and sits on the global assessment panel for PfMP applicants
- Holds a master's degree in strategic management, and is in final year of doctoral studies, researching for a dissertation titled "Complexity and Its Impact on Portfolio Delivery"

Dr. Panos Chatzipanos, P. Eng, D.WRE, RPP, D. CIWEM

Dr. Panos Chatzipanos has been a C-level executive in the construction industry for over 20 years (president, CEO, managing director, and COO in three major construction companies). As a transformational leader, he now consults with the World Bank Group and the European Commission. Entrepreneurial by nature, he is able to implement a holistic approach to organizational strategic objectives. He is also a principal with PMO Advisory Inc., a leading project management training and advisory company. Selective highlights of Dr. Chatzipanos' work include the following:

- Project director of two Olympic Games venues for the Athens 2004 Olympic Games
- Portfolio manager of infrastructure construction projects and large facility projects (industrial complexes, harbors, water and wastewater treatment plants), Olympic Games venues, and energy projects)
- Founding member, American Academy of Water Resources Engineers (A.A.W.R.E.)
- Diplomate, Water Resources Engineer by A.A.W.R.E.
- Charted water and environmental project manager by C.I.W.E.M.—Registered Project Professional (RPP)
- Doctorate of philosophy from London University in Environmental Hydrodynamics. Charted Engineer - Licensed Civil & Environmental Engineer (Dr. Eur Ing)
- Core committee member on committees writing PMI standards, namely: *The Standard for Portfolio Management* – Fourth Edition, *Navigating Complexity: A Practice Guide*, and *Practice Standard for Earned Value Management* – Third Edition

Nick Clemens, DWIA, PMI-ACP, PMP

Nick Clemens is the lead program management instructor at Addx Corporation where he provides support to the U.S. Department of Homeland Security (DHS). Mr. Clemens draws from his extensive experience of over 25 years as a director and program manager delivering in-depth course materials and providing an often-stimulating class experience. His multicultural relational skills gained while managing complex multinational efforts translates well into the classroom environment where he teaches and mentors individuals with a wide range of backgrounds and experiences. Mr. Clemens oversees the delivery of over 35 classes serving some 900 students annually. As the senior courseware subject matter expert, he works with high-level DHS principals and their staffs to support the career and certification training for all DHS program managers. He instructs at all levels of career development to include mentoring of senior-level program and portfolio managers as part of the department's capstone senior class. Selective highlights of Mr. Clemens' work include the following:

- Supervised a dispersed training team of 10 individuals consisting of senior program managers, course development personnel, and a technical editor
- Provided engineering support as a chief systems integration engineer and was a key author of the Joint Tactical Radio System Program Office's strategic plan
- Chaired an aircraft datalink technical working group and the program office's capstone integrated logistics support plan integrated product team
- Directed the establishment of a complex multi-site communication, command and control system involving multicultural management within the North Atlantic Treaty Organization (NATO), Southern Command
- Chaired many high-level multinational coordination boards and technical working groups for NATO and the U.S. government
- Held a U.S. government Level III Acquisition Program Management certification and was a member of the Department of Defense Acquisition Corps

Warren Long, P. Eng, PMP

Warren Long has 40 years of consulting and business experience, including a background in senior management, services operations, strategic/organizational development, capital project management, risk management, and asset management with the Irving Group of Companies. He has utilized strong organizational and implementation skills to transform corporate vision and strategy into reality. He has consistently employed an energized, can-do management style utilizing planning, organizational, leadership, and team-building skills to deliver results. He is fully experienced in managing operations and projects, constantly developing proactive management initiatives that grow profitability and maximize value. Selective highlights of Mr. Long's work include the following:

- Over 40 years of experience in construction, portfolio management, and manufacturing
- Active member of Association of Professional Engineers and Geoscientists of NB (APEGNB), Project Management Institute (PMI), and Saint John Development Corporation
- Served on the core committee for PMI's *The Standard for Portfolio Management* – Fourth Edition

Debbie McKee, PfMP

Debbie McKee has over 25 years of experience in the delivery of IT systems and services to major clients. She has held leadership positions in a number of geographies specializing in enterprise transition/transformation/exit and proactive risk management. She was a member of the core committee for PMI's *The Standard for Portfolio Management* – Fourth Edition, has contributed to Portfolio Management Professional (PfMP)® certification exam development, and has been a subject matter expert reviewer for the forthcoming PMI risk standard. Selective highlights of Ms. McKee's include:

- Leadership of large teams of architects, engineers, and operational personnel on leading-edge infrastructure and client applications solutions within United Kingdom and Ireland and Asia Pacific regions

- Implementation of client server office infrastructures, electronic software distribution, automated testing, management information and reporting, application migration, and remote service management
- Managing a transformation portfolio within Germany and Central Europe, significantly reducing the number of red accounts—signified by cost and schedule overrun
- Assuring major transformation programs globally for HP/HPE/DXC

David Ross, PMP, PgMP

David W. Ross has over 40 years of experience in executive and project management, information systems, communications, and systems test and evaluation for government organizations and commercial companies. He has led the successful start-up of three service and technology businesses and has held senior management positions in major corporations. Mr. Ross received his bachelor's degree in electrical engineering from New Jersey Institute of Technology, and a master's degree in engineering management from Northeastern University. An active member of the Project Management Institute since 1993, he earned his Project Management Professional (PMP)® certification in 1994 and was one of the first to be certified as a Program Management Professional (PgMP)® in 2007. He has been an adjunct faculty member of Antioch University since 2004, teaching a variety of courses in project management and corporate strategy. Selective highlights of Mr. Ross' work include the following:

- Program manager for PMI's first editions of *The Standard for Program Management* and *The Standard for Portfolio Management*
- Member of PMI's Standards Member Advisory Group (SMAG)
- Chair of Project Management Institute's standard committee on *The Standard for Portfolio Management* – Fourth Edition
- Vice chair of Project Management Institute's standard committee on *The Standard for Risk Management in Portfolios, Programs, and Projects*
- Adjunct professor at Antioch University
- President and CEO of Vambrace, Inc., and owner of GW Aviation, Inc.

Gary Sikma, MBA, MSM, CSM, SAFe 4.0 (SA), PMI-ACP, PMP

Gary J. Sikma is a transformational change leader who has provided vision to the strategic planning process and who ties complexity of information technology to business needs. He has more than 30 years of leadership experience in government, for-profit, and not-for-profit organizations in healthcare, insurance, manufacturing, customer service, and intelligence. He has developed and turned around enterprise project management offices (EPMOs) for multiple organizations. He has been an active member of PMI since 2003 when he was instrumental in starting the PMI Sioux Empire, South Dakota Chapter and earned his Project Management Professional (PMP)® certification. Selective highlights of Mr. Sikma's work include the following:

- Author and contributor to a number of PMI publications, including the second and third editions of *Project Manager Competency Development Framework* and *Implementing Organizational Project Management: A Practice Guide*
- Vice chair for Project Management Institute's standard committee for *The Standard for Portfolio Management* – Fourth Edition
- Chair for Project Management Institute's standard committee on *The Standard for Risk Management in Portfolios, Programs, and Projects*
- Multilingual; fluent in English, Czech, French, and German

Dr. Te Wu, PMI-RMP, PMP, PgMP, PfMP

Professor Te Wu is an academic and a professional with over 25 years of work experience helping businesses to improve their strategy execution, over 15 years of teaching experience empowering students with management knowledge and skills, and over 10 years of experience as an entrepreneur. His core belief is that most organizations and people have more ideas than they can successfully tackle. Thus, his recent work has focused on "getting the right things done, in the right way." In his professional journey to date, he grew from the shop floor to leading US$100 million portfolios.

He is a researcher, author, speaker, teacher, and practitioner. Selective highlights of Mr. Wu's work include the following:

- Found and built PMO Advisor into a leading project management training (PMI Registered Education Provider) and consultancy
- Professorship at multiple global universities including China-European Business School and Montclair State University. Also on the Project Management Advisory Board at Stevens Institute of Technology
- Served/serving on two PMI standard committees: *The Standard for Portfolio Management* – Fourth Edition and *The Standard for Risk Management in Portfolios, Programs, and Projects*
- Serving as a U.S. delegate on the International Standard Organization's Technical Committee 258 for project, program, and portfolio management
- International speaker including many PMI chapters around the world, PMI® EMEA Congress; PMI China Congress; and most recently, across multiple cities in China at the invitation of China's State Administration of Foreign Experts Affairs

In addition to this team, we also wish to extend our thanks to John Campbell, Bob Grieser, and the other members of the PMI Global Portfolio Management Core Committees and Subcommittees for their valuable contributions to further the field of portfolio management. Our gratitude also goes to Barbara Walsh and others from the Project Management Institute. Without their support and advocacy, this book would not be possible. Thank you all!

Final Words

Portfolio management is an emerging field, both intellectually and in general adoption. While no book on an emerging topic can come even close to being perfect, this team hopes that we have scratched the surface of portfolio management. To complement this book, we created a website dedicated to advancing the concepts in portfolio management. Please visit us at www.implementppm.com and sign up to receive occasional updates. We also welcome your thoughts and feedback.